# FAITH AND FREEDOM BASIC READERS

# This Is Our Land

### REVISED EDITION

Sister M. Sheila, P.B.V.M.
Sister M. Margaret Michael, O.P.

## GINN AND COMPANY

# Acknowledgments

Grateful acknowledgment is made to the following authors and publishers for permission to use and adapt copyrighted materials:

Abelard-Schuman Limited for "Anita's Gift of Flowers," reprinted from *A New Home for Pablo* by Carol McAfee Morgan, by permission of Abelard-Schuman Ltd., all rights reserved, copyright year, 1955.

W. H. Allen & Company for "Walking Sticks," from *All about the Insect World* by Ferdinand C. Lane.

American Book Company for "God Helps Those" by Mary Ruth Mitchell, from *Widening Horizons* by Ullin W. Leavell, Mary Louise Friebele, and Tracie Cushman, copyright 1956, 1961, and Revised Edition 1964.

Appleton-Century-Crofts and the author for "How Nature Helps Birds to Fly," from *The Travels of Birds* by Frank M. Chapman.

Bank Street College of Education for "Who Built the Bridge?" by Lucy Sprague Mitchell.

The Estate of Hugh F. Blunt for "Mothers" by Rt. Rev. Hugh F. Blunt.

Curtis Brown, Ltd., for "Jonathan Bing," reprinted from *Jonathan Bing and Other Verses*, by Beatrice Curtis Brown, copyright © 1936, by Beatrice Curtis Brown, reprinted by permission of the author.

The Caxton Printers, Ltd., for "A Sea Family," from *Western Wild Life* by Allen Chaffee.

John Ciardi for "A Bookmark," written especially for National Children's Book Week 1963, copyright © — 1963, by John Ciardi.

Alice Curtis Desmond for "Snow Is Your Friend."

The Dial Press, Inc., for "The Flight of Icarus," reprinted from *Stories of the Gods and Heroes* by Sally Benson, copyright © 1940 by Sally Benson and used with the permission of the publishers, The Dial Press, Inc.

Doubleday & Company, Inc., for "Seal Lullaby," from *The Jungle Book* by Rudyard Kipling.

E. P. Dutton & Co., Inc., for "Pooh Goes Visiting and Gets into a Tight Place," from the book *Winnie-the-Pooh* by A. A. Milne, copyright 1924 by E. P. Dutton & Co., Inc., renewal 1952 by A. A. Milne, reprinted by permission of the publishers.

Norma Millay Ellis for "Afternoon on a Hill," from *Renascence and Other Poems*, published by Harper & Brothers, copyright 1917, 1945, by Edna St. Vincent Millay.

Nan Gilbert for her story, "House of Singing Windows," copyright © 1959 by Nan Gilbert, reprinted by permission of the author and the author's agents, Scott Meredith Literary Agency, Inc.

Ginn and Company for "Heidi's Day on the Mountain," from *Heidi* by Johanna Spyri, translated by Helen B. Dole; "The Race," from *Hans Brinker*

2

or the *Silver Skates* by Mary Mapes Dodge and edited by Orton Lowe; "Pinocchio's First Adventure," from *The Adventures of Pinocchio* by C. Collodi and translated by Walter S. Cramp; the song "Our Land" from *We Sing and Blend* by Sister Cecilia, S.C., and others; "The Brave Little Tailor," retold by Doris Gates from *Roads to Everywhere*, Rev. Ed. by David H. Russell, and others.

Miss Norene Carr Grace for "Spring in Hiding" by Frances Frost.

Harcourt, Brace & World, Inc., for "Little Girl, Be Careful What You Say," from *Complete Poems* by Carl Sandburg, copyright 1950 by Carl Sandburg; "Primer Lesson," from *Slabs of the Sunburnt West* by Carl Sandburg, copyright 1922 by Harcourt, Brace & World, Inc., and renewed in 1950 by Carl Sandburg; "The Boy and the Wolf," from *The Magic Circle* edited by Louis Untermeyer, copyright 1952 by Harcourt, Brace & World, Inc. All reprinted by permission of Harcourt, Brace & World, Inc.

Harper & Row, Publishers for the version of "The Lad Who Went to the North Wind," adapted from *East O' the Sun and West O' the Moon* by Gudrun Thorne-Thomsen.

Houghton Mifflin Company for permission to reprint the following selections: "A Song of Greatness," from *Children Sing in the Far West* by Mary Austin; "The First Butterflies," from *The Book of Nature Myths* by Florence Holbrook; "Hiawatha's Childhood," from *The Song of Hiawatha* by Henry W. Longfellow; and "A Nation's Strength," by Ralph Waldo Emerson.

J. B. Lippincott Company for "Dandelion" and "Little Snail," from *Poems by a Little Girl* by Hilda Conkling, copyright 1920, 1947 by Hilda Conkling, published by J. B. Lippincott Company; also for "My Land Is God's Land," from *For Days and Days* by Annette Wynne, copyright 1919, 1947 by Annette Wynne, published by J. B. Lippincott Company.

Little, Brown and Company for "A Pet for Mr. Popper," adapted from *Mr. Popper's Penguins* by Richard and Florence Atwater, by permission of Little, Brown and Co., copyright 1938 by Richard and Florence Atwater.

The Liturgical Press for "Mary, We Greet Thee," the English translation of *Salve Regina*, and the World Library of Sacred Music for the version as it appears in *The People's Hymnal.*

The Macmillan Company for the following selections: "Maybe Today," from *Twig* by Elizabeth Orton Jones, copyright 1942 by The Macmillan Company; "Something Told the Wild Geese," from *Branches Green* by Rachel Field, Copyright 1934 by The Macmillan Company, renewed 1962 by Arthur S. Pederson; "The Potatoes' Dance," from *Collected Poems* by Vachel Lindsay, copyright 1917 by The Macmillan Company, renewed 1945 by Elizabeth C. Lindsay; "The Warm of Heart," from *Five-Bushel Farm* by Elizabeth Coatsworth, copyright 1939 by The Macmillan Company. All reprinted by permission of the publisher.

David McKay Company, Inc., for "New Frontiers," from *The Wild, Wild West* by James Daugherty, copyright © 1948 by James Daugherty, used by permission of David McKay Company, Inc., publishers.

Methuen & Co., Ltd., for "Pooh Goes Visiting and Gets into a Tight Place," from the book *Winnie-the-Pooh* by A. A. Milne.

William Morrow and Company, Inc., for the following selections: "Gardenia and the Pies," from *Eddie and the Fire Engine* by Carolyn Haywood, copyright 1949 by William Morrow and Company, Inc.; "Henry Huggins

4

# FAITH AND FREEDOM

*NIHIL OBSTAT:*
Reverend James J. Kortendick, s.s., CENSOR DEPUTATUS

*IMPRIMATUR:*
† Patrick A. O'Boyle, ARCHBISHOP OF WASHINGTON

Washington, January 6, 1965

COMMISSION ON AMERICAN CITIZENSHIP

THE CATHOLIC UNIVERSITY OF AMERICA

Most Rev. Bishop William J. McDonald, *President of the Commission*
Rt. Rev. Msgr. Joseph A. Gorham, *Director*
Sister Mary Nina, o.p., *Curriculum Consultant*

# Contents

## Our Land Today

PAGE

| | | |
|---|---|---|
| Henry Huggins and Ribsy | *Beverly Cleary* | 12 |
| Maybe Today | *Elizabeth Orton Jones* | 22 |
| Afternoon on a Hill, *a poem* | *Edna St. Vincent Millay* | 30 |
| Hurrah for Danny! | *Mary Synon* | 31 |
| Ellen Rides Again | *Beverly Cleary* | 39 |
| Primer Lesson, *a poem* | *Carl Sandburg* | 50 |
| Little Girl, Be Careful What You Say, *a poem* | *Carl Sandburg* | 51 |
| Gardenia and the Pies | *Carolyn Haywood* | 52 |
| Books to Enjoy | | 62 |

## Tales of Long Ago

| | | |
|---|---|---|
| The Lad Who Went to the North Wind | *Gudrun Thorne-Thomsen* | 64 |
| The Hare and the Tortoise | *Aesop* | 72 |
| The Man, the Boy, and the Donkey | *Aesop* | 73 |
| The Boy and the Wolf, *a poem* | *Louis Untermeyer* | 75 |
| The First Butterflies | *Florence Holbrook* | 76 |
| Hiawatha's Childhood, *a poem* | *Henry Wadsworth Longfellow* | 79 |
| The Brave Little Tailor | *Jacob and Wilhelm Grimm* | 80 |
| The Flight of Icarus | *Sally Benson* | 90 |
| The Pea Blossom | *Hans Christian Andersen* | 95 |
| Limericks | *Edward Lear* | 101 |
| Books to Enjoy | | 102 |

# Building Our Land

PAGE

Keep Up Your Courage               Alice Dalgliesh   104
New Frontiers, *a poem*           James Daugherty   113
A Boy on a Raft                        Mary Synon   114
The Answered Prayer        Sister Mary Henry, O.P.   125
Knowest Thou Isaac Jogues? *a poem*   Francis W. Grey   131
The Big Boy, *a play*             Katherine Rankin   132
Stagecoach to Santa Fe                 Mary Synon   142
God Helps Those                Mary Ruth Mitchell   152
A Song of Greatness, *a poem*          Mary Austin   163
    Books to Enjoy                                   164

# Wonders of Nature

Earth's Litany, *a poem*         Sister Maryanna, O.P.   166
A Wise King and a Tiny Bee        Retold by Rose Dobbs   168
Something Told the Wild Geese, *a poem*   Rachel Field   174
How Nature Helps Birds to Fly   Frank Michler Chapman   175
A Sea Family                            Allen Chaffee   181
Seal Lullaby, *a poem*                 Rudyard Kipling   187
Big Tree                         Mary and Conrad Buff   188
Dandelion, *a poem*                    Hilda Conkling   197
Little Snail, *a poem*                 Hilda Conkling   197
Walking Sticks                       Ferdinand C. Lane   198
Flat Tail Meets Danger     Alice Gall and Fleming Crew   201
Spring in Hiding, *a poem*              Frances Frost   209
    Books to Enjoy                                     210

7

# Storybook Treasures

PAGE

A Bookmark, *a poem* — John Ciardi 212

Pooh Goes Visiting and Gets
  into a Tight Place — A. A. Milne 213

Jonathan Bing, *a poem* — Beatrice Curtis Brown 222

Pinocchio's First Adventure — C. Collodi 223

The Little Juggler, *a play* — Ruth Sawyer 234

Heidi's Day on the Mountain — Johanna Spyri 245

The Race — Mary Mapes Dodge 255

A Pet for Mr. Popper — Richard and Florence Atwater 264

Someone, *a poem* — Walter de la Mare 276

The Potatoes' Dance, *a poem* — Vachel Lindsay 277

Books to Enjoy 280

# God Speaks

The Word of God, *a poem* — Sister M. Sheila, P.B.V.M. 282

A Humble Servant — Old Testament 283

Christmas Morning, *a poem* — Elizabeth Madox Roberts 290

The Shepherd's Coat — Caryll Houselander 292

The Prodigal Son, *a parable* — New Testament 301

The Reward of Love — Janice Holland 303

Mary, We Greet Thee, *a hymn* 316

Song of the Swallows — Leo Politi 318

Prayers from the Ark, *three poems* — Carmen Bernos de Gasztold 326

The Bishop Rides on Horseback — Mary Synon 328

Whatsoever Things Are True, *a poem* — Emilie F. Johnson 337

Books to Enjoy 338

# Americans All

PAGE

The Warm of Heart, *a poem*     *Elizabeth Coatsworth*    340

Who Built the Bridge?     *Lucy Sprague Mitchell*    341

A Nation's Strength, *a poem*     *Ralph Waldo Emerson*    348

Anita's Gift of Flowers     *Carol Morgan*    349

House of Singing Windows     *Nan Gilbert*    358

Mothers, *a poem*     *Rt. Rev. Hugh F. Blunt*    372

Maile's Lei     *Mary Dana Rodriguez*    373

Snow Is Your Friend     *Alice Curtis Desmond*    382

Our Land, *a song*     *Ethel Crowninshield*    395

Books to Enjoy    396

Glossary    397

Illustrations are by Bette Darwin, Phoebe Erickson, Ati Forberg, Mamoru Funai, Denver Gillen, Leslie Goldstein, Paul Granger, David Jonas, Elizabeth Orton Jones, Ray Keane, Gordon Laite, Charles Mikolaycak, Jo Polseno, David Stone, Phero Thomas, and Ed Young.

# My Land Is God's Land

**By Annette Wynne**

My land is God's land—mountains, rivers wide;
God built it, blest it, gave it, to be the whole
   earth's pride,
With lofty silent places and prairies for the free—
My land is God's land that goes from sea to sea.

My flag is God's flag and God will see it through;
It shines on sea and mountain, the Red, the White,
   and Blue—
It has no need of terror, it lives close to the sky—
My flag is God's flag and He will keep it high!

# Our Land Today

# Henry Huggins and Ribsy

**By Beverly Cleary**

## A Dog for Henry

Every Wednesday after school Henry Huggins rode downtown on the bus to go swimming at the Boys' Club. Then he rode the bus back home.

Henry thought it was fun but not really exciting. Nothing very exciting ever happened to him—at least not until one Wednesday afternoon in March.

On that afternoon, Henry left the Boys' Club and went to the store to buy a chocolate ice-cream cone. He thought he would eat the ice-cream cone, get on the bus, and ride home.

That is not what happened.

Henry bought the ice-cream cone. Then on his way out of the store he heard a thump, thump, thump. He turned, and there behind him was a dog, scratching himself.

The dog was hungry. When Henry licked, he licked. When Henry swallowed, he swallowed.

"Just one bite," the dog's brown eyes seemed to say.

"Go away," Henry ordered, but he wasn't very firm about it. He patted the dog's head.

The tail wagged harder. Henry took one last lick. "Oh, all right," he said. "If you're that hungry, you might as well have it."

12

The ice-cream cone disappeared in one quick swallow.

"Now go away," Henry told the dog. "I have to catch a bus for home."

He started for the door. The dog started, too.

"Go away, you skinny old dog." Henry didn't say it very loudly. "Go on home."

The dog sat down at Henry's feet. Henry looked at the dog, and the dog looked at Henry.

"I don't think you have a home. You're so thin that your ribs show right through your skin. And you haven't got a collar," said Henry.

He began to think. If only he could keep the dog! He had always wanted a dog of his very own, and now he had found a dog that wanted him. He couldn't go home and leave a hungry dog on the street corner. If only he knew what his mother and father would say!

13

He fingered the two dimes and the nickel in his pocket. That was it! He would use one of the dimes to phone his mother.

"Come on, Ribsy. Come on, Ribs, old boy. I'm going to call you Ribsy because you're so thin."

The dog trotted after the boy to the telephone booth. Henry pushed him into the booth and shut the door.

"Hello—Mom?" said Henry as his mother answered the telephone.

Ribs began to scratch. Thump, thump, thump.

"My goodness, Henry, what's that noise?" his mother demanded. Ribs began to whimper and then to howl. "Henry," Mrs. Huggins shouted, "are you all right?"

"Yes, I'm all right," Henry shouted back. He never could understand why his mother always thought something had happened to him when nothing ever did. "That's just Ribsy."

"Henry," his mother cried, "will you please tell me what is going on?"

"Mother," said Henry, "I've found a dog. I wish I could keep him. He's a good dog, and I'll feed him and wash him and everything. Please, Mom."

"I don't know, dear," his mother said. "You'll have to ask your father."

"Mom!" Henry cried. "That's what you always say! Mom, please say yes, and I'll never ask for another thing as long as I live!"

"Well, all right, Henry. I guess there isn't any reason why you shouldn't have a dog. But you'll have to bring him home on the bus. Your father has the car today."

14

After Henry hung up, he said, "Come on, Ribs. We're going home on the bus."

When the big blue bus stopped in front of the store, Henry picked up his dog. Ribsy was heavier than he expected.

Henry had a hard time getting him into the bus. He was wondering how he would get a dime out of his pocket when the driver said, "Say, sonny, you can't take that dog on the bus."

"Why not?" asked Henry

"It's a company rule, sonny. No dogs on buses," said the driver. "No animal can ride on a bus unless it's inside a box."

"Well, thanks anyway," said Henry as he lifted Ribsy off the bus.

He went back into the store followed closely by Ribsy. "Have you got a big box I could have, please?" he asked the clerk behind the counter. "I need one big enough for my dog."

The clerk pulled a box out from under the counter. "I guess this is big enough," he said.

Henry thanked the clerk, carried the box out to the bus stop, and put it on the sidewalk. Ribsy trotted after him.

"Get in, fellow," Henry ordered.

Ribsy stepped into the box and sat down just as the bus came around the corner. Henry had to kneel to pick up the box. It was not a very strong box, and he had to put his arms under it. Ribsy lovingly licked Henry's face with his wet pink tongue.

The bus stopped at the curb. When it was Henry's
turn to get on the bus, he had trouble finding the step
because he couldn't see his feet. He had to try several
times before he hit it. Then he discovered he had forgotten to take his dime out of his pocket.

He turned sideways to the driver and asked politely,
"Will you please take the dime out of my pocket? My
hands are full."

The driver pushed his cap back and exclaimed, "And
just where do you think you're going with that animal?"

"Home," said Henry in a small voice.

"Not on this bus, you're not!" said the driver.

"But the man on the last bus said I could take the dog
on the bus in a box," said Henry.

"He meant a big box tied shut—a box with holes in it for the dog to breathe through," explained the driver.

Ribsy began to scratch his left ear, and the box began to tear. Ribsy jumped out of the box and off the bus, and Henry jumped after him.

Soon people were stopping on the corner to wait for the next bus. Among them Henry noticed a lady carrying a large shopping bag full of apples. The shopping bag gave him an idea. He ran back into the store.

"You back again?" asked the clerk. "What do you want this time? String and paper to wrap your dog in?"

"I want one of those big nickel shopping bags," he said, laying his last nickel on the counter.

The clerk handed the bag across the counter. At once, Henry opened the bag and set it up on the floor. He picked up Ribsy and pushed him into the bag. A lot of Ribsy was left over.

The clerk was leaning over the counter watching.

"I guess I'll have to have some string and paper, too," Henry said, "if I can have some free."

"Well! Now I've seen everything." The clerk shook his head as he handed a piece of string and a big sheet of paper across the counter.

Ribsy whimpered, but he held still while Henry wrapped the paper loosely around his head and shoulders and tied it with the string. The dog made a lumpy package, but Henry was able to carry it to the bus stop. He didn't think the bus driver would notice him.

It was getting dark and many people were waiting at the corner.

## A Wild Bus Ride

Henry stood behind the woman with the bag of apples. Ribsy wiggled and whined, even though Henry tried to pet him through the paper.

When the bus stopped, Henry climbed on behind the lady, quickly set the bag down, dropped his dime into the box, picked up the bag, and squirmed through the crowd to a seat beside a fat man near the back of the bus.

Now, if he could only keep Ribsy quiet for fifteen minutes, they would be home and Ribsy would be his for keeps. Crackle, crackle, crackle went the bag. Henry tried to hold it more tightly between his knees.

The passengers at the back of the bus began to stare at Henry and his package. Crackle, crackle, crackle. Henry tried to pat Ribsy again through the paper. The bag crackled even louder. Then it began to wiggle.

Ribs began to whimper and then to howl. Crackle, crackle, crackle. Ribsy scratched his way out of the bag. The bus turned quickly around the corner and started to go uphill. Henry was thrown against the fat man. The frightened dog wiggled away from him, squirmed between the passengers, and started for the front of the bus.

"Here, Ribsy, old boy! Come back here," called Henry, starting after him.

"E-e-ek! A dog!" cried the lady with the bag of apples. "Go away, doggie, go away!"

Ribsy was scared. He tried to run and crashed into the lady's bag of apples. The bag tipped over, and the apples began to roll toward the back of the bus. They rolled around the feet of the people who were standing. Passengers began to slip and slide.

Crash! A high-school girl dropped an armload of books. Rattle! Bang! Crash! A lady dropped a big paper bag. The bag broke open, and pots and pans rolled out.

Skree-e-etch! The driver threw on the brakes and turned around in his seat just as Henry made his way through the apples and books and pans to catch Ribsy.

The driver pushed his cap back on his head. "All right, sonny," he said to Henry. "Now you know why dogs aren't allowed on buses!"

"Yes, sir," said Henry. "I'm sorry."

"You're sorry! A lot of good that does. Look at this bus! Look at those people!"

"I didn't mean to make any trouble," said Henry. "My mother said I could keep the dog if I could bring him home on the bus."

The fat man grinned. Then he laughed until tears streamed down his cheeks. All the other passengers were laughing, too, even the lady with the apples.

The driver didn't laugh. "Take that dog and get off the bus!" he ordered.

Henry didn't know what he was going to do. He guessed he'd have to walk the rest of the way home. He wasn't sure he knew the way in the dark. Just then a siren screamed. It grew louder and louder until it stopped right beside the bus.

A policeman appeared at the bus doorway. "Is there a boy called Henry Huggins on this bus?" he asked.

"I'm Henry Huggins," said Henry in a very small voice.

"You'd better come along with us," said the policeman.

Henry and Ribsy followed the policeman off the bus and into the squad car, where Henry and the dog sat in the back seat.

"Are you going to arrest me?" Henry asked timidly as the squad car started off.

"We-e-ell, I think we might let you off this time," answered the policeman jokingly. "Your mother must be pretty worried about you if she called the police. I don't think she'd want you to go to jail."

The driver of the squad car pushed a button, and the siren screamed again. Ribsy raised his head and howled. Henry began to enjoy himself. Wouldn't this be something to tell the kids at school! Cars pulled over to the curb as the police car went faster and faster. Up the hill it went and around the corner to Henry's house.

Henry's mother and father were standing on the porch waiting for him. The neighbors were looking out of their windows.

"Well!" said his father after the policeman had gone. "It's about time you came home. So this is Ribsy! I've heard about you, fellow. There's a big bone and some strong soap waiting for you."

"Henry, what *will* you do next?" sighed his mother.

"Oh, I didn't do anything, Mom," said Henry. "I just brought my dog home on the bus like you said."

## Matching Titles and Paragraphs

Each title below could be used with a paragraph in this story. Find the paragraph that matches each title and write the number of the page and of the paragraph. On your paper make three rows like those below and fill the blank spaces.

| Title | Page | Paragraph |
|---|---|---|
| Henry Discovers a Dog | . . . . | . . . . |
| A Homeless Dog | . . . . | . . . . |
| Wrapping Ribsy | . . . . | . . . . |
| On the Bus at Last | . . . . | . . . . |
| Spilled Apples | . . . . | . . . . |
| A Fast Ride Home | . . . . | . . . . |

# Maybe Today

**By Elizabeth Orton Jones**

*Twig was a plain everyday sort of little girl, but one hot summer's afternoon she found magic in her own backyard. You, too, can find magic if you do what Twig did. Use your imagination!*

It was a Saturday morning in summer. A little girl named Twig stood on the back porch which belonged to the fourth floor of a high sort of house in the city. That was where she lived with her Mama and her Papa. Her Papa drove a yellow taxi.

Twig stood leaning against the porch's wooden railing, with her chin pressed down on the top of it. She was looking down into the backyard. The backyard was her little world. It was a square little world, with houses on three of its sides and a high fence on its other side. Outside the fence was an alley.

Down in the backyard no grass grew. But a dandelion stood there, all by itself. It had long leaves that were bent over like the branches of a tiny tree. And it had a tall stalk. At the top of its stalk was a little round bud— just a plain little round bud. Inside of it was a beautiful flower. Someday—maybe *today*—the little bud would open and let the flower show. Twig could see the dandelion from where she stood. It looked very green, away down there against the bare brown ground.

22

23

Along the ground, near the dandelion, ran a little stream of drainpipe water. The drainpipe had a leak. Drip-drip-drip! it went most of the time. Twig had dug a little pathway with a stick for the drainpipe water to run in. That made a good little stream. Twig could see it now from where she stood. It looked no wider than a piece of string away down there on the ground.

Next to the dandelion, not far from the stream, stood an empty tomato can, upside down. Twig had found it yesterday, out in the alley. Somebody had thrown it away. There were pictures of bright red tomatoes all around it, and there was a place at the side of it where somebody's can opener had made a mistake. When it was upside down, it looked like a little house—with the can opener's mistake for its door. It looked just the right size for a fairy.

Twig had washed the can clean with drainpipe water. She had stood it—just so!—upside down, next to the dandelion, not far from the stream. There it had been ever since yesterday.

Twig hadn't told her Mama and her Papa because they might think it was silly, but . . . ever since yesterday she had been expecting a fairy to come and live in the little house, and keep her company, and belong to her world. She had been expecting a pretty little fairy to come at any minute—all this time! But she hadn't seen a sign of one yet.

Well . . . maybe *today* a fairy would come!

That afternoon Twig's Mama was sweeping the porch which belonged to the fourth floor at the back of the house where Twig lived. She was sweeping around the old, old sofa. Out of the bottom of the old, old sofa hung several of its old, old springs. On top of the old, old sofa Twig's Papa lay, taking a snooze, with his big handkerchief over his face.

"*Honk . . . whee!*" snored Twig's Papa. "*Honk . . . whee-ee-ee!*"

Every time he snored his handkerchief flew up from his face and floated gently down again. Every time he snored the old, old springs of the old, old sofa rattled.

Twig was going down the steps to the backyard. They were zigzag steps and there were a good many of them. Halfway down the first flight of steps she stopped and called to her Mama, "Did you say something, Mama?"

"Sh!" whispered Twig's Mama, shaking the broom over the railing. "Don't disturb your Papa! I only said it's a hot day—hotter than yesterday, even!"

Yes, it was hot, but Twig didn't mind. She waved good-by to her Mama and went skipping down the steps. She had several things in her pocket. They rattled when she skipped.

At the bottom of the first flight of steps was another back porch, just like the higher one except that it was lower. It belonged to the third floor and on it were a broom, a mop, a big broken box, and a clothesbasket. Twig tiptoed to the clothesbasket and peeked in.

"Dear!" she whispered very, very softly so as not to wake Mrs. Webb's little baldheaded baby. For there he lay, inside the basket, sound asleep.

Twig leaned down close and smiled at Mrs. Webb's little baldheaded baby. "Dear!" she whispered very, very softly, again. Then she went tiptoeing down the next flight of steps.

At the bottom of the next flight of steps was another back porch. It belonged to the second floor, and there stood Blondie Buzzle hanging up some wash. Blondie was a grown-up girl—oh! a lady, really. She surely was beautiful. Her eyes were blue, and her hair was as yellow as Papa's taxi.

Twig looked and looked at Blondie.

"Hello, Twig!" said Blondie with a clothespin in her mouth.

"Hel-lo!" said Twig, smiling very sweetly because Blondie was so beautiful.

26

Squa-a-a-w-w-k! Squa-a-a-w-w-k! went Mrs. Buzzle's radio inside the house. Somebody shouted, "Make your old coat new—by magic!—with a smart fox fur!—"

"HELLO THERE, SWEETIE PIE!" screamed somebody else. Then Mrs. Buzzle's radio went squa-a-a-w-w-w-k! again and was still.

Twig looked some more at Blondie. Then she waved good-by and went skipping down the *next* flight of steps.

At the bottom of the *next* flight of steps was *another* back porch. It belonged to the first floor, and there sat old Mr. Cobb, the landlord, reading the newspaper, as usual.

"How-do, Mr. Cobb, sir!" said Twig. "How's the world?" She didn't really want to know how it was. But everybody tried to be polite to old Mr. Cobb because he was the landlord. And that was a question Twig's Papa always asked.

"Well . . ." began Mr. Cobb, behind the newspaper, as usual.

And, as usual, Twig had to wait for him to think of a word that was big enough to take in the whole world at once. She waited . . . and waited . . . and waited.

She slipped her hand into her pocket and felt the things that were there. She looked down at her feet. She turned her toes in. Then she turned them out. Then she turned them in and out, in and out, fast, like a little dance.

The little dance took her closer—closer to the railing of Mr. Cobb's porch, until she was looking over it into the backyard. My, but the backyard was near now!

It was so near that Twig could see the very tomatoes in the pictures all round the little house. It was so near that she could hear the very drip-drip-drip of the water from the drainpipe's leak. It was so near that she could hear something else! Something . . . quite surprising! It sounded like somebody whistling a careless little tune!

Was somebody there? . . . Was it a fairy? . . . Was it the pretty little fairy that Twig had been expecting ever since yesterday?

She didn't wait any longer for Mr. Cobb to think of his word. She ran down the last flight of steps, two at a time, to the ground. Then she went tiptoeing to the little house. She looked all around, but she didn't see a sign of a fairy. She listened, but she didn't even hear the whistling any more.

Maybe the pretty little fairy was hiding!

Twig leaned away down close to the little house. "Hoo-hoo!" she called very, very softly. "You don't need to be afraid!"

28

Afraid! . . . Out through the doorway marched a little, tiny fellow with his arms folded grandly in front of him and his knees going wobble-wobble. Afraid!

Twig had to hold both her hands over her mouth for a minute to keep from laughing. Then she sat down on the ground, doubled up her legs, and said, "Well?"

The little tiny fellow just stood there with his arms folded and his knees going wobble-wobble . . . Well, what?

"Well, for goodness sakes!" said Twig. "Who are you?"

"I'm Elf!" said Elf.

And his voice sounded like the little squeak which was in Twig's Papa's Sunday shoes.

## Could It Happen?

Read these sentences. Could these things *really* happen or could they happen only in the imagination? Number your paper from 1 to 10 and write *real* or *make-believe* after each number.

1. In the tomato can lived an elf.
2. Twig had no brothers and no sisters.
3. Mother was sweeping around the old sofa.
4. The broom looked over the porch railing.
5. Twig stood on the back porch way up high.
6. "Hello, Twig," called the drip-drip of the drainpipe.
7. The dandelion winked at Twig.
8. Mr. Cobb was the landlord.
9. Somebody had made a mistake with the can opener.
10. The elf's voice had a squeak in it.

# Afternoon on a Hill

**By Edna St. Vincent Millay**

I will be the gladdest thing
    Under the sun!
I will touch a hundred flowers
    And not pick one.

I will look at cliffs and clouds
    With quiet eyes,
Watch the wind bow down the grass,
    And the grass rise.

And when lights begin to show
    Up from the town,
I will mark which must be mine,
    And then start down.

# Hurrah for Danny!

By Mary Synon

"Strike three! You're out!" Father James called. "Danny, you're doing some fine pitching."

There was a big smile on Danny Wood's face as he walked away from the pitcher's mound. Praise from Father James meant a lot to Danny. He and all the other boys knew that their pastor had played ball and coached teams most of his life. They were always happy when the priest came out to the field to help their team.

Today was the last day of tryouts for the Rocket Nine, the fourth-grade team of St. Joseph's School. Soon the Rockets would play real games against all the other fourth-grade teams in town.

Shortly after Father James had praised Danny's pitching, Paul Long came to the pitcher's mound. He was the only other boy trying out for pitcher. Paul was a quiet boy, but everyone knew he loved to play ball.

Danny stood on the sidelines watching Paul pitch. There was no question about it—Paul was good.

As soon as the tryouts were over, Danny ran to George Porter, captain of the Rockets. During the week of tryouts, George had chosen all the players—all except the pitcher.

"George," Danny asked, "have you decided who will be pitcher? You have to decide soon. You know we can have only nine players."

"I think Paul Long would make a good pitcher," George said slowly.

"You're joking!" cried Danny in a hurt way. "I've been practicing all winter. Paul's not as good as I am."

"I think he might be a little better," George said softly.

Perhaps because Danny was his best friend, George gave Danny a chance to practice with the team for the next week. But George was fair, and he wanted his team to win games. So he kept Paul in the practices, too.

Sister William, their fourth-grade teacher, noticed how hard both boys worked. She realized that the children in the class were beginning to take sides. Some of them wanted Danny for their pitcher, and others wanted Paul.

"We cannot let this go on," Sister Willam told Father James one day.

"Why not let the children decide for themselves?" Father James asked. "They could hold an election and vote for their pitcher."

At once Sister spoke to George about this. "That would be fine, Sister," he said, thankful for the help.

When Sister Willam told the children about the election, Danny thought, "We do not need an election. I am a better pitcher than Paul."

That afternoon the voting began. Each child wrote either Danny's or Paul's name on a piece of paper. Sister William picked up the votes and started counting them.

The spring day was warm, but Danny felt cold as he waited for Sister to announce the winner. "What if they do not vote for me!" he thought. "What if Paul wins!"

Sister William was counting the votes very carefully. Finally she stood up and announced, "Danny Wood wins by seven votes."

"Hurrah!" someone shouted. "Hurrah for Danny!"

Paul Long walked up to Danny. "I am glad for you," he said, shaking Danny's hand.

"Thank you, Paul," Danny said quietly, but inside he was ready to shout for joy.

The first game of the season was with the Flying Eagles. Danny walked up to the pitcher's mound. The Eagles' first batter came up. Danny threw two low balls across home plate. The next two were outside, and so the batter was allowed to walk to first base.

Danny was trying hard, but he walked the next two batters, and bases were loaded. Now, Danny knew that he had to pitch well.

The next batter hit the first ball Danny threw. Quickly the first baseman caught the ball, touched first base, and threw the ball to home plate just as an Eagle player was sliding into home. The Rockets had put out two men quick as a wink. "But," Danny sadly thought, "it wasn't because of my pitching."

The Rockets won their first game of the season, but it wasn't a good game. Danny was not happy over it. He knew that he was not playing as well as Paul had played during practice. No one said anything about it, but Danny felt that George knew it, too.

"I'll be all right for our next game," Danny promised George.

The Rockets won the next game, but again Danny was not playing well. He knew good teamwork had won the game, not his pitching.

It was then that George talked to him. "We have one more game before the big game with the Shooting Stars," he said. "I am going to use Paul Long for the game. Watch him closely, Danny. He has been pitching well when he helps out at practice."

There were many school children and their parents standing around the field when the next game began. Danny knew at once that the Jet Streams had a better team than the other two teams that they had played.

Danny sat on the sidelines, wishing that he was in the game. Still he had to tell himself that Paul was doing a good job of pitching.

"I could not have done better," Danny thought at the end of the second inning.

By the fourth inning Paul had really warmed up. He threw a fast ball to the first batter. "Strike one!" called the umpire. Two more fast balls. "Strike two! Strike three! You're out!" yelled the umpire.

Two more batters came up. Paul threw even faster balls across the plate. Both boys struck out. The Rockets were shouting and slapping Paul on the back as they walked off the field.

Now, Danny had to tell himself that he could not pitch as well. Paul Long was a born pitcher. He was better, far better, than Danny Wood had ever been or ever would be. Danny swallowed a lump in his throat and then took a long breath.

35

For the rest of the innings, Paul pitched a great game. None of the Jet Streams got more than a first-base hit. The Rockets won easily. Everyone cheered wildly at the end of the game. It was easy to see that the Rockets had played their best game of the season.

After the crowd left, Danny walked over to George. "You have your pitcher," he said. "Paul is better than I am. Keep him for the big game. The Rockets can't lose with him pitching."

"But you were elected," George said.

"Maybe I shouldn't have been," Danny sighed.

On the way home Danny stopped by the church. There was no one there when he went in. For several minutes he knelt at the altar rail. "Please, God, help me," he prayed. "Show me the way to do what is right."

Danny had no answer as he came out of the church, but the next morning he knew what he should do. As soon as he got to school he went to Sister William.

"Can someone who is elected to a place leave it?" he asked her.

"I suppose so," she replied, "if he has a good reason."

"Then may I talk to the class this morning, Sister?" he asked.

"Of course," Sister William answered quietly.

Just before lunch Sister rang the desk bell. "Danny has something to tell you," she said to the class.

Danny walked to the front of the room. "You elected me to be the Rocket pitcher," he said. "I was proud of that. I did the best I could, but my best was not as good as Paul Long's.

36

"Paul is a better pitcher than I am. George and the other boys on the team know it. They have said nothing because they like me. But they would not keep on liking me and I would not like myself if I kept the job when I know Paul should have it. So will you please elect Paul as your pitcher?"

For a moment the children only stared at Danny in silence. Then suddenly someone cheered, "Hurrah for Danny!" Someone else echoed the cheer. Then all the children were clapping and shouting, "Hurrah for Danny!"

Father James heard the cries as he passed the room and came to the door.

"What's going on?" he asked Sister William.

"A celebration, Father," she answered proudly, "a celebration of real victory. Danny has asked the children to elect Paul Long in his place because he thinks that Paul is a better pitcher."

"Well, he may be," Father James said, "but no one is a better man than Danny."

That is why Paul Long pitched the big game for the Rocket Nine. He won the big game. But Danny Wood won a bigger victory, for now he knows that sometimes a boy wins more by giving up something he wants.

## Using Your Imagination

Choose one of these things to do. Find your ideas in the story, but try to say them a little differently instead of copying them exactly as they are in the story.

1. Imagine that you are Danny and that you are telling your father what happened to you at school. Tell him each thing that happened to make you feel more and more that Paul should be the pitcher. Write this on paper and be ready to share it with the class.

2. Paul Long was a quiet boy, but he loved to play ball. He wanted very much to be a good pitcher and to help his team. Write some of the things that Paul may have been thinking

    *a.* when Danny won the election,

    *b.* when he pitched the game with the Jet Streams, and

    *c.* when Danny asked the children to elect Paul.

3. Imagine that you are George Porter. Write a letter to your best friend, telling him about the problems you have in trying to decide who should be the pitcher of the team.

# Ellen Rides Again

**By Beverly Cleary**

## How It All Began

It all started one warm spring afternoon as Ellen Tebbits was walking home from the library with her very best friend, Austine Allen. At the library Austine had been lucky enough to find two horse books. "I wish I could ride a horse sometime," she said.

"Haven't you ever ridden a horse?" asked Ellen.

"No. Have you?" Austine sounded excited.

"Oh, yes," Ellen said, not in the least bit excited. "Several times."

It was true. She had ridden several times. If she had ridden twice, she would have said a couple of times. Three was several times, and so she had told the truth.

"Where? What was it like? Tell me about it," begged Austine.

"Oh, different places." That was also true. She had ridden at the beach. Her father had rented a horse for an hour and had let Ellen ride behind him with her arms around his waist. She had bounced harder than was comfortable, but she had been able to hang on.

Then she had ridden at Uncle Fred's farm. Uncle Fred had lifted her up onto the back of his old plow horse, Lady. He led her twice around the barnyard. Lady didn't bounce her at all.

Then there was that other time when her father had paid a dime so that she could ride a pony around inside a fence. It hadn't been very exciting. The pony seemed tired, but Ellen had pretended it was galloping madly.

Yes, it all added up to several times.

"Why haven't you told me you could ride?" asked Austine. "What kind of saddle do you use?" Austine knew all about different kinds of saddles because she read so many horse books.

"Oh, any kind," said Ellen, who did not know one saddle from another. "Once I rode bareback."

That was true because Lady had no saddle.

"Goodness," said Austine. "Bareback!"

Ellen was beginning to feel uncomfortable. She had not meant to mislead Austine. She really did not know how it all started.

"Oh, Ellen, you have all the luck," exclaimed Austine. "Imagine being able to ride horseback. And even bareback!"

"Oh, it's nothing," said Ellen, wishing Austine would forget the whole thing.

40

The next day at school Austine did not forget about Ellen's horseback riding. She told Barbara and George. Barbara and George told other boys and girls. Each time the story was told, it grew.

The next morning at ten o'clock Ellen ran down Tillamook Street and around the corner to Austine's house. Since it was a holiday, Mr. and Mrs. Allen were taking the two girls on a picnic.

They had driven a number of miles along the highway when Austine saw some horses. "Look, Daddy! Horses for rent! Please stop," she begged.

Mr. Allen drew over to the side of the road near some horses in a corral. Austine scrambled out of the car and ran to the horses, while the others followed.

"Daddy, please let us go horseback riding. All my life I've wanted to ride a horse. Please, Daddy."

"Would it be safe for the girls to ride alone?" Mrs. Allen asked the man with the horses.

"Sure. Kids do it all the time," answered the man. "They ride up that dirt road as far as the old sawmill and turn around and come back. The horses know the way. They are as gentle as kittens."

"We'll be safe," said Austine. "Ellen has ridden a lot, and I know all about riding from books."

Ellen wished Austine would keep quiet. She was not at all sure she wanted to ride.

"I suppose it would be safe to let the girls ride," said Mrs. Allen.

Austine watched eagerly and Ellen watched uneasily while the man saddled and bridled two horses.

Ellen walked over to the brown horse and patted him gingerly. He seemed very big when she stood beside him. When he looked down at her with large gentle eyes, Ellen felt braver.

The man held out his hand, palm up.

"Oh, I wonder if he wants me to give him some money," thought Ellen. "It must be that, but I'm sure Austine's father paid him. Maybe he wants to shake hands."

"Come on, girlie. Step up," said the man. "Don't be scared. Brownie isn't going to hurt you."

"My goodness," thought Ellen. "I guess he expects me to step in his hand. I suppose it's all right. His hand is dirty anyway."

She put her foot into his hand, and he boosted her onto the horse. The ground seemed a long way below her. Ellen had forgotten how wide a horse was.

Then the man helped Austine onto a pinto.

"Look," cried Austine. "I'm really on a horse!"

## Giddap!

Ellen knew that she was expected to go first. "Giddap," she said uncertainly. Brownie, her horse, did not move.

The man gave each horse a light slap. They walked slowly out of the corral and down the dirt road as if they were used to going that way. Ellen carefully held one rein in each hand. As she looked at the ground so far below, she hoped Brownie wouldn't decide to run.

When Austine's horse moved in front, Ellen took hold of the saddle horn. It wasn't so much that she was scared, she told herself. She just didn't want to take any chances.

Then when they had gone around a bend in the road, Brownie decided it was time to go back to the corral. He turned around and started walking in the direction from which they had come.

"Hey," said Ellen anxiously. She pulled on the right rein, but Brownie kept on going. "Stop!" she ordered, more loudly this time.

"What are you going that way for?" asked Austine.

"Because the horse wants to," said Ellen crossly.

"Well, turn him around."

"I can't," said Ellen. "He won't steer."

Austine turned Old Paint, her horse, and drew up beside Ellen. "Don't you know you're supposed to hold both reins in one hand?" Austine scolded.

Ellen didn't know. "I just held them this way to try and turn him," she said.

Austine reached over and took hold of Brownie's bridle with one hand. "Come on, Old Paint," she said, and turned her horse forward again. Brownie followed.

"Thanks," said Ellen. "My, you're brave."

"Oh, it's nothing," said Austine. "You don't steer a horse," she added gently. "You guide him."

"Oh . . . I forgot," Ellen said.

"Let's gallop," suggested Austine, digging in her heels. Old Paint began to trot. At first Austine bounced, but soon she rode smoothly. Then her horse began to gallop.

When Old Paint galloped, Brownie began to trot. Ellen began to bounce. She hung onto the saddle horn as hard as she could. Still she bounced. Slap-slap-slap.

"Goodness, I sound horrible," she thought. "I hope Austine doesn't hear me slapping this way."

Austine's horse, after galloping a few yards, slowed down to a walk. "Whoa, Old Paint," cried Austine anyway, and pulled on the reins. Old Paint stopped, and Austine panted a minute.

"I did it, Ellen!" she called. "It was just a few steps, but I really, truly galloped. I hung on with my knees and galloped just like in the movies."

"Wh-wh-oa-oa!" Ellen's voice was jarred out between bounces. Brownie trotted on. Slap-slap-slap.

Austine laughed. "Oh, Ellen, you look so funny!"

Slap-slap-slap. Ellen didn't think she could stand more bouncing. It was worse than a spanking.

"Ellen Tebbits! I do not think you know a thing about horseback ·riding," cried Austine.

"Wh-wh-oa-oa-oa!" When Brownie reached Old Paint, he stopped. After Ellen got her breath, she gasped, "I do, too. It's just that the other horses I rode were tamer."

45

The horses walked on until the road curved down to the edge of a stream.

"I wonder if the poor horses are thirsty," said Austine.

There was no doubt about Brownie's wanting a drink. He left the road and picked his way down the rocky bank to the water.

"Poor horsie, you were thirsty," said Ellen, patting his neck.

Brownie did not stop at the edge of the stream. He waded out into it.

"Whoa," yelled Ellen, above the rush of the water. "Austine, help!"

Brownie waded on.

"Austine! What'll I do? He's going swimming!"

"Here, Brownie! Here, Brownie!" called Austine from the bank.

When Brownie had picked his way to the middle of the stream, he stopped.

"Look, he's in over his knees!" Ellen looked down at the water. "Giddap, Brownie!"

"Kick him in the ribs," yelled Austine from across the stream.

"I don't want to hurt him," called Ellen, but she kicked him gently. Brownie did not appear to notice.

"Slap him with the ends of the reins," directed Austine from the bank.

Ellen slapped. Brownie only turned his head and looked at her. By this time some hikers had stopped on the bridge above the stream. Looking down at Ellen, they laughed and pointed. Ellen wished they would go away.

"Yippee!" yelled one of the hikers, and everyone laughed. "Ride 'em, cowboy!"

"Do something, Austine," Ellen called across the water.

One of the hikers climbed down the bank to the edge of the water. "Need some help, little girl?" he called.

47

"Oh, yes, please," answered Ellen gratefully.

"Come on, old fellow," the man said, pulling the reins. Meekly Brownie began to pick his way toward the bank.

"Oh, thank you," said Ellen when they reached dry ground. "I guess I would have had to stay out there all day if you hadn't come for me."

"That's all right," said the man. "The trouble is, you let the horse know you were afraid of him. Let him know you're the boss, and you won't have any trouble."

"Thank you, I'll try," said Ellen, taking a firm grip on the reins. "Good-by."

The girls headed their horses toward the corral. Ellen was so ashamed she didn't know quite what to say to Austine. What would Austine think of her after this? What would she tell the kids at school?

Finally, Ellen said in a low voice, "I guess I didn't know quite as much about horseback riding as I thought I did."

48

"Your horse was just hard to manage, that's all," said Austine kindly.

"Austine?" said Ellen timidly.

"What?"

"You won't tell anybody, will you?"

Austine smiled at her. "Of course, I won't tell. We're best friends, aren't we? Giddap, Old Paint."

"Thank you, Austine," said Ellen gratefully. "You're a wonderful friend. And you know what? I'm going to look for some horse books the next time we go to the library."

Ellen held the reins firmly. Brownie was going to know who was boss. Ellen began to enjoy herself. She pretended she was returning to a ranch after a hard day riding on the range.

## Telling Why

After reading each sentence, ask yourself if it is *true* or *false*. Then think of *why* it is true or false. Write the numbers from 1 to 10 on your paper. Beside each number write *True* or *False* and a sentence that proves your answer.

1. Austine knew more about horses than Ellen did.
2. Ellen had ridden three times all by herself.
3. Mr. Allen decided to take the girls horseback riding.
4. The man thought that the horses were wild.
5. The man wanted to shake hands with Ellen.
6. Austine was eager to ride the horses.
7. Ellen said that her horse was hard to manage.
8. Austine thought that she was brave.
9. Austine proved that she was a good friend.
10. Ellen decided it was a good idea to read about horses.

# Primer Lesson

**By Carl Sandburg**

Look out how you use proud words.
When you let proud words go, it is not easy to call
them back.
They wear long boots, hard boots; they walk off proud;
they can't hear you calling—
Look out how you use proud words.

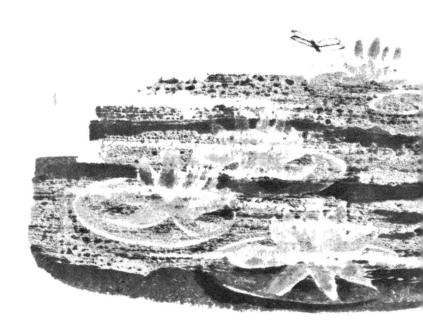

# Little Girl,
# Be Careful What You Say

By Carl Sandburg

Little girl, be careful what you say
when you make talk with words, words—
for words are made of syllables
and syllables, child, are made of air—
and air is so thin—air is the breath of God—
air is finer than fire or mist,
finer than water or moonlight,
finer than spider-webs in the moon,
finer than water-flowers in the morning:
   and words are strong, too,
   stronger than rocks or steel,
stronger than potatoes, corn, fish, cattle,
and soft, too, soft as little pigeon-eggs,
soft as the music of hummingbird wings.
   So, little girl, when you speak greetings,
when you tell jokes, make wishes or prayers,
   be careful, be careless, be careful,
   be what you wish to be.

# Gardenia and the Pies

### By Carolyn Haywood

As soon as school closed for the summer vacation, Eddie Wilson set to work building a wagon that his pet goat, Gardenia, could pull. His brothers Joe and Frank, who were twins, helped him.

Gardenia did not seem too pleased with the idea of being put to work. She had been leading a very easy life, just eating and sleeping. It took a little time to get her to pull the wagon.

Finally the day came when Gardenia pulled the wagon all the way around the block with Eddie sitting in it. Eddie was delighted.

The following day Eddie and the twins offered to go to the store for their mother and bring home the week's groceries. While they hitched up Gardenia to the wagon, Mrs. Wilson made out a long list. Joe put it in his pocket, and the boys started off.

The boys took turns riding in the wagon all the way to the market. When they reached the big building, Eddie took the goat and wagon around to the parking lot behind the market, and the twins went inside to do the shopping.

Eddie stood beside Gardenia in the parking lot and watched baked goods being unloaded from a large truck. The driver carried one large tray after another into the store. There were iced cakes and plain cakes. There were cup cakes and cookies. There were cinnamon buns and coffee cakes, rolls and pies.

Suddenly Eddie heard a sound that always filled him with excitement. It was the sound of fire sirens, and they were coming nearer.

Eddie looked at Gardenia. She was quietly nibbling at a patch of grass that grew beside the parking lot. Eddie ran around the building just in time to see the first of the fire engines swing into the main street.

Joe and Frank had left the store and were standing beside Eddie. Even the driver of the bakery truck was there, looking at the fire engines.

The three boys, forgetting all about Gardenia and their marketing, started to run after the fire engines. The driver of the bakery truck ran, too. He had such long legs and ran so fast that he was soon out of sight.

Meanwhile, Gardenia grew tired of eating grass. For some time she had been smelling a very delicious odor, and now she moved toward the bakery truck. She poked her nose inside the truck and ran it along the edge of a large tray of pies. In a moment she had the tray between her teeth and it was easy to give it a jerk. *Wham* went the tray and at Gardenia's feet lay one dozen blueberry pies, knocked very much out of shape.

Gardenia did not care about the shape of the pies. It was the flavor that interested her, and the flavor of those blueberry pies made Gardenia feel very happy indeed. Twelve pies were never eaten faster than Gardenia ate them.

When she had finished most of the last pie, she went back for more. Again she stuck her head into the truck and clamped her teeth on another tray and pulled. There was a shower of pies, and twelve more broke into pieces on the ground in front of Gardenia. These were cherry pies.

Out on the street the boys had run about three blocks when they saw the fire engines coming back.

The firemen waved to them and called, "False alarm!" Riding on the back of one of the fire trucks was the bakery man.

Gardenia was eating the cherry pies when the driver of the bakery truck appeared. When he saw Gardenia, he let out such a yell that Gardenia galloped off, pulling the wagon after her. She ran out of the parking lot, past the market, and lickety-split up the street, with the bakery man after her.

Eddie and the twins were walking toward the market when they saw Gardenia coming head on. Eddie shouted, "Here comes Gardenia! I forgot all about her!"

The boys ran toward her, but Gardenia rushed right past them with a great clatter. The bakery man rushed past them, too. Eddie and the twins joined the chase after Gardenia.

At the next corner Gardenia ran up on the sidewalk, knocking the wagon against a fireplug. Off went one of the wheels.

Now that the wagon had only three wheels, it was harder for Gardenia to pull it, so she had to slow down. Presently she stopped and began nibbling at the grass on the edge of a lawn. The bakery man stopped, too, and took hold of Gardenia's harness.

"Whose goat is this anyway?" said the bakery man.

"She's mine," said Eddie.

"Well, you come along with me," said the man. "Just wait until you see what this goat did!"

At this moment Eddie saw Gardenia's face. "Oh! Oh!" he cried. "Look at her! Look at her! She's done something to her face. She's hurt herself! Oh, Gardenia!" he cried, kneeling down beside the goat. "Look at the blood all over her face. Look! Red blood! And oh, look! Blue blood!"

"Blue blood, my eye!" shouted the bakery man. "Blueberry pie, that is! My blueberry and cherry pies!"

"It is?" said Eddie, sitting back on his heels and looking up at the man.

"It certainly is!" said the man. "And you're going to have to pay for them. You just come along with me."

When they reached the market, the bakery man, Eddie, the twins, and the goat marched back to the parking lot.

"Just look at that!" cried the man, pointing to the ground where cherries and blueberries and broken pieces of pie still lay.

"Oh, that's too bad!" said Eddie.

"I'll soon tell you how bad it is," said the man. He looked at the trays that had held the pies.

"Two trays!" cried the man.

"Two trays?" Eddie repeated.

"Two trays is right! That's twenty-four pies," said the bakery man.

"Twenty-four pies!" gasped Eddie. "That's a lot of pie! Did Gardenia eat all of them?"

"All but those two on the ground," said the man. "And they're no good to me."

"Gee!" said Eddie. "That sure is too bad."

"You mean it's twenty-two bad and too bad the other two are broken on the ground," said the man. "Let's see. That's twenty-four pies at seventy cents each. That lunch your goat just ate will cost you exactly sixteen dollars and eighty cents."

"Gee!" said Joe. "That's more than Mother gave us to do the marketing. She gave me a ten-dollar bill."

"Well, hand over the ten-dollar bill and give me your name and address. I'll stop around later and collect the six-eighty," said the bakery man.

Joe sadly handed the ten-dollar bill to the man. The man wrote their name and address in a little book.

The three boys walked home with the goat without saying a word. When the reached the house, they put the goat in her house and went indoors.

Mrs. Wilson was in the living room, hanging curtains. "Well!" she called out. "Did you get everything?"

Joe looked at Frank, and Frank looked at Eddie. Eddie gulped.

"You tell her," said Frank, giving Eddie a poke.

Eddie gulped again. Then he said, "We couldn't."

"Why not?" his mother asked.

"The wheel came off the wagon," said Eddie.

"Oh, that's too bad," said Mrs. Wilson.

"The bakery man said it was twenty-two bad," said Frank.

"Twenty-two what?" asked his mother.

"Twenty-two pies," said Frank.

"I didn't tell you to get twenty-two pies," said Mrs. Wilson.

"We didn't," said Joe.

"What are you talking about?" said Mrs. Wilson, sitting down.

"Gardenia," said Eddie.

"Well, what about Gardenia?" his mother asked.

"She ate some pie," said Eddie.

"Oh!" said Mrs. Wilson. "How much pie did Gardenia eat?"

"Well," said Eddie, "she didn't eat all of it. Did she?" he asked, turning to the twins.

"No," said Joe, and Frank added, "Not all."

"Well, how much did she eat?" Mrs. Wilson asked.

58

"She ate all but two," said Eddie.

"*All but two!*" said his mother. "Just how many pies did Gardenia eat?"

Eddie swallowed very hard and said, "Only twenty-two."

"*Twenty-two!*" cried Mrs. Wilson. "Gardenia ate twenty-two pies? And where were you while Gardenia was eating twenty-two pies?"

The three boys hung their heads. "Running after the fire engines," said Eddie.

"I might have known there would be a fire engine in this," said Mrs. Wilson. "It seems to me that no matter what you do, Eddie, you always get mixed up with a fire engine." Then she added, "I suppose you paid for the pies?"

"We didn't have enough money," said Frank. "It came to sixteen dollars and eighty cents. We gave the man the ten-dollar bill, and he took our name and address. He said he would come over and collect it."

Mrs. Wilson shook her head. "Sixteen dollars and eighty cents!" she said. "Sixteen dollars and eighty cents for pies for a goat!"

The three boys sat on three chairs, looking very unhappy.

Then the doorbell rang and Mrs. Wilson got up and went to the door. The boys looked out of the window and saw the bakery truck. Very quietly they all started to tiptoe upstairs.

"Well," said Mrs. Wilson when she opened the door, "I hear our goat had quite a pie feast and that you have come to collect six dollars and eighty cents."

"No," said the bakery man. "My boss told me to stop over and give you back your ten dollars. He said I shouldn't have left the truck."

60

"Where were you while Gardenia was eating all those pies?" asked Mrs. Wilson.

The bakery man turned bright pink and looked very sheepish. "Well," he said, "ever since I was a boy I've been crazy about fire engines. Can't leave 'em alone. Just let me hear a fire siren and I have to run."

Mrs. Wilson laughed. "Your name ought to be Eddie."

"Matter of fact, it is," said the bakery man. "Eddie Murphy. That's me."

## Reading between the Lines

You found out much about Eddie Wilson and his family when you read this story. But did you read between the lines? Without the author telling you in so many words, did you discover what a character was like by something he did or said? Make your answers to the following questions look like this: *page 52, paragraph 6.*

1. In no place does the author say, "Gardenia was a lazy goat." But one paragraph in the story shows you that Gardenia was lazy. Which paragraph is it?

2. In no place does the author say that the goat was very dear to Eddie. Which paragraph shows this?

3. The author doesn't say that the boys didn't want to tell their mother what had happened, but you can tell that this is true. Which two paragraphs prove this?

4. Nowhere are you told that Eddie Murphy's boss was a fair man. Which paragraph shows this?

5. You are not told that the bakery man was ashamed of chasing fire engines. Which paragraph shows that he is?

# Books to Enjoy

*Henry Huggins*, by Beverly Cleary.

This book, in which Henry finds his dog, is the first of several books about Henry. Others are *Henry and Ribsy*, in which more amusing things happen to the boy; *Henry and Beezus*, in which Henry tries to earn enough money for a bicycle; and *Henry and the Paper Route*, in which Henry goes into business.

*Twig*, by Elizabeth Orton Jones.

Twig's backyard is small and closed in by a fence, but her imagination is large and knows no boundaries as you will find out when you read this delightful book.

*Dot for Short*, by Frieda Friedman.

Crowded New York City is the setting for this story about the poor, but lovable, Fleming family. Grandma Fleming at the beginning of the book correctly predicts that exciting things will happen to Dot, the youngest Fleming girl.

*A Dog Named Penny*, by Clyde Robert Bulla.

Mike and his sister Emmy Lou want very much to have a pet of their own. A man lets them keep his collie dog, and all goes well until the man's nephew comes to claim the dog.

*Cotton in My Sack*, by Lois Lenski.

Before writing this book the author lived and worked with the people of the Arkansas cotton fields. She gives a true and interesting picture of the sorrows, the joys, and the hardships of one family who worked in the cotton fields.

*Cowboy Boots*, by Shannon Garst.

A boy from the city spends the summer at his uncle's cattle ranch and learns what it means to be a cowboy.

# Tales of Long Ago

# The Lad Who Went to the North Wind

By Gudrun Thorne-Thomsen

Once upon a time there was an old widow who had only one son. Because she was feeble and weak, she asked her son to go out to the storehouse and fetch flour for cooking. After the lad had got the flour, he walked outside the storehouse. As he was going down the steps, the North Wind came puffing and blowing. It caught up the flour and carried it away through the air.

The lad went back into the storehouse for more. When he came out again on the steps, the North Wind came again and carried off the flour with a puff. More than that, he did it a third time.

By this time the lad had grown very angry. It was hard for him to believe that the North Wind should behave so. The lad decided to go in search of the North Wind and ask him for the flour that he had taken.

So off he went, but the way was long. He walked and walked. At last he came to the North Wind's house.

"Good day," said the lad. "Thank you for coming to see us the other day."

"Good day," said the North Wind. His voice was loud and gruff. "Thanks for coming to see me. What do you want?"

64

"Oh," answered the lad, "I only wished to ask you to be so good as to let me have back the flour you took from me on the storehouse steps. My mother and I haven't much to live on. If you're to go on snapping up the morsel we have, there'll be nothing for us to do but starve."

"I don't have your flour," said the North Wind. "Since you are in such need, I'll give you a tablecloth which will get you everything you want. You need only say, 'Cloth, spread yourself, and serve up all kinds of good dishes!'"

With this, the lad was well content.

As the way was long, the lad could not get home in one day, so he turned into an inn on the way. When he was sitting down for supper, he laid the cloth on the table and said, "Cloth, spread yourself, and serve up all kinds of good dishes!"

He had scarcely said this before the cloth did as it was bid. All who stood by thought it was a fine thing, but most of all the landlord thought so.

That night, when all were fast asleep, the landlord took the lad's cloth. In its place he put another like it, but this cloth could not so much as serve up a bit of dry bread.

When the lad woke, he took the cloth and went off with it. That day he got home to his mother.

"Now," said he, "I've been to the North Wind's house. A good fellow he is, for he gave me this cloth. When I say to it, 'Cloth, spread yourself, and serve up all kinds of good dishes,' I get every sort of food I please."

"All very true, I dare say!" said the mother. "But seeing is believing."

The lad drew out a table, laid the cloth on it, and said, "Cloth, spread yourself, and serve up all kinds of good dishes!"

But not even a bit of dry bread did the cloth serve up.

"Well," said the lad, "there is nothing I can do except go to the North Wind again."

Away he went. Late in the afternoon, he came to where the North Wind lived.

"Good evening!" said the lad.

"Good evening!" said the North Wind.

"I want my rights for that flour of ours which you took," said the lad. "That cloth you gave me isn't worth a penny."

"I have no flour," said the North Wind, "but you may have this ram which will coin gold pieces when you say to it, 'Ram, ram! Make money!'"

The lad thought this a fine thing.

As it was too far to get home that day, he turned in for the night at the same inn where he had slept the first time.

Before the lad asked for anything at the inn, he said to the ram, "Ram, ram! Make money!" Sure enough, the ram coined the pieces of gold just as the North Wind had said he would do.

When the landlord saw this, he thought it a fine ram. When the lad had fallen asleep, the landlord got another ram which could not coin even a penny. He exchanged it for the lad's ram.

The next morning, off went the lad. When he got home, he said to his mother, "After all, the North Wind is a jolly fellow, for now he has given me a ram. It will coin gold pieces if I only say, 'Ram, ram! Make money!'"

"All very true, I dare say!" said his mother. "But I shan't believe it until I see the coins made."

"Ram, ram! Make money!" said the lad. But not even a penny did the ram coin.

So the lad went back to the North Wind and scolded him. He said the ram was worth nothing, and that he must have his rights for the flour.

"Well!" said the North Wind. "I've nothing else to give you but that old stick in the corner. Still, it's a stick of such a kind that if you say, 'Stick, stick, lay on!' it beats until you say, 'Stick, stick, now stop!'"

The lad thanked the North Wind and went his way. As the road was long, he turned in this night also at the same inn. By this time he could guess pretty well what had happened to the cloth and the ram. So he lay down at once on a bench and began to snore as if he were asleep.

Now, the landlord thinking surely the stick must be worth something, hunted up one which was like it. When he heard the lad snore, the landlord started to exchange the two sticks. Just then the lad called out, "Stick, stick, lay on!"

At once the stick began to beat the landlord. It beat him until he jumped over chairs and tables and benches, yelling and roaring, "Oh, my! Oh, my! Bid the stick to be still, or it will beat me to death. You shall have back both your cloth and your ram!"

When the lad thought the landlord had had enough, he said, "Stick, stick, now stop!"

At once the stick stopped beating the landlord, and the lad soon had his cloth and ram. Then the lad started home, with the cloth in his pocket and the stick in his hand, leading the ram by a cord tied around its horns.

And so it was that the lad got his rights for the flour he had lost.

## Saying It Another Way

Words and phrases that we would not use today are often used in old tales. Today we would not say that someone *hunted up a stick*. We would say that someone *looked for and found a stick*. The underlined parts of the sentences below show the way things are said in the old tale about the lad and the North Wind. Write the sentences, changing the underlined parts to show how we would say these things today.

1. The lad went to the storehouse to fetch flour.
2. The wind caught up the flour.
3. Off he went, but the way was long.
4. You are snapping up the morsel we have.
5. Cloth, serve up all kinds of dishes.
6. The lad was well content.
7. The lad turned into an inn on the way.
8. His mother said, "All very true, I dare say."
9. I want my rights for the flour.
10. This ram will coin gold pieces.
11. The lad called out, "Stick, lay on."
12. "Bid the stick to be still," cried the landlord.

# The Hare and the Tortoise

**An Aesop Fable**

A hare was once boasting about how fast he could run. A tortoise overheard him boasting and said, "I'll run you a race."

The hare laughed and laughed and said, "Done!" They asked the fox to be the judge, and the race was on.

The hare quickly outran the tortoise and, seeing how far ahead he was, lay down to take a nap.

"I can soon catch up with that old slowpoke when I wake up," he boasted.

But, unluckily, the hare overslept. When he awoke, the tortoise was far, far ahead. Though he ran his best, the hare found the tortoise already at the goal.

As the fox gave the race to the tortoise he said, "Slow and steady wins the race many times."

# The Man, the Boy, and the Donkey

**An Aesop Fable**

A man and his son were once driving their donkey to market to sell him. As they were going along a country road, they passed some girls.

"Look at that silly man and boy," said one of the girls. "How foolish they are to trudge along in the dust while their donkey walks along so freely!"

The man heard what they said and boosted his boy up on the donkey's back, and they went on their way. They had not gone far when they came to a group of old men.

"See here, now," said one of the men to the others. "This shows that what I say is true—the young no longer take care of the old. See this lazy boy riding while his poor old father has to walk by his side."

Upon hearing this, the man told his son to get down, and he got on the donkey himself. In a little while they

passed a couple of women. "For shame," cried the women. "How can you ride like a king and let your poor son trudge along beside?"

The man then took the boy up behind him on the donkey, and they rode on. Just before they got to the town, some young men stopped them and cried out, "How awful of you to load that poor animal so! You look more able to carry him than he to carry you."

So the man and the boy got off the donkey and thought of what they might do next. Finally, they took rope and tied the donkey's legs and fastened them to a pole. Then they each took one end of the pole and carried the donkey. As they trudged along, everyone they met laughed and laughed at the strange sight.

By and by they came to a bridge. Then the donkey began to struggle and kick, breaking the ropes as he did so. The poor animal fell off the pole, over the bridge, and into the water and was drowned.

The old man and his son started their long trip home, thinking all the while to themselves, "Try to please everybody, and you please nobody."

## Drawing Pictures to Show Main Ideas

The six titles below show things that happen in the fable. Using simple stick figures, draw a picture for each title. Put your drawings in the order in which they happen.

The Man and Boy Ride       The Donkey Falls into the River
The Man and Boy Walk      The Boy Rides
The Man Rides                   The Donkey Is Carried

# The Boy and the Wolf

**From the Greek of Aesop, adapted by Louis Untermeyer**

A boy employed to guard the sheep
Despised his work. He liked to sleep.
And when a lamb was lost, he'd shout,
"Wolf! Wolf! The wolves are all about!"

The neighbors searched from noon till nine,
But of the beast there was no sign.
Yet "Wolf!" he cried next morning when
The villagers came out again.

One evening around six o'clock
A real wolf fell upon the flock.
"Wolf!" yelled the boy. "A wolf indeed!"
But no one paid him any heed.

Although he screamed to wake the dead,
"He's fooled us every time," they said,
And let the hungry wolf enjoy
His feast of mutton, lamb—and boy.

THE MORAL's this: The man who's wise
Does not defend himself with lies.
Liars are not believed, forsooth,
Even when liars tell the truth.

# The First Butterflies

**By Florence Holbrook**

The Great Spirit thought, "By and by I will make men, but first I will make a home for them. It shall be very bright and beautiful. There shall be mountains and prairies and forests. About it all shall be the blue waters of the sea."

As the Great Spirit had thought, so he did. He gave the earth a soft cloak of green. He made the prairies beautiful with flowers. The forests were bright with birds of many colors, and the sea was the home of many wonderful sea creatures.

"My children will love the prairies, the forests, and the seas," he thought, "but the mountains look dark and cold. They are very dear to me, but how shall I make my children go to them and so learn to love them?"

Long the Great Spirit thought about the mountains. At last, he made many little shining stones. Some were red, some blue, some green, some yellow, and some were shining with all the lovely colors of the beautiful rainbow.

"All my children will love what is beautiful," he thought. "If I hide the bright stones in the seams of the rocks of the mountains, men will come to find them, and they will learn to love my mountains."

When the stones were made and the Great Spirit looked upon their beauty, he said, "I will not hide you all away in the seams of the rocks. Some of you shall be out in the sunshine, so that the little children who cannot go to the mountains shall see your colors."

Then the South Wind came by. As he went, he sang softly of forests flecked with light and shadow, of birds and their nests in the leafy trees. He sang of the moonlight and the starlight. All the wonders of the night, all the beauty of the morning, were in his song.

"Dear South Wind," said the Great Spirit, "here are some beautiful things for you to bear away with you to your summer home. You will love them, and all the little children will love them."

At these words of the Great Spirit, all the stones before him stirred with life and lifted themselves on many-colored wings. They fluttered away in the sunshine, and the South Wind sang to them as they went.

And so it was that the first butterflies came from a beautiful thought of the Great Spirit. In their wings were all the colors of the shining stones that he did not wish to hide away.

## Finding the Author's Words

The author uses some very descriptive words to help you see the things that she writes about. Skim through the story and find and write

1. the sentence that tells that the Great Spirit covered the earth with green trees and grass.

2. two words that tell how the mountains looked before the shining stones were put there.

3. the sentence that tells all the colors of the stones.

4. the word that the author uses to mean holes or spaces between the rocks.

5. the word that tells that the forests were *spotted* with light and shadow.

6. the words that tell what was in the South Wind's song.

7. part of a sentence that tells that the stones moved and then began to fly.

8. the word that tells how the first butterflies *flew*.

# Hiawatha's Childhood

**By Henry Wadsworth Longfellow**

At the door on summer evenings,
Sat the little Hiawatha;
Heard the whispering of the pine-trees,
Heard the lapping of the water,
Sounds of music, words of wonder;
"Minne-wawa!" said the pine-trees,
"Mudway-aushka!" said the water.
Saw the fire-fly, Wah-wah-taysee,
Flitting through the dusk of evening,
With the twinkle of its candle
Lighting up the brakes and bushes,
And he sang the song of children,
Sang the song Nokomis taught him:
"Wah-wah-taysee, little fire-fly,
Little, flitting, white-fire insect,
Little, dancing, white-fire creature,
Light me with your little candle,
Ere upon my bed I lay me,
Ere in sleep I close my eyelids!"

# The Brave Little Tailor

By Jacob and Wilhelm Grimm

## Seven at One Stroke

One fine summer morning, as a little tailor sat by his open window sewing, a farmer's wife came down the street. She was calling, "Good jam! Good jam! Buy my jam!"

The little tailor put his head out of the window and cried, "Come here, my good woman. This is the place to sell your jam."

The woman climbed the three steps to his shop and uncovered the basket in which was a large jar of his favorite jam.

"That smells so good," said the tailor. "I must have a fourth of a pound."

The woman, who had hoped to sell much more, gave him what he wished and went away grumbling. The tailor spread some of the jam on a piece of bread. He placed the bread on a chair near him and began to sew, with his heart full of joy.

"Before I take even one bite," he said, "I must finish this fine woolen coat."

In the meantime the smell of the jam brought many flies to feast upon the sweet. The tailor tried to drive them away, but it was no use. So he ran to the chimney corner and got a piece of cloth.

"Wait and see what I will give you!" he cried, hitting at the flies with the cloth.

In a minute he stopped and counted. To his surprise no fewer than seven flies lay stretched out with their legs in the air. They were quite dead.

"What a fellow am I!" he exclaimed. "Seven at one stroke! The whole town shall hear of this."

Quickly the little tailor cut out a wide belt and sewed on it these words: *Seven at one stroke*. Then snipping the thread, he put on the belt.

"Why not tell the whole world about it?" he asked himself. "Why stop at this town?" He now thought himself much too brave to be a tailor.

Before leaving the house, he looked for something to take with him. All he found was a soft cheese, which he stuck in his pocket. As he went out the door, he spied a bird caught by a bright thread in a clump of bushes. This the tailor placed in his pocket with the cheese. Then he set out, light of heart and of foot.

The road he took led him up a high mountain. When he reached the top, he met a giant.

"Good morning, my friend," said the tailor. "I am out looking for adventures. Will you go along with me?"

The giant was scornful. "Go adventuring with such a wee thing as you! A likely idea!"

"Not so fast," cried the tailor. He unbuttoned his coat and pointed to the belt. "If you can read, that will show you what a man I am."

The giant read, "Seven at one stroke," and thought it must be seven men the tailor had killed.

"Well, now I shall test you," said the giant. "Look here, can you do this?" He took up a large stone and squeezed a drop of water from it.

"Oh, that is nothing!" exclaimed the tailor.

He reached into his pocket and took out the cheese. He squeezed and squeezed until thin milky water ran out of it, crying at the same time, "Beat that, if you can."

The giant knew not what to say. However, he took up another stone and threw it so high that the eye could hardly follow it.

"That is very clever," said the tailor, "but the stone will fall somewhere. I will throw you one that will not come down to earth again."

82

He put his hand into his pocket and, taking out the bird, threw it into the air. The bird soared overhead and soon flew out of sight.

"What do you think of that?" asked the tailor.

"You can throw very well," said the giant. "But can you lift as easily as you can throw?"

He led the little tailor to a forest in which lay a huge tree that had fallen to the ground.

"Now then," he said scornfully. "I'll test you again. If you are as strong as you say, just help me to carry this tree out of the forest."

"Most willingly," answered the little man. "You take the trunk on your shoulders, and I'll take the leaves. They are the heaviest."

The giant lifted the trunk on his shoulders, but the clever little tailor crouched in the branches. The giant started off, not knowing that he was carrying the tailor. He had not gone far, however, when he cried feebly, "I can't take another step."

Then the giant started to put down his heavy load. At this, the little tailor jumped down, seized the tree with both hands, and exclaimed, "Well, you can't be so very strong. I should think you would be able to carry such a tree as this."

The giant was not happy with the outcome of this test but could do nothing about it just then. So he took the tailor home with him to spend the night.

84

Now, the giant lived with many other giants in a great cave, and all the beds were huge. The little tailor didn't like the big bed where he was to sleep. When all was quiet, he crept out of it and curled up in a corner.

In the middle of the night the giant, thinking the tailor was asleep, seized an iron pole. With this he struck a blow at the bed, breaking it.

"Ah," thought he, "I must have killed the little grasshopper. He'll play no more tricks now."

The next morning, when the giants went out into the woods, the tailor walked up to them as brave as ever. It so frightened the giants to see him alive again that they took to their heels, remembering he had killed seven at one stroke.


## More Danger Ahead

The tailor traveled on until he came to the gates of the king's palace. There he lay down on the grass and went to sleep. People passing by him could see the words, *Seven at one stroke,* on his belt. They thought he must be a great soldier, and so they told the king. Then the king sent for the little tailor and asked him to come to the palace.

The tailor was given a fine apartment in the king's palace, but the other servants were afraid of him. They wished him a thousand miles away.

"What might become of us if he were angry with us?" they asked in great excitement. "He can kill seven at one stroke."

They went to the king and told him they were leaving. They would not stay with a man who could kill seven at one stroke. This worried the king, but how could he get the newcomer to leave without making him angry? At last an idea came to him, and he sent for the little tailor.

"In a forest not far from here," he told the tailor, "live two giants so fierce that no one will go into that part of my kingdom. If you can destroy these giants, I will let you marry my daughter and give you half of my kingdom. You shall have a hundred soldiers armed with spears to help you."

The tailor rode off to the forest, the hundred soldiers following after him. When they reached a cottage at the edge of the forest, he asked them to stay behind while he looked for the giants. This they were quite willing to do.

The tailor found the two giants fast asleep under a tree. He ran quickly and filled both his pockets with large stones. Then he climbed up into the tree and let fall one stone after another upon one of the giants.

The giant woke up and gave his friend a rough push. "What do you mean by hitting me?"

"You are dreaming," said the other. "I never touched you."

Grumbling, they went to sleep again, and the tailor threw a heavy stone at the other giant. He woke up in a rage.

"Now it is you who are striking me," he cried gruffly. "What do you mean by it?"

"I never struck you," the first giant growled.

As soon as their eyes were closed again, the tailor threw his largest stone at the first giant, who jumped up in great rage and seized his friend roughly.

"This is too much," he cried, landing a fierce blow on his sleeping friend. So they began to fight in such a rage that they pulled up whole trees by the roots. The battle lasted until both giants lay dead.

The little tailor crept forth from the woods to the cottage where the hundred soldiers waited. "I have made an end of them both," he said.

Then the little tailor went before the king, who said, "There is a fierce unicorn in my forest. It spreads fear over the whole kingdom. You must kill this creature."

"One unicorn will be nothing after two giants," said the tailor, not the least discouraged. "Seven at one stroke, that is the way I work."

He went to the forest, taking with him a rope and an ax. The unicorn was not long in coming. As soon as it saw the tailor, it rushed forward to run him through with its one horn.

The tailor stood quite still and waited for the animal to come nearer. Then he jumped lightly behind the trunk of a large tree. The unicorn ran at the tree with all its might, sticking its horn tightly into the trunk and making itself a prisoner.

The tailor put the rope around the unicorn's neck and chopped off the horn with his ax. Then he led the animal to the king.

The king was still not content. The tailor must now kill a boar that was destroying the forest. The king's hunters would help him.

Off went the tailor, the hunters following him. When they came to the woods, the little man made the others wait as before and went on alone. As soon as the boar caught sight of the tailor, it flew at him, but he was too quick for it. He jumped through the open window of a chapel that stood nearby, and out through another on the other side.

The boar was soon after him, racing into the chapel through the doorway. The tailor, now on the outside, quickly closed the door, and the wild boar found itself a prisoner, for it was unable to jump out of the chapel window.

The little tailor called the hunters and showed them the prisoner. Then he went as before to the king. This time the king had to keep his promise, and the little tailor married the princess. As king and queen, they ruled over half the kingdom and lived happily ever after.

## When Did It Happen?

The following sentences are not in the same order as they are in the story. Can you put them into the correct order? Number your paper from 1 to 9. After each number write the letter of the sentence that should be first, second, and third. Continue until you put all the sentences into the correct order.

a. A king invited the tailor to live in the palace.
b. The king promised to let the tailor marry the princess if he killed the giants.
c. The tailor caught the fierce unicorn.
d. The tailor killed seven flies in one stroke.
e. The tailor trapped the fierce boar that was destroying the forest.
f. The tailor made the two giants destroy each other.
g. The tailor married the princess.
h. A giant decided to test the tailor's strength.
i. The tailor decided to tell the whole world about killing seven with one stroke.

# The Flight of Icarus

**By Sally Benson**

Once upon a time, when the world was young, there lived a very clever man by the name of Daedalus. Now, it happened that Daedalus angered the king of an island and was made a prisoner in a high tower.

Because he was so clever, Daedalus was able to escape from the tower, but he could not escape from the island. The king had every ship that put out to sea watched to make sure that Daedalus did not leave.

Daedalus was not discouraged by this. "The king may rule the land and sea," he said, "but he does not rule the air. I will try that."

Daedalus had a son, a young boy named Icarus. He called Icarus to his hiding place and asked him to gather all the feathers he could find on the rocky shore. As thousands of gulls flew over the island, Icarus soon had a huge pile of feathers.

His father then went to work. He melted some wax, shaped it into a large pair of bird's wings, and covered the wax with large feathers. Then he pressed the smallest feathers into the soft wax with his fingers.

When the wings were finished, Daedalus fastened them to his own shoulders. After one or two efforts, he found himself lifted into the air for one glorious minute. Then down he came. Filled with excitement, he made another pair of wings for his son. They were smaller than his own, but strong and beautiful.

One clear windswept morning the wings were finished, and Daedalus fastened them to the boy's shoulders.

"Watch the gulls in flight, my son," he said. "See how they soar and glide overhead. See how they beat the air steadily without fluttering. What the birds are able to do, surely we can learn to do, now that we have wings like theirs."

Soon Icarus was sure that he could fly. He raised his arms up and down. He ran along the shore, beating his wings as he had seen the gulls do when they wanted to fly into the air. In the next moment he was lifted above the sands and flew out over the shining water.

Daedalus watched the youth proudly, but he was very much worried for the safety of his daring son. He called Icarus to his side and put his arm around him.

"Icarus, my son, we have a good chance to escape, and we are about to make our flight to freedom," he said. "No man has ever traveled through the air before, and I want you to listen carefully to what I am about to tell you. Remember and follow these rules for our flight.

"Do not fly too high, and do not fly too low. If you fly too low, the fog and spray will make your wings heavy and weigh you down. If you fly too high, the blazing sun will melt the wax that holds them together. Keep near me, and you will be safe."

He fastened the wings more tightly to the youth's shoulders. He thought that Icarus looked like a lovely bird, standing in the bright sun, the shining wings on his shoulders. His golden hair was wet with spray, and his eyes dark with excitement.

Daedalus' eyes filled with tears. Then, turning away, he soared upward into the sky, calling to Icarus to follow. From time to time he looked back to see that the boy was safe and to watch how he used his wings in his flight.

They flew across the land to test their wings before setting out across the dark wild sea. Farmers in the fields below stopped their work, and shepherds watched in wonder. They thought Daedalus and Icarus were gods. One of them surely must be Apollo, the sun god.

92

Soon father and son were ready to start out over the sea toward freedom. Icarus, beating his great wings joyfully, felt the cool wind fill them and lift him in glorious flight. He forgot the islands and the sea below him as he flew higher and higher.

His father, flying lower, looked up and called out in fear. He made an effort to follow the boy, but he was heavier, and his wings would not carry him so high. He could not stop, either, because he would have dropped into the sea. He could only fly on and hope that the boy would follow him.

Up and up Icarus soared, through the soft clouds and out again into the blue sky. He was filled with a sense of glorious freedom. He beat his wings wildly so that they would carry him ever higher and closer to the blazing sun.

As Icarus came nearer and nearer to the sun, the air around him grew warmer and warmer. The wax wings became soft and began to melt. Small feathers fell off and floated down, warning Icarus that he was flying too high. But the delighted boy did not notice until

the blazing sun had melted the wax that held all the largest feathers to his wings.

Icarus himself began to fall. Wildly he fluttered his arms, but no feathers were left to hold the air. Down, down he fell with one frightened cry for help.

Daedalus, having lost sight of his son, but hearing the faraway cry, called, "Icarus, my son, where are you?"

Then he turned back in time to see his son falling, straight as an arrow shot from the clouds above, into the sea. Daedalus hurried to save him, but it was too late. Icarus drowned before his father could reach him. Only a few soft feathers floated on the water.

With a sad flutter of wings Daedalus flew on, but the joy of his flight was gone. There was only grief in his heart for the birdlike son who had dared to fly so high in the excitement of his freedom from the earth.

## What Would Have Happened?

Many other things could have happened to Icarus and Daedalus. Read the following questions and write what you think would have happened. You may get ideas from the story. Be ready to share your answers with the class.

1. What do you think would have happened if Icarus had flown very low?

2. What do you think would have happened if Icarus had followed all of the rules that his father gave him?

3. What do you think would have happened if Daedalus had followed his son?

4. What do you think Daedalus would have done if the king had not kept such a careful watch over the island?

# The Pea Blossom

**By Hans Christian Andersen**

There were once five peas in one shell. They were green, and the shell was green, and so they thought that the whole world must be green, and that was just as it should be.

The shell grew, and the peas grew all in a row. The sun shone and warmed the shell. It was pleasant and mild in the bright day and dark at night, just as it should be. The peas, as they sat there, grew bigger and bigger. They became more and more thoughtful, for they felt there must be something for them to do.

"Are we to sit here in this pod forever?" asked one. "It seems to me there must be something outside. I feel sure of it."

Weeks went by. The peas became yellow, and the shell became yellow, too.

"All the world is turning yellow," said they—and perhaps they were right.

Suddenly they felt their shell being pulled from the plant. It was torn off and held in human hands. Then it was slipped into the pocket of a jacket along with other full pods.

"Now we shall soon be let out," said one, and that was just what they all wanted.

"I should like to know which one of us will travel farthest," said the smallest of the five.

"What is to happen will happen," said the largest pea.

"Crack!" went the shell, and the five peas rolled out of the pod into the bright sunshine. There they lay in a child's hand. A little boy was holding them. He said they were fine peas for his pea-shooter. At once, he put one in and shot it out.

"Now I am flying out into the wide world," cried the pea. "Catch me if you can." And he was gone in a moment.

"I shall fly straight to the sun," said the second. And away he went.

"We shall go to sleep wherever we find ourselves," said the next two, "but we shall roll on all the same."

And they did fall to the floor and roll about, but they got into the pea-shooter for all that. "We will go farthest of any," said they.

"What is to happen will happen," exclaimed the last one as he was shot into the air.

Up he flew against an old board under an attic window and fell into a little crack, which was filled with soft earth. The earth covered him, and there he lay—a prisoner indeed, but not unnoticed by God.

"What is to happen will happen," said he to himself.

Within the little attic room lived a poor widow. Each day she went out to do hard rough work to provide for herself and her child. The little daughter had been ill in bed for a whole year. It seemed as if she could neither die nor get well.

"She is going to her little sister," sighed the mother wearily. "I had only two children, and it was not easy to provide for them. The good God provided for one of them by taking her home to Himself. The other was left to me, but I suppose my sick child will go to her sister in heaven."

All day long the sick girl lay quietly and patiently, while her mother went out to earn a little money.

Spring came, and early one morning the sun shone pleasantly through the little window. The sick girl fixed her eyes on the window.

"Oh, Mother!" she exclaimed. "What can that little green thing be that peeps in at the window? It is moving in the wind."

The mother stepped to the window and half opened it. "Oh," she said, "there is a little pea that has taken root and is putting out its green leaves. How did it get into this crack? Well, now, here is a little garden for you to look at."

She moved the sick girl's bed nearer to the window so that the child might see the budding plant. Then the mother went out to her work.

"Mother, I believe I shall get well," said the sick child in the evening. "The sun has shone in here so bright and warm today. The little pea is growing so fast that I feel better too. I think I shall soon be able to go out into the warm sunshine again."

"God grant it!" said the mother, but she did not believe it would be so.

She took a little stick and propped up the green plant so that it would not be broken by the wind. She tied a piece of string to the windowsill and to the upper part of the frame so that the pea might have something around which it could twine as it grew. Indeed, the plant shot up so fast that one could almost see it grow from day to day.

"Look! Here is a flower coming!" said the mother one morning.

At last the widow was beginning to hope that her sick child might indeed get well. She remembered that for some time the child had spoken more cheerfully. During the last few days she had raised herself in bed in the morning to look with sparkling eyes at her little garden which had but one plant.

A week later the child sat up for the first time by the open window. For a whole hour she sat there happily and content in the warm sunshine. The window was open, while outside grew the little plant and on it a pink pea blossom in full bloom. The little maiden bent down and gently kissed the delicate leaves. This day was like a festival to her.

"Our heavenly Father Himself has planted that pea and made it to grow to bring joy to you and hope to me, my blessed child," said the happy mother. She smiled at the flower as if it had been an angel from God.

But what became of the other peas? Three of them were, in time, eaten by the pigeons. The fourth fell into a gutter and lay there in the water until it burst.

But the fifth—well, at the open window of the little attic room stood the young girl, with sparkling eyes and the rosy glow of health upon her cheeks. She folded her delicate hands over the pea blossom and thanked God for what He had done.

## Thinking about the Story

Think carefully about each of the following questions and then write your answers.

1. Read page 95, paragraph 6. What two words show you that a *person* pulled the pod off a vine?

2. Now read page 96, paragraph 2. Who do you imagine this little boy was?

3. Why would the peas think that the world was yellow? Do you think they were right?

4. What did the largest pea say three times? What do you think he meant by this?

5. Read page 97, paragraph 1, to find out how long the little girl had been ill. What do you think could have been wrong with her?

6. The author does not give the little girl a name. What name would you give her?

7. What do you think happened to the little girl after she was well and able to go outside?

# Limericks

There was a Young Lady of Norway,
Who casually sat in a doorway;
    When the door squeezed her flat,
    She exclaimed, "What of that?"
This courageous Young Lady of Norway.

**By Edward Lear**

There was an Old Man with a beard,
Who said, "It is just as I feared!—
    Two Owls and a Hen,
    Four Larks and a Wren
Have all built their nests in my beard."

**By Edward Lear**

There was an old man of Peru,
Who dreamt he was eating his shoe.
    He woke in the night
    In a terrible fright—
And found it was perfectly true!

**Author Unknown**

101

# Books to Enjoy

*East of the Sun and West of the Moon and Other Tales,* collected by P. C. Asbjornsen and Jorgen E. Moe.

If you like the story about the North Wind, you will enjoy these twelve tales from Norway. You will not find fairies in any of the tales, but you will find an enchanted world of witches, giants, kings, queens, and magic in many forms.

*Fables from Aesop,* retold by James Reeves.

Here old fables are told in a simple way that makes them fun to read. There are many lessons to be learned from the greedy fox, the patient crow, and the wise old mouse.

*Tales from Grimm,* retold by Wanda Gág.

Many of these seventeen fairy tales will be new to you; others you will enjoy reading again. *Favorite Fairy Tales Told in Germany,* by Virginia Haviland is a smaller and more simply told collection of tales from the Grimm brothers.

*Seven Tales by H. C. Andersen,* retold by Eva Le Gallienne.

Here are stories such as "The Ugly Duckling" and "The Steadfast Tin Soldier." The stories are simply told and are beautifully illustrated by the well-known artist, Maurice Sendak.

*Hans Andersen, Son of Denmark,* by Opal Wheeler. ·

The lanky, awkward Hans grows to become one of the world's greatest storytellers. Here is his life story, as well as six of his own lovely tales.

*Favorite Fairy Tales Told in England,* by Virginia Haviland.

Six old favorites, such as "Dick Whittington," and "Jack and the Beanstalk," and "Cap o' Rushes," are retold in a lively and easy-to-read way.

# Building Our Land

# Keep Up Your Courage

**By Alice Dalgliesh**

Sarah lay on a quilt under a tree. The darkness was all around her, but through the branches she could see one bright star. It was comfortable to look at.

The spring night was cold, and Sarah drew her warm cloak close. That was comfortable, too. She thought of how her mother had put it around her the day she and her father started out on this long, hard journey.

"Keep up your courage," her mother had said, fastening the cloak under Sarah's chin. "Keep up your courage, Sarah Noble!"

And, indeed, Sarah needed to keep up her courage, for she and her father were going all the way into the wilderness of Connecticut to build a house.

Finally they had come to the last day of the journey. The Indian trail had been narrow; the hills went up and down, up and down. Sarah and her father were tired, and even Thomas, the brown horse, walked wearily.

By late afternoon they would be home. Home? No, it wasn't really home, just a place out in the wilderness. But after a while it would be home; John Noble told Sarah it would be. His voice kept leading her on.

"Now we must be about two miles away."

"Now it is surely a mile . . . only a mile."

Sarah's tired feet seemed to dance. She picked some wild flowers and stuck them in the harness behind Thomas's ear.

"You must be well dressed, Thomas," she said. "We are coming home."

She put a pink flower on her own dress and her feet danced along again. Then suddenly she stopped.

"Father, if there is no house, where shall we live?"

Her father smiled down at her. "I have told you. . . ."

"Then tell me again. I like to hear."

"I hope to find a cave in the side of a hill," he said. "I will make a hut for us, and a fence around it. Then you and Thomas and I will live there until the house is built. Though Thomas will have to help me with the building."

Sarah laughed. "Thomas cannot build a house!" She had a funny picture in her mind of solemn, long-faced Thomas carefully putting the logs in place.

"He can drag logs," her father said. "Soon we shall have a fine house."

Now they had come to the top of a long, steep hill and they stopped at a place where there were not many trees, only bushes and coarse grass.

"This is one of the bare places," John Noble said.

"The Indians have cleared it for a hunting ground."

Sarah looked around her fearfully. Behind the bushes something stirred. . . .

"A deer," said her father, and raised his gun. But Sarah clung to him.

"No, Father, no! Do not shoot it!"

"But we must have meat. . . ."

"Not now, not now," Sarah begged. "Its eyes are so gentle, Father."

"Well . . ." said John Noble. But he did not shoot. The deer rushed away, its white tail showing like a flag. Then Sarah drew a long breath and looked down.

Below there was a valley. "And you would see the Great River if it were not for the trees," her father said.

Sarah looked and looked and filled her mind with the beauty of it. It was a beauty that would stay with her all her life. Beyond the valley there were green hills, and beyond . . . and beyond . . . and beyond . . . more hills of a strange, soft, and misty blue.

The trees were the dark green of firs and the light green of birches in springtime. And now they were friendly. They were not like the angry dark trees that had seemed to stand in their path as they came.

"I do like it," Sarah said. "And I do not see any Indians."

"The Indians are by the Great River," her father said. "And I have told you, Sarah, they are good Indians."

John Noble took Sarah's small, cold hand in his.

"There are people in this world who do not help others along the way, Sarah, while there are those who do. In our home all will be treated with kindness— always, Sarah. The Indians, too, and they will not harm us."

Now Sarah held her courage a little more firmly. She also held tightly to her father's hand. And so they came, with Thomas, down the long hill into the place that would be their home.

It was a fair piece of land with the trees already cleared. Men had come over from Milford, on the coast, to buy the land from the Indians. They had cleared it and divided it into plots for the houses. The land sloped down to the Great River, and beyond the river were the Indian fields.

It was in the hill across the river that Sarah and her father found a place hollowed out, that would do for the night.

"And tomorrow I will make it larger and build a shed and a fence," John Noble said.

They took from Thomas the heavy load he had been carrying—bedding and pots, seeds for planting, tools, and warm clothes for the weather that would be coming.

For some days John Noble was busy making the cave a good place to live. He built a shed with a strong fence around it. He made, too, rough beds of logs, and a table and stools. Sarah took delight in it all.

But after it was done, he said to her, "I must begin the work on the house. It should be finished before winter. You will not mind staying here, Sarah, while Thomas and I work?"

Sarah did mind, but she did not say so. There was still the question of Indians. On the hill and along the river they could see the bark-covered houses. People

moved about among the houses, but no Indians had come near the cave. She knew, though, that her father had spoken with some of the men.

She did not want her father to go, but the house must be built. So she looked at him steadily and said, "I will stay here, Father." But to herself she was saying, "Keep up your courage, Sarah Noble. Keep up your courage!"

Then John Noble and Thomas went across the river at a place where it was not deep. They went on up the hill, and Sarah was alone. For a little while she did not know what to do. Then she took out the Bible they had brought with them. It was a book full of wonderful stories. Which should she read? She liked the story of Sarah, whose namesake she was. Sarah had a son named Isaac. That was a scary story, but it came out all right in the end.

Then there was the story of David and how he killed the giant. . . . Oh, it was hard to choose.

Sarah sat on a stool at the entrance to the shed, the Bible on her lap. So she had often sat and read to her doll, Arabella, and to her little sister, who never *would* listen. Here there was not anyone to listen—not anyone, not even Arabella, for there had been no room to bring her.

The early June air was mild, but Sarah felt suddenly that she needed her cloak. So she got it, and sat down again.

No one to listen—but she would read to herself. She opened the Bible and there was one of the stories she loved best of all.

It was the story of the boy Samuel and of how the Lord called to him in the night. Sarah thought of the Lord as a kind old man like her grandfather. Her mother said no one knew how He looked, but Sarah was sure *she* knew. She wished He would speak to her as He had to Samuel. That would be exciting. What in the world would she answer?

Sarah read on and on. And then the sounds began. There was a rustling and a sound of feet coming quietly nearer and nearer. . . .

Sarah held tightly to the book and pulled her cloak around her. Rustle—rustle. . . . Suddenly Sarah saw a bright eye peering at her through a chink in the log fence.

INDIANS! They were all around her; some of them crowded in the opening of the palisade. But they were young Indians, not any older than she was. Still, there

110

were many of them. . . . Sarah kept as still as a rabbit in danger. The children came in, creeping nearer, creeping nearer, like small brown field mice, until they were all around Sarah, looking at her.

Sarah closed the book and sat very still. Then she remembered what her father had said as they stood on the hill.

"Good morning," she said politely, "you are welcome to our house."

The Indian children stared at her. Then they came nearer. Soon Sarah found that all around her was a ring of children, standing and sitting, staring, staring with their dark eyes.

The children stared; Sarah began to feel as if their eyes were going all the way through her.

*Keep up your courage, Sarah Noble.* She thought the words to herself. Here she was in the wilderness with all these Indians around her. She wished the Lord would speak to her as He had to young Samuel. He would tell her what to do.

The Lord did not speak out loud, or at least Sarah did not hear Him. But all at once she knew what to do. She opened the book and began to read to the children. They came nearer and nearer.

*They like the story*, Sarah thought. *They will not hurt me because they like the story.*

She read and read, and the children listened, because the sound of her voice was strange and pleasant.

Then the story was over and Sarah closed the Bible. Still the children sat and stared and said not a word.

"My name," said Sarah clearly, "is Sarah Noble."

One of the boys said something; then another spoke. Sarah did not understand a word of their strange talk.

"How foolish," she said aloud, "why can't you speak English?"

Perhaps some of her impatience crept into her voice, for the spell was broken. Like the deer when her father lifted the gun, the children were off and away.

Sarah sat there by herself and now she really felt alone.

"Oh," she said to herself. "I wish they would come again!" And she shook her head. "For shame, Sarah Noble, I fear you were not polite. Perhaps they will never come back."

The Indian children did come, again and again. Sarah soon lost all fear of them, and they of her.

## Reading between the Lines

Without the author telling you in so many words, can you discover what characters are like by what they do or say? The author does not exactly tell us the following things, but by reading between the lines, you can tell that they are true.

1. Nowhere in the story does the author say that Sarah liked animals very much. Write two things that she did to show that this is true.

2. The author does not say that Sarah's family was a good Christian family. Write at least two things that show that they were.

3. The author does not say that there were many hardships in these early days. Write at least two things that show that this is true.

112

# New Frontiers

**By James Daugherty**

Trapper and plainsman and wrangler,
Rustlers and mountain men
Have ridden into the sunset
And pass not this way again.
Let us pause where you passed, to remember,
Let us not too soon forget:
There are new frontiers of freedom,
High goals that are not won yet.

# A Boy on a Raft

**By Mary Synon**

## Indians

Day after day, as the raft went down the Ohio River, Tom Fay stood at its bow with a gun in his hand.

"Looking for Indians?" the men on the raft would ask him.

"Looking for Indians," the boy would answer.

The men laughed. There was so little danger of the Indians firing on the raft while the boat stayed in the wide Ohio River. The danger would come, they knew, when they turned into the narrow Salt River.

The raft was taking a load of iron kettles to Kentucky. There, on the Salt River, the kettles would be used in making salt, which the settlers needed so badly.

They passed many other rafts on the wide Ohio. In those days many people traveled on rafts. With them they carried furniture, tools, horses, and cattle. Like Tom and his father, the people were going to settle in new country—the frontier, as Tom's father called it.

As they passed the other rafts the men waved and shouted. Tom waved harder than anyone else, but he never let go of his gun. Even when he slept, he kept it beside him.

"Whom are you guarding?" teased one of the men.

"My father," Tom answered.

All the men laughed except Tom's father. "The boy is right," he said. "We are partners. I guard him, and he guards me. Tom's mother died many years ago. Now we have no one but each other and God."

"That makes a big army," one of the men said.

"There is no bigger army," replied Tom's father.

God would save them from the Indians, Tom was sure. He was so sure that he was a little disappointed that they had heard no war cry as they went down the Ohio.

"Why would the Indians want to shoot at us?" Tom asked Jim Hawkins, the man who steered the boat.

"Some white men have lied to them and have stolen from them," explained Jim. "They imagine we are all alike, and so they shoot first now."

Tom frowned. "If the Indians shoot at us, I will certainly shoot back."

"That is big talk for a little boy," one of the boatmen joked.

"I am a big boy!" cried Tom angrily.

Soon the raft came to the Salt River. It was narrow and flowed between banks covered with bushes. Early one morning Tom heard a strange sound.

"Turkey's gobble," one of the men exclaimed.

Tom's father shook his head. "That does not sound to me like a turkey's gobble."

The other men laughed at him as they headed the raft nearer the riverbank. A fat turkey would make a good dinner. Two men jumped from the raft to the shore and ran up the bank. The others tied the raft to a tree.

116

Suddenly the sound of shots rang out. "Turkeys!" shouted the men on the raft. Then more shots sounded.

"Indians!" cried Tom's father as he drew Tom close to him. "Do not shoot until they come near."

The two men who had gone after the turkeys raced down the riverbank, followed by howling Indians. The two men were killed before they could reach the raft. The men on the raft began to fire their rifles. Tom lifted his rifle and fired, too.

The bullets of the Indians began to strike near the raft. A man fell. Another fell. The other men and Tom kept firing, but the Indians kept coming nearer to the raft. Inch by inch, they came through the water. In another moment, Tom thought, they would jump up on it.

"O dear God, save us," he kept praying.

Suddenly the Indians fell back. They gathered on the shore and kept on firing. The raft was still tied to the tree on the shore. Someone must cut the rope that held it to the tree. Unless they could get the raft away, everyone on it would be killed.

Jim Hawkins looked at the line of empty kettles between the men and the rope. "No chance," he sighed. "The kettles are so low that anyone who crawled behind them could be seen and killed before he reached the rope."

"I could do it," exclaimed Tom.

"No, no," his father said quickly.

"Please, Father," begged the boy, "let me do it. I am so much smaller than anyone else that the Indians may not see me. Let me try!"

Tom's father could see that his son was right. It was their only chance. "God keep you!" he whispered.

Tom put down his rifle and slipped the long knife from his belt. Slowly he crawled along the deck behind the kettles. The Indians saw him, and shots whistled over his head. Tom knew that as long as he stayed behind the kettles, the Indians could not shoot low enough to hit him. Just beyond the last kettle there was an open space which must be crossed before he could reach the rope.

Could he finish his task before the Indians shot him?

With a knife in his hand and a prayer in his heart, he crawled out into the open space. It was better, he thought, not to move in a straight line. He crawled, zigzagging across the space, until he reached the rope.

Quickly he cut it. Then he began to creep back toward the safety of the kettles.

Shots rang over him. Bullets rattled against the iron kettles. Bullets ripped up the wood of the boat deck. Bravely the boy moved forward until he came to the kettles. Then he crawled faster to where the men waited.

"Good boy!" they cried.

"Thanks be to God!" said his father.

Slowly the raft began to move away from the shore. Jim took a pole and used it to speed the raft. Tom's father took another pole and pushed with all his might. The raft slowly moved up the river.

# Alone in the Woods

For a while the Indians kept firing. Then they stopped suddenly.

"Are we safe?" Tom asked.

"I am afraid we are not," said Jim wearily. "There is a very narrow bend in the river just beyond those trees. The Indians have gone there to wait for us. There is only one way we can escape them. We can take a chance by running the raft to shore here. Then we can try to make our way by foot through the woods to the settlement."

"Let us try," said Tom's father.

As the raft came close to the shore, Jim Hawkins said, "We cannot go together. Each one of us must find his way."

"God keep you," said Tom's father as they left the boatmen.

"And you," replied Jim.

Tom and his father crept up the steep riverbank and moved into the dark woods. For a little while Tom thought he saw an Indian behind every tree. Then they heard a single shot fired nearby and more firing to the east. Tom turned and saw that his father had suddenly become very pale.

"What is the matter?" he asked him.

"They hit me," said his father.

"The Indians?" Tom exclaimed. "You mean they shot you?"

"Yes, Tom," his father gasped feebly. "I cannot go any farther." He opened his coat, and Tom saw that his shirt was red with blood. "I shall have to rest."

He sank down beside a tree. His hands trembled, and his head drooped. "Tom," he said, "you were a brave boy today on the raft. You must prove once more that you are brave.

"In the settlement there is a missionary priest called Father Francis. You must find your way to him. Tell him that a man needs him. He will come back with you."

"How far is the settlement?" Tom asked his father.

"I do not know." His father shook his head weakly and pointed toward the south. "Go that way."

Tom turned so that his father would not see that he was crying. He set off toward the south, leaving his partner behind. He had to go slowly, for there was no path to follow.

He trudged on and on. Sometimes he wondered if he were going the right way. He trembled at every sound he heard. After a while his feet ached so badly that he took off his moccasins and tied them on his knees. Then he crawled along the ground.

It began to grow dark in the woods. There were many sounds among the trees—birds flying, squirrels running, branches snapping in the wind. Each sound frightened Tom until he knew what it was. Any sound might be an Indian moving through the forest.

Peering through the trees, Tom saw fires. There must have been a hundred fires burning in the darkness. They were the fires at the salt licks, the places where men were getting the salt. The fires were still a long way off, and Tom was too weak to go farther.

Then, near him, he heard the sound of a horse's hoofs. They were beating down upon the forest trail. He must be near that trail. He moved as fast as he could toward the sound and shouted. The sound stopped.

"Who is it?" a voice asked.

"Tom, I'm Tom Fay," the boy called. "Can you tell me where I can find the priest, Father Francis, for my father?"

"I am Father Francis," the voice replied. A big man, leading his horse, came through the darkness. "Where are you?" he asked.

"Here, Father," Tom cried.

The missionary bent down over him. "You poor lad," he said. "Where is your father?" He shook his head when Tom told him.

"We must tell the men at the salt licks about the Indians," Father Francis said. "Then I will take you back with me to find your father."

He boosted Tom up on his horse and jumped up behind him.

"Everything is going to be all right, Tom," he promised as they rode toward the blazing fires.

The rest of the night was like a dream to Tom. The crowd at the fires shouted as Father Francis told them Tom's story and rushed off to rescue the men at the river. Father Francis turned his horse and rode back through the woods.

It was almost morning when they found Tom's father. He was weak and cold. He was very, very ill, but Father Francis said he would get well.

In a little while the men who had come from the salt licks arrived. They made a stretcher of pine branches for the wounded man and started out through the woods toward the settlement.

"People are good to one another here," Tom said as Father Francis boosted him once more upon the horse.

"Yes, people are good," smiled Father Francis. "That is what makes the frontier a good place to live. We are building a nation, Tom, and the only way to build a great nation is by the goodness of its people."

## Using the Pictures

1. There are five pictures in this story. Study the pictures and think about the main idea of each picture. Now number your paper from 1 to 5. Write a good title for each of the five pictures. Remember that your title should tell the main idea of each picture.

2. Look carefully at the picture on pages 114 and 115. The people on the raft are carrying with them tools, furniture, and all the things that they will need to make a new home in the wilderness. Make a list of all of these things that you can see. Then write sentences telling how each of these things might be used by the early settlers in the new frontier.

3. In the picture on pages 114 and 115, you can not see *all* the things the settlers are carrying. The following things may have been important to some of these settlers: a clock, quilts, seed corn, medicines, a treasured book, or a rose bush. Write a sentence for each of these six things, telling why each may have been very important to early settlers.

# The Answered Prayer

By Sister Mary Henry, O.P.

"Good night, Mother!"

"Good night, Isaac!"

The door closed softly, and Isaac's mother left him. The boy turned back to his studies. As he worked, the soft spring breeze which came through the open window made his candle flicker.

He rose to shut the window and stopped for a minute to look at the town below. The little French village lay sleeping in the moonlight. The steeple of the church seemed to be tipped in silver.

The boy wished he could stay to admire the beauty, but both his time and the candle were precious. He closed the window and returned to his books.

As time passed, the candle burned low. When his lessons were ready for the next day, Isaac blew out the light and knelt to say his prayers. He held a little wooden crucifix in his hands and often bent to kiss the Sacred Wounds.

Isaac Jogues prayed with all his heart, "Oh, my God! How much You suffered for our souls! Dear Jesus, teach me how to suffer for You. Take my soul, my hands, my head, and my heart for Your work!"

Isaac Jogues was in many ways like other boys of his age, but in one way he was very different. He had a secret wish, which only his mother knew. He wanted to be a missionary. His goal was to travel to North America to teach the Indians about God. He knew that a missionary must be brave and kind and able to stand great hardships, and so he tried to train himself for this in his daily life.

The years passed quickly. Isaac became a Jesuit priest, and at last the day came when he was to offer his First Holy Mass. How happy his mother was to receive Holy Communion from her son's hands! But the good woman was sad, too, for she had learned that her son was to sail at once far, far across the sea, to the Jesuit mission in North America.

Father Jogues wrote a letter to his mother once each year from the New World. In his first letter he told her about the journey to the mission where he was to stay until he had learned the languages of the Huron Indians. At this time there were only twenty priests to work among thirty thousand Huron Indians.

126

On the journey to the mission, Father Jogues met with many hardships. He had to sit for hours in the canoe without moving. Mush, unsalted and without sugar, was the only food. At night he slept on the hard ground or on the rocky shore.

The Huron mission was called St. Joseph's. Here the missionaries lived in a bark-covered house with an opening in the roof to serve as a chimney and as a window. When it was closed at night, the smoke filled the house and made their eyes ache.

There was much sickness among the Indians, and many children died. The priests tried to baptize all of these little ones. Long afterward it was a comfort to Father Jogues to recall how many of these souls he had helped to reach heaven.

It was a good thing that Father Jogues knew how to study because the Huron language is very difficult. He learned it at last and was then able to begin his work of visiting and teaching the Indians.

One day, when he was traveling through the forest with a group of Christian Indians and a couple of young Frenchmen, the party was attacked by a band of Iroquois Indians. French traders had fought the Iroquois, and from that day the Iroquois had been the enemies of the French. The priest could have escaped, but he stayed to help the young Frenchmen and was taken prisoner.

Father Jogues was beaten and tortured. His fingers were torn, and a spear was run through the palms of his hands. He was dragged from one Indian village to another. He suffered from cold, and most of the time he was hungry.

Through all that time, the good priest prayed. When the Indians made him run between two lines of warriors who beat him with clubs, he prayed. He called the lines of cruel Indian warriors "the narrow road to Heaven."

For months the Iroquois held Father Jogues prisoner. As he went through the woods he carved the Sign of the Cross and the name of Jesus upon the trees. He made many efforts to win the cruel Indians for Christ, but they would not even listen to the holy priest.

At last the prisoner was brought to a Dutch settlement in what is now the state of New York. Kindhearted people heard of the sufferings of the French priest and found a way to help him to escape to a boat in the Hudson River.

After a long and dangerous journey, Father Jogues reached the French coast. Dressed in rags, weak and ill from the hardships he had suffered, he made his way on foot to a Jesuit school. His Jesuit brothers did not recognize him when he knocked at the gates, but they took him in.

When they heard that he came from the New World, they asked, "Do you know Father Isaac Jogues?"

"I am he," he answered humbly.

That night was a night of joy and thanksgiving in the Jesuit school.

The next spring, Father Jogues was happy to be sent again to his Indians in the New World. He lived there in great danger for several years, visiting many parts of the country and helping traders as well as Indians.

Once again he was taken prisoner by the Iroquois and held as a slave for a long time. He was beaten and wounded and suffered much until one day an angry Indian killed him.

The work of Saint Isaac Jogues was done. God had heard the prayer of the little boy who had once asked Him to take his soul, his hands, his heart, and his head to do His work on earth.

## Using the Alphabet

The alphabet can be said in special ways, as:

A is for the APRON that Mother wears.

B is for the BABY that smiles in his crib.

Try to write something like this, using the letters in the name of Isaac Jogues. You may choose ideas from the pairs of words listed below or you may think of your own words. You may wish to start like this:

I is for the IROQUOIS for whom Isaac Jogues prayed.

I (Indians, Iroquois)  J (Jesuit, journey)
S (souls, Sacred Wounds)  O (offering, order)
A (adventure, America)  G (God, goodness)
A (attack, anger)  U (unkindness, understanding)
C (Christ, Crucifix)  E (enemies, escape)
S (slave, Sign of the Cross)

# Knowest Thou Isaac Jogues?

**By Francis W. Grey**

A wayworn pilgrim from a distant shore
　　Knocked at the convent gate at early day,
　　Then waited patiently: "Whence com'st thou, pray?"
The brother asked. "From Canada"; the door
Was opened wide in welcome; faint and sore
　　With many a toil he seemed, and long the way
　　That he had journeyed; greatly marveled they
To see the cruel wounds and the scars he bore.

"Com'st thou from Canada?" the Rector said,—
　　Vested was he for Mass, yet came to see
The traveled guest, who answered, "Yes"; they led
　　To welcome food and rest; then asked, "Maybe
Thou knowest Isaac Jogues?" He bowed his head,
　　As one who shunneth honor—"I am he."

# The Big Boy

**By Katherine Rankin**

## THE PLAYERS

NARRATOR      CARL
THE BIG BOY      CARL'S MOTHER

## Act I

NARRATOR. Learning to read and write was a hard task in a frontier school. One child might never have learned without the help of *the big boy*.

Carl was the child. He went to school in Indiana—the ABC school which stood in a clearing surrounded by deep woods. Carl had told himself that he was not afraid of anything, but he always ran fast through the forest. He had heard stories of the dangerous bears and wolves that might be lurking there. When he came to the clearing and near the school, he went slowly. Carl was more afraid of school than he was of animals that might be in the forest.

One day Carl was walking home from school. He was walking—not running—through the forest. His head was held low, and he was thinking about what had happened to him in school that day.

VOICE OF THE BIG BOY (*shouting*). Get back, get back!

NARRATOR. A large tree fell with a crash almost at Carl's feet. It would have struck him if he had not heard the warning and jumped back. Then Carl saw the big boy. Carl had seen him before, always working with the ax, but Carl had never spoken to him.

THE BIG BOY (*swinging the ax over his shoulder*). You had better take care, young one. Keep your eyes open or you may be hurt.

CARL. I had my eyes open, but I was thinking about something else.

THE BIG BOY. What were you thinking about?

NARRATOR. There was something about the boy's voice that made Carl want to tell him the truth.

CARL. I was thinking about school.

THE BIG BOY (*looking very interested*). Oh, that's fine, just fine.

CARL (*scornfully*). It is *not* fine. You don't understand. I do not like school. I would rather be whipped than go to school.

THE BIG BOY. Well, you are a strange young one. You should be glad you have the chance to go to school. I wish I could have gone longer than I did.

CARL. It might be simple or easy for one who can read English printing and write English letters. I can't!

THE BIG BOY. Do you mean that you can't read or write at all?

CARL. Oh, I can make the German letters that my father and mother know. I can read only one book—a German book that my father brought with him from the old country.

THE BIG BOY. Oh! Are you German?

CARL. I'm American now.

THE BIG BOY. Do your folks read or write English?

CARL. They speak English, but they cannot read it or write it.

THE BIG BOY. Why do you not learn to read and write in school?

CARL. Oh, I try. I try my best to do all that the schoolmaster tells me to do. But I can't. Just today a horrible thing happened to me. A very, very little boy was reading. When he finished, the schoolmaster called on me. I looked at the strange English printing, and not one word could I read. It was awful! All the children stared and laughed at me until I could no longer keep tears from my eyes. Oh, I shall never go back to that school again.

THE BIG BOY (*seeing the tears swelling again in Carl's eyes*). You *really* want to learn to read, don't you?

CARL. Oh, yes, more than anything else, but I will never learn in that school. The schoolmaster has so many to teach that he cannot take time for me.

THE BIG BOY. Well, now, that's too bad. (*He pauses to swing his ax down and leans on it.*) I taught myself most of what I can read. Maybe you could teach yourself.

CARL. No, I cannot. I do not know enough English to even begin.

THE BIG BOY. Then, maybe I can teach you.

135

CARL. You could? Could you teach me how to read books and to write letters?

THE BIG BOY. I could try. Where do you live?

CARL (*pointing to the trail that ran to a little clearing*). Just beyond these woods.

THE BIG BOY. Run home now. I shall come to your house as soon as I have chopped this tree into logs.

CARL (*anxiously*). Today?

THE BIG BOY (*laughing and shaking his head*). I do not work that fast. No, young one! Tomorrow.

## Act II

NARRATOR. Just as he said he would, the tall, thin boy came to Carl's cabin the very next day. It was soon after Carl had come home from school.

CARL (*to his mother*). He has come to teach me how to read and write English.

CARL'S MOTHER. Oh, thank you, thank you. He has so much trouble with the reading and writing, but I know that he is not a dull boy.

THE BIG BOY. I am sure of that, ma'am. Now we shall get to work.

CARL. Shall we sit at the table?

THE BIG BOY. There is no light on the table. Why don't we sit on the floor by the fire? This is the way I read. (*He flings his long body down on the cabin floor and sets a book against a log.*) Come on, Carl. Let us attack it before it attacks us. Do you know this word?

CARL. No.

136

THE BIG BOY. Well, that word is "basket." B–a–s–k–e–t. It was what Red Riding Hood carried when she went to her grandmother's house.

CARL. Oh, my mother told me that story, but I cannot read it.

THE BIG BOY. You will. Now, you look hard at the page. I shall put my finger on each word as I read. I shall say the word. You say the word after me. Then you will remember that the word you say and the word on the page are the same.

NARRATOR. For more than an hour they lay on the floor before the fire. The big boy read the words on each page slowly, carefully, and Carl said them after him.

THE BIG BOY. Now, you say a line by yourself.

CARL (*reading very slowly*). The—young—lad—looked—at—his—mother.

THE BIG BOY. That is good. You will learn, young one. You will learn. It is getting dark outside now, and I must go. Tomorrow I will come back.

NARRATOR. Almost every school day the big boy came to Carl's cabin. He came after he had finished chopping wood in the forest. In the cabin he read with Carl by the fire. Every day Carl could read a little better, for he studied his reading after the big boy had gone home.

After a while he could read alone some of the easy stories. Whenever he found he could read a whole page without help, he would run to his mother and read it for her. In time, he could read from a book of stories that the teacher gave him. One day he was reading one of the stories for the big boy.

CARL (*reading from the book*). George Washington was the first President of the United States. (*He pauses and peers up from his reading.*) What is a President?

THE BIG BOY. He's the man who runs our nation, the way Mr. White runs the woolen factory near the river.

CARL. Does he tell everyone what to do?

THE BIG BOY. Not exactly. He tells people what the nation *should* do.

CARL. Is it hard to be President?

THE BIG BOY. Well, the first hard thing is to be elected.

CARL. Could I be President?

THE BIG BOY. No, Carl, you were not born in this country.

CARL. But I am an American!

THE BIG BOY. You *will be* an American as soon as your father can make himself a citizen.

CARL. He is making himself a citizen now. In a little while he will be able to vote. Even before he votes, he is a good American. He does what Americans do. He believes like Americans.

THE BIG BOY. So do you, Carl. That's what counts.

CARL. Were you born in this country?

THE BIG BOY. Yes, I was born in Kentucky. I came here to Indiana when I was seven years old. That was only two years before my mother died.

CARL. Are you going to stay here?

THE BIG BOY. I don't know. After my mother died my father married again. My new mother is a kind woman. She takes good care of the family. We are poor, and so I have had to work to help my family. But soon I will be able to go out to earn my own living.

CARL. What do you want to do when you are a man?

THE BIG BOY. I do not rightly know yet. But I should like to do something to help people.

CARL. Could you be President?

THE BIG BOY (*laughing*). What chance would I have?

CARL'S MOTHER. You would make a good President.

THE BIG BOY (*politely*). Thank you, ma'am.

NARRATOR. Carl enjoyed these talks with the big boy almost as much as he did his lessons. The older boy had done far more for Carl than just teaching him to read. He had also made Carl feel that he really belonged to this new country.

139

Perhaps, because the big boy was such a good teacher, as well as a friend, Carl had learned fast. The schoolmaster once told Carl that he was one of the best students in the school. The children no longer laughed at him. He was very happy.

Only one thing bothered him. He knew that his friend would be leaving sometime soon. Carl no longer needed his help in reading and writing, but he did need his friendship. Carl was thinking about this when his friend walked up to the cabin one day.

THE BIG BOY (*slowly*). I have come to say good-by. I am going away early tomorrow morning.

CARL (*looking at his mother and then at his friend*). Maybe I can go with you.

THE BIG BOY. You are not big enough, young one, or old enough. You must stay here with your own folks. Perhaps, I shall come back sometime. But now I think it is time that I should go out in the world.

CARL. What shall you do?

THE BIG BOY. I shall work. I shall keep on reading and studying. A man cannot get far without study.

CARL'S MOTHER. We shall miss you. Carl will never forget you.

THE BIG BOY (*putting his hand on Carl's head*). Keep on with your studying, young one. Maybe someday you'll be the governor of this state, even if you cannot be President.

NARRATOR. The tall boy walked off through the woods. Carl and his mother stood in the doorway and watched him as long as they could see him.

CARL. He will be a great man.

CARL'S MOTHER (*shaking her head*). He is already great, that Abraham Lincoln.


## What Do You Think Happened?

You know what happened to one of the characters—Abraham Lincoln. Do you wonder what happened to Carl? Perhaps you think he became a farmer or head of the woolen factory. Maybe you think he went to college and then became a teacher or the governor of the state. Do you suppose he ever saw Abraham Lincoln again? How do you suppose Carl felt when Lincoln became President of the United States?

Write a short story telling what you think happened to Carl. Your story may begin like this:

"Oh, I'll never be able to read," said Billy.

"At one time I thought I would never be able to read," said Master Carl, the head teacher of the ABC school. "This is the way I learned to read. . . ."

# Stagecoach to Santa Fe

**By Mary Synon**

Molly was happy and excited as she waited for the stagecoach to Santa Fe. The young girl had no idea of the adventure that awaited her on the trip. That was not the reason she was excited. It was because she was going to join her parents.

Her father, an officer in the Army of the United States, had been sent to Santa Fe. Her mother had gone there earlier, and now Molly was going on the long trip by herself.

As Molly waited on the street corner in Trinidad, a mining town in Colorado, she watched all the people who had gathered around. She wondered which ones were going to Santa Fe and which ones were only there to say good-by to friends.

In the crowd there were two Catholic Sisters whom everyone but Molly seemed to know. One of the Sisters was tall and blue-eyed. Although she smiled at those who spoke to her, she spoke very little.

The other Sister was little and dark-eyed. She talked most of the time, waving her hands as she did. People kept greeting her, and Molly wondered how this Sister knew so many people. She wondered why these people all wished to talk with her.

The girl was staring at the Sister when an old man near her spoke. "You are a stranger here, aren't you?" he asked. When Molly nodded, he said, "That is why you do not know Sister Blandina."

"Sister Blandina?" Molly repeated.

"She's the little Sister. She's leaving Trinidad. The town won't be the same without her," the old man said.

"Why? What has she done?" the girl asked.

"What has she *not* done!" exclaimed Molly's new friend. "She has taught in the Sisters' school, but that has been only part of her work. I am not a Catholic, but I would vote any day to make Sister Blandina the mayor of Trinidad. So would all our leading citizens—the doctors, the lawyers, and the judges, and even the Indian chief. The doctors would certainly vote for her. She saved their lives, all four of them."

"Do you mean she nursed them?" Molly asked.

"She did not nurse them," the old man said. "She nursed another man. He was one of the gang of Billy the Kid, and. . . ."

"Billy the Kid!" Molly exclaimed.

It was a name greatly dreaded by travelers in the West. Billy the Kid had killed many men and had robbed many more. He and his gang held up stagecoaches and covered wagons all over the West.

Now Molly was looking at a woman, a Catholic Sister, who had met some of Billy's gang.

Looking at his watch, the man said, "The coach is coming. I'll tell you the whole story as we ride along."

The stagecoach, drawn by four horses, clattered along the street. People were shouting, "Good-by, Sister Blandina! Come back soon!" The little dark-eyed Sister waved to them as she climbed into the coach, and she kept waving from the window.

Molly climbed in and took a seat next to the old man. He took out his heavy gold watch again as the coach driver shouted to the horses. "On time to the minute!" he said as the stagecoach started on its journey to Santa Fe.

The coach jolted off along the mountain road. From the window the girl saw little ranch houses set in the valleys. Sometimes in the distance she saw a rider moving alone across the range.

"Now, I'll tell that story," said the man to Molly.

As he talked, Molly became so interested in the story about Sister Blandina that she forgot the world outside.

"One day," the old man began, "Sister Blandina heard that a man in Billy's gang had been badly hurt. He had crept to a cave near the town and had sent for a doctor.

"Although we have four doctors in Trinidad, not one of them would go near the man. But Sister Blandina went. She took a man and woman with her, and she walked right into the cave. She was afraid, of course, but she told the wounded man that she would take care of him. She gave him food and cared for his wound.

"The man had his gun in his hand. He put it down as Sister Blandina talked kindly to him. Sister Blandina and the friends she chose to go with her went every day to care for the man.

"Then one day he told her that Billy the Kid and the rest of the gang were coming to Trinidad the next day. They were planning to hang the four doctors who had refused to help the wounded man. He warned her to stay away.

"The next day Sister went to the cave anyway. She left her friends outside and walked in alone. There were four other men in the cave with the wounded man. Sister could see that the young one was the leader—the wildest leader this part of the country has ever known.

146

"The young man took off his hat when he spoke to Sister Blandina. He told her that he was grateful to her for what she had done for the wounded man. He said that he would grant any favor she asked of him.

"It was then that Sister asked him not to harm the four doctors. The men grumbled against her. But Billy said, 'She is game. I made a promise and it stands. If we can ever serve you, you will find us ready.'

"Then Billy and his gang rode off. Sister Blandina helped the wounded man to get back to his home in California. It is too bad that Billy and the rest of the gang did not go with him," the old man added.

"Are they still around here?" Molly asked.

"They have not come back to Trinidad," the man answered. "But I hear that they sometimes try to hold up the stagecoaches running into Santa Fe."

"Do you mean they might attack us?" exclaimed Molly.

"Maybe we shall see them," said the old man.

His voice showed a hope that Molly did not share.

"How soon shall we get to Santa Fe?" she asked.

The man looked at his watch again. "Not until late tomorrow, if we are on time," he said.

All day the stagecoach followed the winding mountain road. Molly stared out of the window at the mountains which were beginning to turn red in the late afternoon sunlight.

Suddenly the coach jolted to a stop. The old man, who had been snoozing, awoke and pulled out his watch. "This is not the place for a stop," he grumbled.

The driver called down to the passengers in the coach, "Everybody out!"

Molly and the old man got out of the coach behind the other passengers. The Sisters stayed in their seats.

The stagecoach had stopped just before a bend in the mountain road. The reason for the stop was clear. Three men, with very large handkerchiefs tied over their faces and wide hats pulled low over their eyes, were sitting on horses at the turn of the road. All of them held guns in their right hands.

"Is it Billy the Kid?" Molly whispered to the old man.

"I do not see Billy," he said in a low voice, "but this might be his gang."

One of the men rode forward a little. "Give us the express box," he demanded. The driver quickly obeyed

148

him. "Hold up your hands," he ordered the others. "If you make no trouble, you will not be hurt. If any man moves. . . ." He lifted his gun. No one moved.

"There is someone in the coach," he said to the driver. Then he demanded that they come out.

The driver opened the coach door. "You'll have to come out, Sisters," he said.

Sister Blandina and the other Sister came from the coach just as a fourth rider came around the turn of the road. He wore no handkerchief over his face, and Molly could see that he was young. He was gayly dressed in dark velvet trousers and a jacket trimmed with silver. His wide hat was pushed to the back of his head.

"Billy himself!" whispered the old man.

The young rider looked over the line of passengers. Suddenly his gaze fell on the Sisters. Swiftly he pulled up his horse until it stood on its hind legs. He took off his hat and made a low bow toward the two Sisters. Sharply he shouted an order to his men. They stared at him as if they did not believe what he had said. He repeated the order. The men turned, leaving the express box, and galloped away.

Billy the Kid was the last to go. At the bend in the road he pulled his horse up on its hind legs again, took off his hat, and waved. It was a salute, but no one but Molly saw its answer. She saw Sister Blandina raise her hand swiftly and drop it before she got into the coach.

Sister Blandina glanced up as Molly entered the coach. Molly gave her a look which said, as Billy the Kid had once said, "You're game."

150

Sister Blandina winked.

When the old man came back to his seat, he said, "That was something. Did you see what he did? Called off his gang when he saw Sister Blandina! I guess that after this everyone will be wishing they could have her on the stagecoach to Santa Fe."

"Why did he do it?" Molly asked.

"Sister Blandina once did an act of kindness in Christian charity," the old man said. "Perhaps, even a bad man can understand that." He took out his watch again. "I wonder," he said, "if this will make us late getting into Santa Fe."

## Thinking about the Characters

The phrases below tell about these people: Molly, Sister Blandina, the old man, the four doctors, and Billy the Kid. Write the names of the five persons on your paper. Then below each name write the phrases that tell about that person.

had a dreaded name
liked to know the time
was "a good sport"
kept a promise
was a good listener
liked to snooze
liked gay clothing

went on a long trip alone
showed charity in her actions
didn't help the wounded man
was excited about a trip
waved her hands as she talked
was the youngest on the trip
had their lives saved

Here is an example to show how you should write the first phrase about Molly.

Molly
1. was a good listener

151

# God Helps Those

**By Mary Ruth Mitchell**

Mary Jane heard the knock on the door and was glad that her mother went to answer it.

Mary Jane was busy with her figuring. "New strap for Old Bush's harness, two dollars," she said to herself. "I'll add it to this column. Oh, dear! That makes fifty-six dollars already that we owe to Mr. Peters, and there's still this whole pile of bills to be added to that! We'll *never* have enough money left. Never!"

The sound of voices came to Mary Jane from the doorway, where Ma had just opened the door for Mrs. Samson, a neighbor from a nearby farm.

"Well, good evening, Mrs. McLeod," Mrs. Samson said. "I'm sorry to trouble you on a nice spring evening like this, but I wonder if Mary Jane could help me for a few hours? I've all these bills that need figuring, and I can't make heads or tails of them!

"Everyone's been telling me that your Mary Jane can count now, and I thought maybe she wouldn't mind adding the bills for me."

Mary Jane's pencil stopped in the air and she held her breath, listening for her mother's answer.

Mrs. McLeod hesitated for a moment. She turned toward Mary Jane, sitting at the long table by the window. In the flickering light of the McLeod's only oil lamp, their eyes met. Mary Jane's lips did not move,

but her eyes were begging, "Not tonight, Mother. Any other time—tomorrow, the next day, any other time—but please not tonight!"

Her mother's eyes read the message. She knew that Mary Jane's chances for more schooling depended on the outcome of her figuring. An hour before, the family had agreed that if any money were left from the harvest after paying the bills, it would be spent on Janie's schooling.

The McLeods were proud of their Janie. She was one of the first Negro children in that part of South Carolina to learn to read and write and count. She was the only one in her family who had ever gone to school. When Emma Wilson's little one-room school was opened, it was decided that only one of the seventeen McLeod children could leave the farm work. Mary Jane was chosen because she had always had a great longing to learn to read and write.

Her family had helped her, but Mary Jane had helped herself, too. She had studied hard, and for six years she had walked the five long miles to school. Now she had finished her first schooling and wanted to go on to high school.

Going to high school in these times took money, and extra money was something that the McLeod family did not have.

Would there be any money left for Mary Jane's schooling after the harvest this autumn? That was what Mary Jane was trying to find out this evening. The crop had not even been planted yet, but she would be able to tell, from her figuring.

Mary Jane's mother smiled understandingly and turned back to Mrs. Samson. "I'm sure that Mary Jane will be glad to help you, Mrs. Samson," she said. "But would you mind waiting until tomorrow evening? Mary Jane is working hard tonight on something that is important to all of us."

Mary Jane gave a sigh of relief and turned back to her figuring. Of course she would be glad to help Mrs. Samson as soon as she could. Ever since she had learned to count, she had tried to make use of what she had learned by helping others.

The neighbors—both white and colored—were glad to have someone to whom they could bring their arithmetic problems.

Mary Jane could help them to figure how much cotton weighed by the number of bags they had picked. She could figure for them how much they owed the village store or what their share of this year's crop should be.

On the evenings when Mary Jane did not have any arithmetic problems to do for her neighbors, she would teach her family to read. As soon as supper was finished and the dishes were cleared away, the whole family would gather around Mary Jane for a reading lesson.

"It seems that," she would declare, "the nicest thing about learning is being able to pass on to others what I learn myself." Mary Jane loved to teach as much as she loved to learn.

But tonight was different. Tonight she had a very special job to do, and she was thankful that her mother was so understanding.

Much later that evening, a tired but happy Mary Jane put down her pencil and jumped up from the table. "I think we can make it, Ma!" she cried, running to hug her mother. "If we are ever so thrifty and the harvest is good, there will be enough money left for me to go to high school!"

Her father looked up from where he was sitting, and his tired eyes seemed to catch the glow from Mary Jane's. "We will all do our part to help, Janie," he said. "God will help us, for God always helps those who help themselves."

How good her father was! Mary Jane was remembering his words as she watched him walking toward her in the field the next morning. "We'll all do our part," he had said. Here they were, all getting ready to do their part to prepare the soil for the planting.

It was springtime now, and springtime was planting time. One of the boys had gone to fetch Old Bush, the family mule. The rest of the children, with Ma and Pa, had walked to the field.

"Wonder what can be keeping Sam?" Mary Jane thought, drawing her bare arm across her forehead to wipe off the sweat.

Just then her brother appeared at the edge of the field, waving his arms and shouting, "Pa, come quick! Some-

thing's wrong with Old Bush!" Even at that distance, Sam's frightened voice sent cold chills racing through Mary Jane and started strange, fluttery feelings in her stomach.

Pa shot across the field toward the shed, and the others followed. By the time Mary Jane arrived, Pa was kneeling beside Old Bush.

"What's wrong with him, Pa?" Mary Jane cried, breathless with fear and the effort of running in the hot sun. By now, all of the McLeods were crowding around, looking at Pa and then at Old Bush.

"Is he sick, Pa?" Mary Jane asked.

"No, Janie," answered Pa, swallowing hard. "I'm afraid he's not just sick. He's dead."

Pa's hand was trembling as he ran his fingers over the furry neck of the faithful mule that had plowed their fields so many seasons.

"Dear Old Bush," he said. "You were a good mule, and we will miss you. But I'm glad that you died in your sleep, so nice and peaceful-like."

"Oh, Pa," Mary Jane whispered, "how will we plow the fields without Old Bush?"

"Have to buy another mule, I guess," one of her brothers spoke up.

"Buy a mule!" cried Mary Jane. "But mules cost money, Pa! If we have to buy a mule. . . ." She couldn't go on. With a sob she covered her face with her hands.

Pa was standing now, looking at his children. His tired eyes moved from face to face.

"If we can't plow," he said with a crack in his low voice, "we can't plant. If we don't plant, then we don't harvest. If we don't harvest, we all starve. So we've *got* to plow. It's not a question of *if* we plow. It's a question of *how* we plow.

"If we borrow the money to buy another mule, high school for Janie is out for sure. There are lots of farmers in this world that are poorer than we are, children. Some of them never owned a horse or a mule to begin with, and I reckon we are as strong as they are.

"Seems to me for Janie's sake it would be worth the sacrifice of getting along without a mule for a few seasons. . . ."

Mary Jane and her older brother were already stepping forward. The others followed them silently as they dragged the plow out of the shed.

Taking their places before the plow, Mary Jane and her brother lifted the straps of the harness and fitted them over their shoulders.

Summer passed. The field was plowed and planted, and harvest time was drawing near. One day Mary Jane looked up from her work in the field and saw her schoolteacher, Miss Emma Wilson, coming toward her.

"I have such good news for you, Mary Jane!" she called happily to her favorite pupil.

Mary Jane ran to meet Miss Wilson. "Is it about school?" she cried.

"Indeed it is!" said Miss Wilson, giving Mary Jane a hug. "I've just received some money from a kind and generous lady in Colorado. She said that the money is to be spent to send one student to a high school in North Carolina. You have been chosen to receive the money!"

"A lady in Colorado?" Mary Jane repeated in amazement.

Miss Wilson went on to explain. She said that the lady in Colorado, a dressmaker, had decided to give her life's savings to help some Negro child to get more education.

Mary Jane could scarcely believe her ears. Pa would be able to buy another mule after all! With the help of this gift, she would be able to earn her own way. God would help her as He had helped Pa—as He had helped them all.

"God helps those who help themselves," she murmured.

"What did you say, Mary Jane?" asked Miss Wilson.

"I was just thinking about something Pa said to me," Mary Jane answered. "Oh, Miss Wilson, I'm so proud! I am going to make you and my family and the lady in Colorado proud of me, too! Someday you will all be glad that you gave me a chance to learn!"

When Mary Jane McLeod finished high school, she still had a desire to learn. To satisfy this desire, she worked her way through college. By the time she had finished college, her old love of teaching was burning to express itself again.

After she married Albertus Bethune, Mary McLeod Bethune started a new school for Negro girls in Florida. Believing always that God helps those who help themselves, she spent her life showing others how an education could help them to help themselves. In her efforts, she served not only her own people, but the whole country.

## Can You Prove It?

Skim through the story and find what the characters did or said that prove that each of the following sentences are true.

1. Mary Jane showed that she was very willing to help herself. Write at least two things that Mary Jane did to prove that this is true.

2. The McLeod family showed their willingness to sacrifice so that Mary Jane could go to high school. Find and write two things that persons in her family did to prove that this is true.

3. Mary Jane's mother was very understanding. What did she do to prove that this is true.

4. Mary Jane's father showed that he had faith and trust in God. Write what Mary Jane's father said to show that this is true.

5. Mary Jane was willing to help others. Write two things that Mary Jane did to prove that this is true.

162

# A Song of Greatness

**By Mary Austin**

When I hear the old men
Telling of heroes,
Telling of great deeds
Of ancient days,
When I hear them telling,
Then I think within me
I too am one of these.

When I hear the people
Praising great ones,
Then I know that I too
Shall be esteemed,
I too when my time comes
Shall do mightily.

# Books to Enjoy

*The Columbus Story*, by Alice Dalgliesh.

This is an easy story to read about the life of Columbus from the time he was a young boy until he made his famous voyage across the Atlantic Ocean.

*Squanto, Friend of White Men*, by Clyde Robert Bulla.

An Indian boy of Massachusetts becomes a friend of the Pilgrims and travels to Europe for some thrilling adventures.

*The Courage of Sarah Noble*, by Alice Dalgliesh.

You have already read of Sarah's first meeting with the Indians. You will want to read the whole book to find out what happens when Sarah was left alone with an Indian family.

*George Washington's Birthdays*, by Wilma Pitchford Hays.

This is the story of Washington from his eleventh birthday—the day his father gave him a frisky colt—to his sixteenth birthday when he earned his first job. You may also enjoy his life story in *George Washington*, by Ingri and Edgar d'Aulaire.

*Little House in the Big Woods*, by Laura Ingalls Wilder.

Here you will be given a true picture of frontier life of a family that really lived many years ago in a small log cabin in the Wisconsin forests.

*Abraham Lincoln*, by Ingri and Edgar d'Aulaire.

You will enjoy this excellent picture biography which gives many interesting facts about Lincoln.

*Becky and the Bandit*, by Doris Gates.

This is an exciting story of the gold rush days in California and a girl who meets a frightening bandit.

# Wonders of Nature

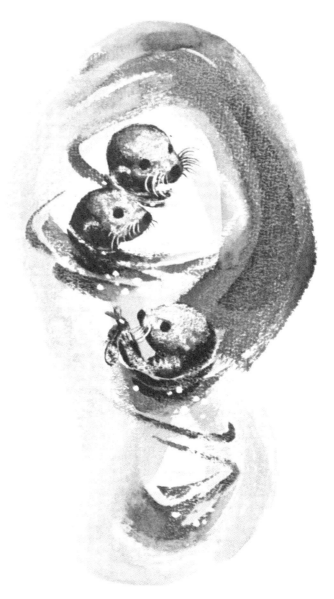

# Earth's Litany

**By Sister Maryanna, O. P.**

I passed a laughing brook today
And as it wound its woodland way,
I thought I heard its waters say:
"We thank Thee, Lord!"

The fallen leaves, pine needles sweet,
A green-gold carpet 'neath my feet,
Stirred by each passing breeze repeat:
"We thank Thee, Lord!"

Across the sky, star after star
Sends out its jeweled gleams afar—
The words they seem to twinkle are:
"We thank Thee, Lord!"

Each sharp-eyed, bright-eyed, furry thing,
All forest folk, afoot, awing
In woodland language mutely sing:
    "We thank Thee, Lord!"

Much more should children every day
In time of prayer, or work, or play,
For all God's gifts, the blessings say:
    "We thank Thee, Lord!"

*To each of His creatures God has given*
*a very special kind of wisdom.*

# A Wise King and a Tiny Bee

**Retold by Rose Dobbs**

Many, many years ago there lived in the holy city
of Jerusalem a mighty king whose name was Solomon.
God had given Solomon a wise and understanding heart.
He was wiser than any man who lived before him and
any man who came after. Many people came to hear
his wisdom, and he always judged wisely and well.

Now, suppose I were to tell you that a little bee, a little, tiny bee, once proved itself to be wiser than this wisest
of men? You would not believe it. Yet it is true. There
is an old, old story to prove it. Because Solomon was
humble as he was wise, the story has a happy ending.
And here it is:

It happened that one of the countries which rang
with the fame of Solomon's wisdom was ruled by the
proud and beautiful Queen of Sheba. She longed to
prove to everyone that Solomon was not the wisest man
in the world. She wanted to give him some difficult task
which he could not do. Better still, she wanted to ask
him a simple question which he would not be able to
answer. She thought and she thought. At last an idea
came to her.

She called together all the most skilled craftsmen in the land. She ordered them to make for her a bouquet of flowers. It was to be of roses and lilies of the valley. The flowers were to be made so perfectly that no one standing within a few inches of them would be able to tell if they were real or false.

The craftsmen went to work. Shortly afterward, they brought the bouquet to the queen. The little bells of the lilies of the valley and the pink blossoms of the roses were so perfect that the queen could not believe they were false. Her skilled workmen had worked long and hard to make a perfume that matched perfectly that of the real flowers.

The queen was more than pleased. "Now we shall see," said she, "how wise Solomon truly is."

The Queen of Sheba announced that she would pay King Solomon a visit—to do him honor, she said. She came to Jerusalem with many friends and servants. She brought with her camels loaded with much gold and with boxes full of precious stones.

King Solomon welcomed her warmly. The best rooms in the palace were offered to her and her friends. The finest musicians and dancers entertained her, and a great feast was planned for her.

On the evening of the feast, the queen sent her oldest servant to get a bouquet of real roses and lilies of the valley. When the merry-making and feasting were in full swing, the queen left the gay company. She soon returned with the two bouquets—the real one and the one designed by her skillful craftsmen. Everyone gasped. Never had they seen such beautiful bouquets, such perfect flowers. And each bouquet was the exact copy of the other.

170

"O great and mighty king," said the Queen of Sheba, standing at a little distance from Solomon and holding out the two bouquets. "The whole world rings with stories of your wisdom. Tell me, you who can always see the truth, which of these bouquets is made of real flowers and which of false flowers?"

There was a deep silence in the great hall. Not one person there could see any difference between the two bouquets. The little white bells of the lilies of the valley swayed gently in each. The lovely pink blossoms of the roses sent out a faint perfume from each.

The deep silence was broken by a whispering and murmuring which started in one corner, traveled to another, and soon filled the great hall. Solomon leaned forward, a puzzled look on his face. He heard the excited and the anxious murmurings of his people. Both bouquets looked exactly alike. Perhaps they were both real? Or, perhaps they were both false?

Suddenly, above the hum in the hall, Solomon's sharp ear caught another sound. It was made by a little bee buzzing outside the window. Solomon smiled. He was wise enough to know that all wisdom comes from God and that God has given to each of His creatures a special wisdom of its own.

The king watched as the small bee started through the window opening. Solomon's eyes followed the bee carefully as it flew into the great hall. Straight and sure it flew to one of the bouquets and was soon lost to sight deep within the blossoms. Everyone was so busy watching the queen or whispering to each other that no one noticed what had happened.

The king sat up very straight and met the queen's eyes. "My honored guest," he said, "the true flowers are those," and he pointed to the bouquet chosen by the little bee.

The queen was amazed.

"Then what I heard in my own land of your acts and wisdom is true," she said. "But I did not believe it until I came and saw for myself. You have wisdom beyond the fame of which I have heard. Happy are your men. Happy are your servants. Happy are all those who stand before you and hear your wisdom."

Then a great shout and roar of praise rang out from all the people. Only the king himself was silent. In his heart he was giving thanks for the little bee that had come to help him.

## Finding the Reason

Read the first paragraph in this story. The last sentence says that many people came to hear Solomon's words of wisdom. The third sentence of the same paragraph tells *why* this happened. Show that you can find reasons by writing a sentence to tell *why* each of the following things happened.

1. It was very easy for the tiny bee to tell which was the real bouquet of flowers.

2. King Solomon was able to hear the low buzzing of the bee even though the great hall was very noisy.

3. Craftsmen designed a bouquet of flowers.

4. The man-made roses had the same lovely perfume as that of the real roses.

5. King Solomon let the tiny bee help him.

# Something Told the Wild Geese

### By Rachel Field

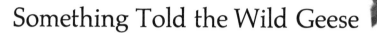

Something told the wild geese
   It was time to go.
Though the fields lay golden,
   Something whispered,—"Snow."

Leaves were green and stirring,
   Berries, luster-glossed,
But beneath warm feathers
   Something cautioned,—"Frost."

All the sagging orchards
   Steamed with amber spice,
But each wild breast stiffened
   At remembered ice.

Something told the wild geese
   It was time to fly—
Summer sun was on their wings,
   Winter in their cry.

*The bird moves delicate wings and soars through the air. With each move the bird mirrors the great wisdom of its Maker.*

# How Nature Helps Birds to Fly

### By Frank Michler Chapman

The bird traveler has no trunk to pack or ticket to buy. But still there are certain things he must do in order to get ready for a trip.

The warbler which nests in Alaska in the summer makes a seven-thousand-mile journey through the air over mountains, plains, and seas to its winter home in South America. The bird cannot begin such a trip unless its engine is in good order and it has enough fuel.

"But," you ask, "what is a bird's engine and where does it carry fuel?"

A bird's engine is really its wings and the muscles which move the wings. It is one of the most perfect engines in the world. It is simple, but strong. It works easily, but is powerful. And it rarely gets out of order.

For many years man tried to make flying machines which would have wings like those of birds, but he never could. He could not even make a feather! Finally he made a plane which has wide stiff wings—wings that cannot be flapped. They in themselves provide no power. So man added an engine to turn a propeller which

175

makes the plane move forward. Then the wings simply hold the plane up.

A bird's wing, we must remember, has the engine in it. The wing holds the bird up as well as giving the power. It is a far more amazing machine than the one made by man.

Not all birds have the same kind of engine. Most of the engines work in much the same manner, but they are very different in shape and size. Most birds which make long journeys have one kind of engine, but those that travel little have quite a different looking engine.

Think of the swallow's engine! The wings alone are as long as the bird itself. The feathers are stiff and strong. When they are moving, they cut the air with graceful, sweeping strokes. The bird is able to move forward easily, but at great speed. A bird having such an engine could make a very long journey quickly without tiring itself. For this reason the barn swallow, which glides and darts about our fields in the summer, goes to Brazil to spend the winter.

Now let us look at the engine of the quail or bob-white. How short and round it is! When the bird flies, it moves its wings very quickly—at least four times as fast as does the swallow. The bird is heavy, and its wings are so small that it is hard work for it to move swiftly. This is why the bird makes only short flights before dropping to the ground again. So we are not surprised to find that the bobwhite spends his life near the place where he is born. He is not a traveler. Most of the time he lives on the ground like a chicken.

Everyone knows that birds' wings, or engines, are made of feathers growing from a very light but wonderfully strong frame of bones. But even the strongest wings wear out. Then the engine must be repaired. This is when molting begins.

It is amazing how the molting takes place. No bird wears a suit of feathers longer than one year. The old and worn feathers drop out and fresh ones grow very quickly in their place.

If the feathers should fall out of one wing faster than they did from the other, the bird's flight would not be balanced. It would be crippled like an airplane with only one wing. If the feathers were to fall out of both wings at once, the engine would be powerless. None of this happens, for the bird's engine is repaired in a most wonderful way.

The feathers begin to drop from the middle of the wing. Only two are lost at a time, and they are from exactly the same place in each wing. New ones at once sprout from the hole left by the falling feathers. When these new feathers are half-grown, two more feathers are lost as before, one from each wing. Again the new ones sprout quickly. Now the third pair is lost.

So the repair of the engine, or the molt of the wings, continues. This repair is slow, for at no time is there more than one pair of feathers missing from the wings. In this way the wing is always balanced, and the bird can fly during the time he is molting.

The molting usually takes place in the summer after nesting is over and the baby birds have learned to take care of themselves. It is not until the molt has been completed and the engine is in perfect order that the bird starts on his travels.

The only thing left to do to prepare for the trip is to take on fuel. With birds the fuel is nothing more than fat. Many birds, when preparing for a long journey, put on a coat of fat. They live on it while they are traveling.

If a bird can get food on the way, he does not need to carry so much with him. Swallows can feed as they fly. The warblers and other birds that fly by night can hunt insects during the day. Other birds that travel over the seas cannot stop for meals. Like bears in winter, they must live on their fat. When they start, their bodies are covered with thick layers of fat, but when they arrive at their journey's end it has disappeared. It was fuel for the engine.

179

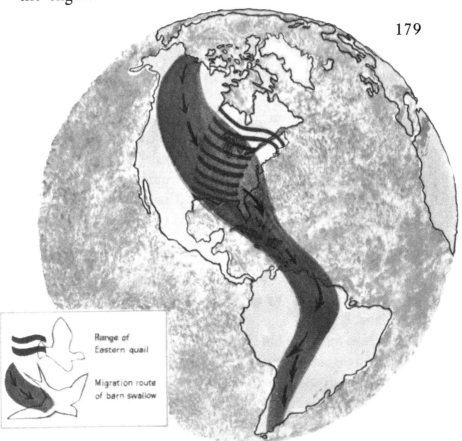

Range of
Eastern quail

Migration route
of barn swallow

Scientists have found that North American birds which were about to start on their long journey to their summer homes were very fat. Other birds, which were not traveling but were only getting ready to nest, were almost without fat.

Still, there they were, living together and eating much the same kind of food. Why this food should make one bird fat and the other thin, it is hard to say. But we may be sure that in each case it was preparing the bird for the work it had to do.

## Thinking about the Story

1. Think of how the bird's engine mirrors the wisdom of its Maker. One way is that its engine is one of the most perfect engines in the world. Find and write five reasons given by the author on page 175 to show that this is true.

2. Look at the map on page 179 and answer these questions:

   a. How far south does the swallow fly?

   b. In what part of our country would you find the quail?

   c. Does the swallow fly mostly over land or over open water? Tell why you think this happens.

3. The bird's wings are repaired by an amazing plan. Reread page 178, and write in your own words the wonderful story of molting. Try to find pictures in an encyclopedia or other books to show the way birds molt.

4. If you would like to find out more about birds, read about them in other books or in an encyclopedia. You may want to write some of the important or interesting facts you learn and share them with the class. You may wish to draw pictures of birds or parts of birds to use with your report.

*God's creatures are not left helpless.*
*They sense danger, and they know how to*
*protect themselves and their young.*

# A Sea Family

**By Allen Chaffee**

Bobry was not a kitten, but his mother could hump her back like a cat, and hiss. She could even wash his soft fur with her tongue. Her face was whiskered like a cat's, too, and she loved to eat fish. Bobry's mother lived in the water most of the time, and she caught her own shellfish.

Bobry's mother used to hold him in her arms, almost as a human mother does her baby. She would lie on her back in the water and sing him to sleep with soft sounds.

Bobry's mother was really an otter. She had shining dark brown fur to keep her warm even when the sea was icy. The baby's fur was brown and shining, too.

Years ago there were a great number of otters in Bering Sea, where Bobry lived. But an otter's fur is so lovely that hunters caught many of them. Now those that still live have learned to hide when people are about.

Bobry was no larger than a squirrel. His father and mother were much larger than cats. Their bodies were long and ended in pointed tails. They could swim faster than anything else on four legs.

181

One of Bobry's early adventures was with a large Snowy Owl. The mother otter had placed her baby on his back in the water to float. Then she started to look for a shellfish for her dinner.

Bobry floated about, sniffing the salt breeze. He held his paws up to shade his eyes from the light. Wide-winged sea birds circled above the waves looking for fish.

Soon a shadow fell across the water. It was the shadow of a bird with wings so softly feathered that it made no sound as it flew near. It was a large Snowy Owl ready to swoop down upon Bobry.

Bobry was frightened by the dark shadow and began to cry. His crying sounded almost like that of a human baby.

Bobry's father was nearby, for he was always alert to danger. Otter babies are never left alone.

"Sssssss! Sssssss! SSSSSSS!" Father Otter hissed fiercely and humped up his back. Then he grabbed the baby otter in his mouth and dived deep into the chilly water.

Before they reached the surface again, Mother Otter came swimming back like a shot. Rising half out of the water, she hissed fiercely at the great bird.

The hungry owl, seeing that he had missed his meal, flew away to hunt for other game.

One day a thick white fog rolled over the Bering Sea. Bobry and his family were hunting for crabs. Mother Otter loved crabs. When she caught one, she would float on her back and crack the shell of the crab on a stone that she had placed on her chest. Then, taking the crab meat out of the shell with her paws, which she used like hands, she washed it carefully. After eating, she would wash her face and paws like a cat.

183

Bobry and his mother were on their way home in the fog when an Eskimo boy, who had seen them one day from the high rock, passed in his boat. He threw the net over a fish and swung it into his boat. Then, as Bobry made a sound, the boy swung his net around and threw it over the little otter.

Quick as a flash, Mother Otter made a dive. The next second Bobry felt her grab him in her mouth from under the water. He felt himself being pulled downward out of the net, and deep, deep into the sea. Water filled his eyes and nose.

Mother Otter had saved him from the net, but Bobry was too young to hold his breath for a long time under water. She had to bring him back to where he could breathe, or he would have drowned.

In the fog the Eskimo boy could not see them, but Bobry would not stay hidden. He was angry at his ducking. No sooner did he get his breath than he began to cry. At that the boy turned and paddled straight toward the sound, but he could see nothing. Not even a head was bobbing to the surface of the Bering Sea. Fog blanketed everything.

Again Mother Otter grabbed Bobry and dived under the waves with him. Had she been alone, it would have been easy for her to stay under water. Then the boy would not have known what had become of her, and he soon would have gone away.

A second time she had to bring Bobry up for air. Once more the little fellow cried so loudly that the boy heard him.

This happened again and again. At last Mother Otter did what seemed like a very mean thing. She had to do it to save her baby's life. When Bobry opened his mouth to cry, she ducked him.

Bobry held fast to his mother, both paws around her neck. His crying was hushed only until she brought him up for air. Again she had to duck him, and again and again. At last the little otter understood. Or if he didn't understand all about the boy and his net, he understood that he was not to cry.

So they hid in the thick fog until the boy gave up trying to catch them and went away. Bobry pressed his furry face deep into his mother's neck, crying softly. Tears ran down his small face, for otters cry real tears just as human babies do. Mother Otter sheltered him in her arms and licked his nose with her warm tongue, while Father Otter swam close beside them.

Time passed, and Bobry was quite happy again. He paddled in slow circles around his mother. Anyone watching him would have thought he was trying to tell her what a very clever young otter her son would turn out to be someday!

## How Does the Author Say It?

Many times the author points out that otters act like people. He also points out that they are like cats in some ways. Most children reading the story would not know much about otters. But most of them would know about cats, and all of them would know about people. The author knows this and tries to help his readers to get a good understanding of the otter family by showing that otters are like things we already know about. Did you notice how the author did this? Write answers to these questions to show that you did.

1. How does the author point out that otters act like people? Skim the story and find at least four examples.

2. What six things show that otters are like cats?

3. How does the author tell you the size of the baby otter and the size of the father and mother otter?

4. The author says otters swim faster than anything on four legs. What other creatures with four legs swim?

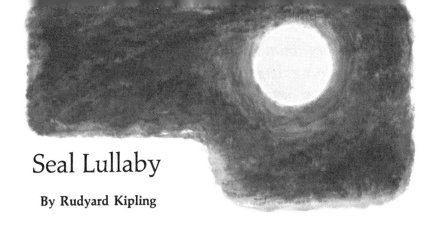

# Seal Lullaby

**By Rudyard Kipling**

Oh! hush thee, my baby, the night is behind us.
    And black are the waters that sparkled so green.
The moon, o'er the combers, looks downward to find us
    At rest in the hollows that rustle between.
Where billow meets billow, there soft be thy pillow;
    Ah, weary wee flipperling, curl at thy ease!
The storm shall not wake thee, nor shark overtake thee,
    Asleep in the arms of the slow-swinging seas.

*From small beginnings come great things*
*. . . things that bring the beauty and wonder*
*of creation before our eyes . . . things to*
*treasure and keep.*

# Big Tree

**By Mary and Conrad Buff**

We, the Giant Trees, are old;
Older than any living thing
On earth.
Long, long before the cave man
Chipped his stone club
In the darkness of his cave,
Long, long before then,
Our fathers lived.
They lived all over the world.

I came from them.
A seed,
A seedling,
A sapling,
A youth,
A tree,
A GIANT

From an ancient clan,
From a forgotten time,
From the morning of the World.

# A Struggle to Live

A big tree, a very big tree, one of the biggest trees in the world, lives today in the mountains of the West. The Indians call this great tree Wa-wo-na.

Even the tallest pine or fir tree in the forest is a dwarf beside him. He is so tall that, to see his top, you must bend your head far back and let your eyes travel up, up, and still up. This tree is taller than the tallest church steeple. He is as big inside as a small house.

Besides being one of the greatest trees in the world, Wawona is one of the oldest trees in the world. He is one of the oldest living things on earth. He is at least five thousand years old.

In the very beginning Wawona was a tiny seed. He was no larger than an ant and no thicker than a sewing needle. He was packed tightly in a small brown cone with two hundred other seeds.

For over a year Wawona slept in his brown cradle-cone at the top of old Father Tree. Then, in the autumn of the second year, the cone began to split. Each day it split open wider and still wider. At last, one very windy morning, Wawona felt himself falling out of his cradle. On each side of his thin red body were tiny stiff wings. The wind carried him along like a glider.

This tiny seed was lucky, for he fell into a mound of black earth which a ground squirrel had piled up when he dug his hole. The earth was fine and just right for a seed to sprout in. But this was not the time for Wawona to sprout. Snow soon fell. The snow covered him with a heavy white blanket many feet deep. He slept. He slept through the short cold days and the long colder nights.

Early in the spring Wawona awoke and sent down a root into the damp earth. He found food. The sun grew stronger and stronger and melted the snow. The ground became warm. Then Wawona sprouted four tiny green fingers upward. Wawona had started to live!

That first summer was full of many dangers. Wawona had one narrow escape after another. One July morning a cutworm wiggled along over the brown earth toward Wawona. His four tiny green fingers shivered. Just then a bird came hopping over the fallen pine needles. The bird spied the cutworm. In a second the worm had disappeared down the bird's throat, and the young tree was saved.

Ten, eleven, twelve years passed by. At the end of each summer, Wawona's green head was several inches taller. As he grew taller, his taproot stopped growing downward, and roots spread outward in all directions, like fingers, drawing up food and moisture from forest and meadow.

When Wawona was twenty-five years old, he was fifteen feet tall. Then his gray bark changed to red bark. He was a handsome, straight, perfect tree. Each year his gray-green head grew more and more like a cone, as his lower branches fell to the ground.

Seventy-five years hurried by. One dry September morning, when Wawona was about a hundred years old,

dark clouds covered the sky. Suddenly, from a black cloud, lightning burst out. It hit the top of an old dead pine. In a few moments the dead tree became a burning torch.

The fire raced along the tops of the trees almost as fast as a mountain lion races after a frightened deer. Burning branches fell to the ground. They fell into the dry needles and the piles of leaves that had covered the ground for years. Soon the forest floor was on fire.

The flames, fanned by the fierce wind, crept nearer and nearer to Wawona. He was helpless, rooted to the ground with his strong roots. But before the first flame reached him, the wind suddenly changed. The black clouds let fall sheets of rain. In a short time the last sparks of fire were out.

As time went on, Wawona lived through other fires, and he began to learn that giant redwood trees are almost unburnable. They all have tannin in their bark which resists fire, and that is why they have outlived all other trees. In this way Nature had protected the giants of the earth.

Some time after this first fire had burned itself out, Wawona burst into bloom. The lovely yellow flowers on his head came as a welcome surprise. How gay he felt! From the flowers would come cones.

Big Wawona was now one hundred fifty years old. Chipmunks and squirrels would soon come to live with him, for the seeds in the cones were good to eat. At last Wawona became the home of many lively animals.

## A Giant among Trees

As the years raced by and Wawona grew taller, his red bark became very thick. He grew great buttresses near the ground, like twisting muscles. They became thicker than a man's body. These buttresses gave him the strength to hold up his great trunk. He was almost eight hundred years old. In those days pyramids were being built in ancient Egypt.

192

Another six hundred years passed by. Wawona grew on, and his trunk became ever thicker. His great gray-green head loomed up three hundred feet into the sky. He was at home among the fog clouds that came in from the Pacific Ocean.

In the Old World, Moses was leading his people out of the land of Egypt toward the Promised Land.

At last Wawona was three thousand years old. He had lived through many forest fires. He knew terrible windstorms. He knew long winters with thirty feet of snow about his great trunk. He knew short chilly summers that were so dry and so cold he did not grow an inch. He was becoming Old Wawona.

In the Old World, about this time, a child was born in a humble stable in ancient Palestine. The child's name was Jesus.

As more years passed, many things happened in the world of man. America was discovered by white men. Pioneers spread westward, pushing back the Indians. And near the middle of the nineteenth century, someone discovered gold on the Pacific coast. Gold, gold, gold! The West began to fill up with men who worked and suffered for the yellow metal.

During the next fifty years men came and went through the forest for different reasons. Some were looking for gold; some were hunters. In the summer cowboys drove their horses and cattle from the valley up into the green pasture of the meadow. All these men were harmless and left the forest as it always had been.

But in the last part of the nineteenth century, men came to destroy. They were men who killed, but did not plant. They were lumbermen. They built platforms around the great trees. They climbed up on the platforms and began to chop at the bodies of the forest giants with sharp axes.

194

They worked away patiently. It took them a long time to chop a wedge in the old red trunks. It was a long slanting wedge, and it made a place for the saws to work in. The lumberjacks took the long saws. A man held each end, and they sawed through the giants' hearts with slow cuts.

The trees fell, one by one, crashing down onto the forest floor and taking younger trees with them in their fall. Closer and closer the men worked toward Wawona.

Soon he, too, would have a platform built around him. Then he would be thrown to the ground and dragged off to the mill. There was enough lumber in his trunk to build a small village.

One day two men rode through the forest on horses. They did not carry axes or guns. They gazed at the great trees. They saw the marks the woodsmen had made —the marks which told the lumberjacks where to start cutting. There was anger in the men's voices as they began talking.

"I don't see how anyone could cut down these trees. Just think how long they must have lived! Take this old fellow here," said one of the men as he placed his hand on Wawona's trunk. "He may have lived five thousand years. I've seen trees cut down that were no larger than he is, and their rings prove they have lived that long."

"Yes, come to think of it, Bill," said the other man, "that old giant was likely a youth when the pyramids were being built in Egypt. He may have been full grown when Jesus Christ was on earth."

Bill said thoughtfully, "I'll never forget what John Muir said about these trees when he was begging for them to be saved—'through hundreds of years God has cared for these trees, saved them from every danger that Nature could send to them. It is left to the American people to save them from the sawmills!' "

"Well, we're saving them," smiled the other man. "There'll be a park here someday, and this old fellow will be one of the finest trees in it."

Wawona was saved. Several years later a park was made of the grove of giant trees where Wawona stood. It became a place to which people came and wondered. Men who know how to care for forests came and planted seedlings. They fought fires. They made the forest a place where deer could graze once more unafraid.

And Wawona, giant of giants, grew more noble with the passing years.

## Using the Glossary

1. Find each of the words listed below in the glossary. Each word will have more than one meaning. To show that you understand the meanings of each word, write a sentence for *each* of the meanings listed in the glossary.

| buttresses | loom | root |
| cone | ring | sprout |

2. Join pairs of the following words to make five compound words. Find each compound word in the glossary and use it in a sentence to show that you understand the meaning.

| cut | wood | saw | lumber | red |
| mill | worm | jack | tap | root |

# Dandelion

**By Hilda Conkling**

O little soldier with the golden helmet,
What are you guarding on my lawn?
You with your green gun
And your yellow beard,
Why do you stand so stiff?
There is only the grass to fight!

# Little Snail

**By Hilda Conkling**

I saw a little snail
Come down the garden walk.
He wagged his head this way . . . that way . . .
Like a clown in a circus.
He looked from side to side
As though he were from a different country.
I have always said he carries his house on his back . . .
To-day in the rain
I saw that it was his umbrella!

197

*God created even the smallest of His creatures in a special way . . . a way which keeps them safe from enemies.*

# Walking Sticks

**By Ferdinand C. Lane**

Someday while in a woodland you may notice a twig moving among the leaves. You may even rub your eyes and wonder if you are seeing things. You would be seeing things, for there are few stranger creatures than those insects that we call walking sticks.

The name is well chosen. They look so much like sticks that they fool even the birds and field mice which might find that they are tasty morsels. Like other insects, walking sticks have six legs.

But these legs are so slender you could easily overlook them. Besides, when they are at rest, walking sticks often push their front legs straight out in front of them and fold the other four close to their bodies.

A favorite trick of theirs is "playing possum" or appearing to be dead. They can stay completely still for several hours. Then they look and act like sticks.

198

These insects are fine examples of Nature's ways of protecting her children. They look so much like the plants they feed upon that their enemies fail to see them. Many of them change color with the season. In spring-time they are green like the young leaves. As the leaves turn brown in the fall, so do the walking sticks.

While in the woodland, you may hear a pattering like drops of rain upon the fallen leaves. As you look up and see the sun shining brightly, you wonder what is happening. This queer sound may be only the female walking sticks laying their eggs. They let the eggs drop upon the ground to be hidden among the leaves.

In the places where there are many "sticks," you might find several dozen eggs upon every square foot of ground. The eggs lie there for months during which time scarcely one in a hundred hatch.

The young insect looks much like his mother, but molts or sheds his skin several times before he is fully grown. If one of his legs breaks off, he can grow another, although it takes him months to do this.

There are several different kinds of walking sticks in America. In the South a fairly large "stick" gives off a bad-smelling liquid that would burn badly if you got some in your eye. The insect does this to discourage hungry birds that may be watching it with interest.

Some walking sticks can only get about on crooked legs. But in very warm countries some "sticks" have wings, and they are much larger. In fact, some giant walking sticks are perhaps the largest of all insects. Some have been reported that were fifteen inches long.

Walking sticks eat the leaves of some trees and bushes. They are otherwise quite harmless as they creep about awkwardly just as they have been doing for millions of years.

## Completing an Outline

When you read a story like this in a science book, you may need to take notes in outline form like the one below. All the main topics are listed for you, and some of the subtopics are listed. Write the outline form on your paper, and complete the outline by filling in the subtopics.

    I. How walking sticks look
       *A.* Like leaves
       *B.*
   II. What walking sticks do to protect themselves
       *A.* Play possum
       *B.*
  III. Enemies of walking sticks
       *A.*
       *B.*

*In God's plan for nature, each creature has its own part to play—a part played alone or with others.*

# Flat Tail Meets Danger

**By Alice Gall and Fleming Crew**

Above the tops of the trees the sky was pink with the last glow of the setting sun. Deep purple shadows climbed higher and higher up the sides of the distant hills.

Flat Tail, the young beaver, paused now and then as he walked along the shore. He stopped to listen to the sound of the little stream as it tumbled down over the stones, on its way to the river. The whole summer lay before him, and so he could travel as slowly as he liked. He could go where he pleased. There was no one to tell him what he should do.

201

It was strange, he thought, this feeling that he had. It made him want to go away from the pond and the family lodge. It made him go away from his mother and father and his little brothers and sisters. He did not understand it, but it was there. It was leading him on beyond the hills.

Now and then he stopped to look back. Through the gathering darkness he could still see the dam and the tops of the beaver houses. He could see his own family lodge with the white birch tree near it. After a while night settled over the valley, and he could see them no more.

When morning came, he found himself in a thickly wooded valley. Here the stream widened into a deep pool, and strange caves formed by great rocks lay all around the pool.

To Flat Tail the place seemed empty and lonely and he wanted to get away from it. But where should he go? Somehow, this morning, he wanted more than ever to see some place that was new.

Back in the hills the frogs were singing. These were voices of the marsh. Suddenly Flat Tail decided to leave the pool and go back among the hills to find the marsh where the frogs were singing.

Keeping himself hidden as well as he could, he started his journey beside a tiny stream that led him away from the pool. Then he stopped and his courage almost failed him. There might be unfriendly creatures lurking about. And now there would be no pool deep enough to give him shelter. But again he heard the frogs, and after a moment he went on.

All that day and all the next, he traveled slowly. He stopped to eat where the food pleased him or to rest when he grew tired.

On the morning of the third day, he could hear the frogs more clearly. He knew that the place he was looking for could not be far away. He was just starting up a hillside when the sound of a twig breaking behind him made him stop and look around.

It was a strange creature that he saw. It was not like any other he had ever seen. It was smaller than he was. But instead of being covered with fur, it had a coat of sharp quills that reached all the way to the tip of its tail.

It was a porcupine. The way the creature's quills bristled, Flat Tail backed away a few steps in fear. He could tell that the porcupine did not want him to come near.

Flat Tail decided to continue on up the hillside. He could tell that the porcupine wanted to be alone.

What an unfriendly fellow the porcupine is, thought Flat Tail, starting to walk away. Suddenly he stopped. He lifted his head and sniffed the air sharply.

He had caught a scent that he knew and feared. It was the scent of a creature that was one of his most dreaded enemies.

What should he do? If he ran away, he would be quickly caught. If he tried to hide, he would be hunted out. He forgot all about the porcupine. He was so frightened that all he could think about was his enemy who was coming nearer to him each moment.

Flat Tail heard a frightened "chir-rup" of a chipmunk as it scurried away to its hole in the ground. There was a rustling in the bushes, and Flat Tail suddenly found himself looking into the yellow eyes of the lynx.

The frightened beaver stood rooted to the spot. He was unable to move or make a sound. He was unable to look away from the eyes that stared back at him.

Overhead a blue jay screamed loudly. A yellow butterfly floated softly down and came to rest on a leaf just above the head of the lynx. From a nearby tree came the peck-peck-peck of a woodpecker.

Life was going on just as it always had there on the hillside. But Flat Tail knew that he was at last face to face with a danger that he could not escape.

The lynx crept slyly out of the bushes and came a step or two nearer. Flat Tail, hardly breathing now, waited for it to spring.

Suddenly the small sharp voice of the porcupine broke the stillness. Flat Tail looked at the little creature in amazement.

The porcupine had changed so much in these few seconds that it looked like a different creature. Every quill on its body stood straight out, making it seem much larger than it really was. It was facing the lynx fearlessly.

The lynx stopped in its tracks and looked at the porcupine uncertainly. Never before had so small a creature had the courage to stand before him like this. But this fierce-looking little thing, with its bristling quills, seemed not at all afraid.

Showing long, sharp teeth, the lynx snarled angrily and began to walk around the porcupine in circles that grew smaller and smaller all the time. The two creatures eyed each other steadily.

Flat Tail, seeing that he was not being watched for the moment, moved quickly back into some bushes. He wondered what would happen next as he shook with fright. How soon would the lynx spring upon the little porcupine?

Almost as he asked himself this question, the porcupine darted toward a great hemlock tree. It stuck its head quickly into a hole among the roots of the tree.

Now all hope for the porcupine was gone, Flat Tail felt. For a moment he forgot his own danger. He only felt pity for the little creature who had stood so bravely before the lynx.

With a spring the lynx hurled himself through the air, straight at the porcupine among the hemlock roots.

Then suddenly a strange thing happened. The little porcupine began to thrash its tail about. It moved so fast that Flat Tail could scarcely see it. It struck the lynx while he was still in the air. With a cry of pain, the lynx rolled over and over on the ground.

There were quills in his nose. There were quills in his paws. They stung and burned. Try as he would, he could not get them out. At last, with a snarl of rage, he tore off headlong through the bushes.

The porcupine, its head still hidden in the hemlock roots, kept on thrashing madly about with its tail. For a moment or two, Flat Tail did not dare to move. Soon, when he could no longer catch the scent of danger in the air, he came out of his hiding place.

At once the porcupine withdrew its head from among the hemlock roots and looked about proudly. The little creature seemed to know that it had filled the lynx with quills and had run the huge cat away.

Flat Tail looked at the porcupine respectfully. He noticed that there were not many quills around the porcupine's head. That's why it could fight better with its head hidden.

Flat Tail was very grateful. He knew the little porcupine had saved his life. He knew that the lynx would have killed him, for he had no place to hide. Flat Tail had always jumped into water if he were in danger, but there was no water around this spot. He could have done nothing but wait for the lynx to spring at him.

He shuddered as he thought of it and looked thankfully at the porcupine. The little creature did not seem at all upset by the adventure. It was biting a piece of bark from the hemlock tree and eating it greedily. It acted again as if it didn't want to be bothered.

Flat Tail wanted to thank the porcupine for chasing the lynx away. He knew that he would never forget it. But the porcupine kept on with its meal of hemlock bark and did not even look up.

In a moment Flat Tail, the young beaver, turned and made his way toward the top of the hill. He was going to find the safe water where the frogs were singing.

## Finding the Author's Words

1. The authors use words well to describe several happenings and scenes. Find and write the words which tell
  *a.* how the sky looked in the evening.
  *b.* what kind of shadows climbed the distant hills.
  *c.* that it was getting darker and darker.
  *d.* how the lynx walked around the porcupine.
  *e.* how the lynx ran away.
  *f.* what Flat Tail was leaving to find.

2. Now skim the pages listed below to find one word answers. Find the word used by the authors to tell
  *a.* that the stream moved hurriedly. (page 201)
  *b.* that the quills stood up. (page 203)
  *c.* that the chipmunk ran fast. (page 204)
  *d.* that the lynx growled. (page 205)
  *e.* that the lynx jumped with force. (page 206)
  *f.* that the porcupine's tail moves fast. (page 207)
  *g.* that the porcupine pulled his head out. (page 207)
  *h.* that the beaver shook with fear. (page 207)

# Spring in Hiding

**By Frances Frost**

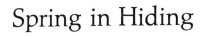

Before I saw the Spring,
I smelled it in the air.
There was no sign of green,
the silver trees were bare.

But strangely, under snow,
the root had told the stalk;
the tangled grasses stirred
around the frozen rock.

The root had told the tree,
the cherry branch was warned;
the pasture, sloped with snow,
dreamed thickety and thorned.

And one dawn when I woke,
I sniffed, I heard, I saw
the Spring in bud, in brook,
in small grass through the thaw!

# Books to Enjoy

*Birds and Planes: How They Fly*, by John Lewellen.

When you finish reading this book, the author says that you will know more about flying than the Wright brothers did when they made their first flight. The book has many drawings to help you to understand how bird and plane flight is possible.

*Sea Pup*, by Archie Binns.

Clint Barlow raises a lovable but unusual pet—a seal. For two years they are constant companions except when the seal is sent 600 miles away only to make the long journey back to Clint.

*The First Book of Trees*, by M. B. Cormack.

Here you will find not only information about trees in general, but also good descriptions of individual trees. There are many pictures to help you identify American trees.

*Insect Engineers: The Story of Ants*, by Ruth Bartlett.

Queens, princes, and slaves; soldiers, hunters, and bridge builders—you will find them all in this amazing story about ants. You will also learn how to observe ants yourself.

*Wagtail*, by Alice Gall and Fleming Crew.

During his first summer of life, a young frog learns many interesting things from the creatures around Blue Pool. But he also learns that there are things about Nature that even the oldest, wisest frog cannot explain.

*Blue Canyon Horse*, by Ann Nolan Clark.

In the wild country of Utah a mare leaves her master, a young Indian boy, to live among the wild horses. The story reads almost as if it were poetry.

# Storybook Treasures

# A Bookmark

**By John Ciardi**

You go out in a ship, up in a plane,
Around in a car, and far in a train.
But every good book that you begin
Goes far, around, up, out, and *in*.
As far in as imagining goes
To time, or to anywhere anyone knows.
Have a good trip! And just in case
You stop to rest, I'll hold your place.

# Pooh Goes Visiting
# and Gets into a Tight Place

### By A. A. Milne

Edward Bear, known to his friends as Winnie-the-Pooh, or Pooh for short, was walking through the forest one day, humming proudly to himself.

He had made up a little hum that very morning, as he was doing his Stoutness Exercises in front of the glass: *Tra-la-la, tra-la-la,* as he stretched up as high as he could go, and then *Tra-la-la, tra-la—oh, help!—la,* as he tried to reach his toes. After breakfast he had said it over and over to himself until he had learned it off by heart, and now he was humming it right through, properly. It went like this:

> *Tra-la-la, tra-la-la,*
> *Tra-la-la, tra-la-la,*
> *Rum-tum-tiddle-um-tum.*
> *Tiddle-iddle, tiddle-iddle,*
> *Tiddle-iddle, tiddle-iddle,*
> *Rum-tum-tum-tiddle-um.*

Well, he was humming this hum to himself, and walking along gayly, wondering what everybody else was doing, and what it felt like, being somebody else, when suddenly he came to a sandy bank, and in the bank was a large hole.

213

"Aha!" said Pooh. (*Rum-tum-tiddle-um-tum.*) "If I know anything about anything, that hole means Rabbit," he said, "and Rabbit means Company," he said, "and Company means Food and Listening–to–Me– Humming and such like. *Rum-tum-tum-tiddle-um.*"

So he bent down, put his head into the hole, and called out, "Is anybody at home?"

There was a sudden scuffing noise from inside the hole, and then silence.

"What I said was, 'Is anybody at home?'" called out Pooh very loudly.

"No!" said a voice, and then added, "you needn't shout so loud. I heard you quite well the first time."

"Bother!" said Pooh. "Isn't there anybody here at all?"

"Nobody."

Winnie-the-Pooh took his head out of the hole, and thought for a little, and he thought to himself, "There must be somebody there, because somebody must have *said* 'Nobody.'" So he put his head back in the hole, and said, "Hallo, Rabbit, isn't that you?"

"No," said Rabbit, in a different sort of voice this time.

"But isn't that Rabbit's voice?"

"I don't *think* so," said Rabbit. "It isn't *meant* to be."

"Oh!" said Pooh.

He took his head out of the hole, and had another think, and then he put it back, and said, "Well, could you very kindly tell me where Rabbit is?"

"He has gone to see his friend Pooh Bear, who is a great friend of his."

"But this *is* Me!" said Bear, very much surprised.

"What sort of Me?"

"Pooh Bear."

"Are you sure?" said Rabbit, still more surprised.

"Quite, quite sure," said Pooh.

"Oh, well, then, come in."

So Pooh pushed and pushed and pushed his way through the hole, and at last he got in.

"You were quite right," said Rabbit, looking at him all over. "It *is* you. Glad to see you."

"Who did you think it was?"

"Well, I wasn't sure. You know how it is in the Forest. One can't have *anybody* coming into one's house. One has to be *careful.* What about a mouthful of something?"

Pooh always liked a little something at eleven o'clock in the morning, and he was very glad to see the Rabbit getting out the plates and mugs. When Rabbit said, "Honey or condensed milk with your bread?" he was so excited that he said, "Both." And then, so as not to seem greedy, he added, "But don't bother about the bread, please." And for a long time after that he said nothing . . . until at last, humming to himself in a rather sticky voice, he got up, shook Rabbit lovingly by the paw, and said that he must be going on.

"Must you?" said Rabbit politely.

"Well," said Pooh, "I could stay a little longer if it—if you—" and he tried very hard to look in the direction of the larder.

"As a matter of fact," said Rabbit, "I was going out myself directly."

"Oh, well, then, I'll be going on. Good-by."

216

"Well, good-by, if you're sure you won't have any more."

"*Is* there any more?" asked Pooh quickly.

Rabbit took the covers off the dishes, and said, "No, there wasn't."

"I thought not," said Pooh, nodding to himself. "Well, good-by. I must be going on."

So he started to climb out of the hole. He pulled with his front paws, and pushed with his back paws, and in a little while his nose was out in the open again . . . and then his ears . . . and then his front paws . . . and then his shoulders . . . and then—

"Oh, help!" said Pooh. "I'd better go back."

"Oh, bother!" said Pooh. "I shall have to go on."

"I can't do either!" said Pooh. "Oh, help *and* bother!"

Now by this time Rabbit wanted to go for a walk too, and finding the front door full, he went out by the back door, and came round to Pooh, and looked at him.

"Hallo, are you stuck?" he asked.

"N-no," said Pooh carelessly. "Just resting and thinking and humming to myself."

"Here, give us a paw."

Pooh Bear stretched out a paw, and Rabbit pulled and pulled and pulled. . . .

"*Ow!*" cried Pooh. "You're hurting!"

"The fact is," said Rabbit, "you're stuck."

"It all comes," said Pooh crossly, "of not having front doors big enough."

"It all comes," said Rabbit sternly, "of eating too much. I thought at the time," said Rabbit, "only I didn't like to say anything," said Rabbit, "that one of us was eating too much," said Rabbit, "and I knew it wasn't *me*," he said. "Well, I shall go and fetch Christopher Robin."

Christopher Robin lived at the other end of the Forest, and when he came back with Rabbit, and saw the front half of Pooh, he said, "Silly old Bear," in such a loving voice that everybody felt quite hopeful again.

"I was just beginning to think," said Bear, sniffing slightly, "that Rabbit might never be able to use his front door again. And I should *hate* that," he said.

"So should I," said Rabbit.

"Use his front door again?" said Christopher Robin. "Of course, he'll use his front door again."

"Good," said Rabbit.

"If we can't pull you out, Pooh, we might push you back."

Rabbit scratched his whiskers thoughtfully, and pointed out that, when once Pooh was pushed back, he was back, and of course nobody was more glad to see Pooh than he was, still there it was, some lived in trees and some lived underground, and—

"You mean I'd *never* get out?" said Pooh.

"I mean," said Rabbit, "that having got *so* far, it seems a pity to waste it."

Christopher Robin nodded.

"Then there's only one thing to be done," he said. "We shall have to wait for you to get thin again."

"How long does getting thin take?" asked Pooh anxiously.

"About a week, I should think."

"But I can't stay here for a *week!*"

"You can *stay* here all right, silly old Bear. It's getting you out which is so difficult."

"We'll read to you," said Rabbit cheerfully. "And I hope it won't snow," he added. "And I say, old fellow, you're taking up a good deal of room in my house—*do* you mind if I use your back legs as a towel-horse? Because, I mean, there they are—doing nothing—and it would be very convenient just to hang the towels on them."

"A week!" said Pooh gloomily. "*What about meals?*"

"I'm afraid no meals," said Christopher Robin, "because of getting thin quicker. But we *will* read to you."

Bear began to sigh, and then found he couldn't because he was so tightly stuck; and a tear rolled down his eye, as he said, "Then would you read a Sustaining Book, such as would help and comfort a Wedged Bear in Great Tightness?"

So for a week Christopher Robin read that sort of book at the North end of Pooh, and Rabbit hung his washing on the South end . . . and in between Bear felt himself getting slenderer and slenderer. And at the end of the week Christopher Robin said, "*Now!*"

So he took hold of Pooh's front paws and Rabbit took hold of Christopher Robin, and all Rabbit's friends and relations took hold of Rabbit, and they all pulled together.

And for a long time Pooh only said "Ow!" . . .

And "Oh!" . . .

And then, all of a sudden, he said "Pop!" just as if a cork were coming out of a bottle.

And Christopher Robin and Rabbit and all Rabbit's friends and relations went head-over-heels backwards . . . and on the top of them came Winnie-the-Pooh —free!

So, with a nod of thanks to his friends, he went on with his walk through the forest, humming proudly to himself. But, Christopher Robin looked after him lovingly, and said to himself, "Silly old Bear!"


## *Hole* Means *Rabbit*

Reread the funny speech Pooh made on page 214 in the first paragraph. Part of it can be written like this:

HOLE means RABBIT,

And RABBIT means COMPANY,

And COMPANY means FOOD.

Try to write something like Pooh said. First, think of one word and what that word means to you. You may want to start with one of these: NIGHT means SLEEP; ICE CREAM means CAKE; CRIB means BABY. You may wish to use something that happened in the story and start like this:

FOOD means EATING-TOO-MUCH,

And EATING-TOO-MUCH means . . . .

# Jonathan Bing

**By Beatrice Curtis Brown**

Poor old Jonathan Bing
Went out in his carriage to visit the King,
But everyone pointed and said, "Look at that!
Jonathan Bing has forgotten his hat!"
(He'd forgotten his hat!)

Poor old Jonathan Bing
Went home and put on a new hat for the King,
But up by the palace a soldier said, "Hi!
You can't see the King; you've forgotten your tie!"
(He'd forgotten his tie!)

Poor old Jonathan Bing,
He put on a *beautiful* tie for the King,
But when he arrived an Archbishop said, "Ho!
You can't come to court in pyjamas, you know!"

Poor old Jonathan Bing
Went home and addressed a short note to the King:
If you please will excuse me
I won't come to tea;
For home's the best place for
All people like me!

222

# Pinocchio's First Adventure

**By C. Collodi**

## Master Cherry's Surprise

Once upon a time there was a piece of wood. It was not fine wood. It was a simple piece of wood—the kind we put in stoves and fireplaces to make a fire and heat rooms.

I do not know how this happened, but one fine day a certain old woodcutter found this piece of wood in his shop. The name of the old man was Antonio, but most people called him Master Cherry for the tip of his nose was so round and red and shiny, just like a ripe cherry.

As soon as Master Cherry saw the piece of wood, he was filled with joy. Rubbing his hands together happily, he murmured to himself, "This piece of wood has come at a good time. I will make from it a leg for the table."

223

He quickly took an ax with which he planned to peel off the bark and shape the wood. But as he was about to strike the wood, he heard a tiny, thin, little voice say, "Do not strike so hard!"

Just imagine how surprised good old Master Cherry was!

He turned frightened eyes about the room to find out where that little voice came from, but he saw no one! He looked under the bench—no one! He peeped inside the closet—no one! He searched in the basket of chips—no one! He opened the door to look up and down the street—and still no one!

"Oh, I understand!" he said, laughing and scratching his wig. "I *imagined* I heard that little voice! I will start to work again."

He took up the ax and again gave the piece of wood a hard blow.

"Oh! You have hurt me!" cried the little voice.

This time Cherry became dumb, with his scared eyes almost popping out of his head, with his mouth open wide, and with his tongue hanging down on his chin.

As soon as he could speak again, he said, trembling and stammering from fright, "Where does that little voice come from? There is nothing alive in this room. Can it be that this piece of wood has learned to cry and scream like a baby? I cannot believe it. This is only an ordinary piece of wood for the fireplace. It is like all other pieces with which we boil a pot of beans. Yet, might someone be hidden in it? If there is, so much for him. I'll fix him!"

Saying this, he grabbed the poor piece of wood with both hands and knocked it around without pity against the stone wall of the room. Then he stopped to listen for the tiny voice. He waited two minutes, and nothing; five minutes, and nothing; ten minutes, and nothing.

"I understand," he said, forcing a laugh and rubbing his wig. "I *imagined* that I heard a voice cry. I will begin to work once again."

Because he was somewhat frightened, he tried to sing a gay song to give himself courage. He stopped working with the ax and picked up a plane to make the wood smooth and even.

As he drew the plane back and forth, he heard again that little voice, laughing and laughing, "Stop it! Oh, stop it! Ha, ha, ha! You're tickling my stomach."

This time poor Cherry fell down as if he had been shot. When he opened his eyes, he found himself sitting on the floor. His face had changed; fright had turned the tip of his nose from red to deepest purple.

At this moment there was a knock at the door.

"Come in," said the woodcutter, not having strength enough to rise.

A lively old man called Geppetto entered the room. He was wearing the wig that he always wore—a wig that was just the color of yellow corn.

"Good morning, Master Antonio," said Geppetto. "What are you doing on the floor?"

"I am teaching the ants their ABC's," the woodcutter answered.

"Good luck to you!"

"What brought you here, friend Geppetto?"

"My legs. Do you know, Master Antonio, that I have come to ask you a favor?"

"Here I am, at your service," answered the wood-cutter, raising himself on his knees.

"This morning I had an idea," said Geppetto.

"Let me hear it."

"I thought that I would make a wooden marionette—a wonderful marionette, one that can dance, walk, and jump. With this marionette I wish to travel through the world and earn for myself a little bread," said the lively old man. "I should like a piece of wood to make the marionette. Will you give it to me?"

Master Antonio gladly took up the piece of wood which had frightened him so. As he was about to hand it to Geppetto, the piece of wood gave a spring, slipped out of his hands, and struck Geppetto's legs.

"Ah! You are very polite when you give presents! Truly, Master Antonio, you have nearly crippled me."

"Oh, I promise you I did not do it," cried the wood-cutter.

"It was *I*, of course!" moaned Geppetto.

"This piece of wood is the guilty one."

"You're right; but remember, you were the one who threw it at my legs," Geppetto added angrily.

"I did not throw it! This piece of wood is guilty," shouted Master Cherry.

"Truly?"

"Truly!"

They shook hands and promised to be friends for the rest of their lives. Then Geppetto took the piece of wood in his arms and, thanking Master Antonio, went home, limping all the way.

# Geppetto's Misfortune

Little as Geppetto's house was, it was comfortable and neat. It was a small room on the ground floor, with a tiny window under the stairway. The furniture could not have been more simple—a broken chair, an old bed, and a nearly ruined table.

On one of the walls there was a fireplace full of bright logs, but the fire was painted on the wall. Over the fire, there was also painted a boiling pot with clouds of steam all around it that made it look quite real.

As soon as he reached home, Geppetto began to make a marionette.

"What name shall I give him?" he said to himself. "I think I'll call him Pinocchio. This name will bring with it good fortune. I knew a whole family called Pinocchio, and they were all lucky."

When Geppetto had found a name for his marionette, he set to work. He quickly made the top of the head, then the hair, and then the eyes. After he had made the eyes, just imagine how surprised he was to see them look around, and finally gaze at him fixedly.

Geppetto, seeing himself looked at by two eyes of wood, said to the head, "Why do you look at me so, eyes of wood?"

There was no answer.

After he had made the eyes, Geppetto made the nose. The nose began to grow, and it grew, grew, and grew until it became a great nose. Geppetto thought it would never stop. He tried hard to stop it, but the more he cut at it, the longer it became. At last he gave up.

Next he made the mouth. No sooner was it finished than it began to laugh and sing.

"Stop laughing!" said Geppetto sternly, but he might as well have spoken to the wall.

"Stop laughing, I say!" he roared.

Then the mouth stopped laughing and stuck out its tongue. Not wishing to start an argument, Geppetto pretended he saw nothing and went on with his work. After the mouth, he made the chin, then the neck, then the shoulders, then the body, then the arms and hands.

Hardly had he finished the hands when Geppetto felt his wig being pulled off. He quickly turned, and what do you think he saw? He saw his yellow wig in the hands of the marionette.

229

"Pinocchio, give me my wig at once," Geppetto said sternly.

But Pinocchio, instead of giving back the wig, hastily put it on his own head and glared at Geppetto.

At this naughty trick, Geppetto looked very sad—sadder than he had ever looked in his whole life.

"Pinocchio, you naughty boy!" he cried. "You are not yet finished, and already you have no respect for your poor old father. Bad, bad boy!"

He brushed away a tear as he spoke.

There were now only the feet and legs to make. As soon as they were finished, Geppetto felt a sharp kick on the tip of his nose.

"I should have thought of all this before I made him," Geppetto murmured unhappily. "Now it's too late!"

Then he took the marionette in his arms and placed him on the floor to teach him to walk. Pinocchio behaved at first as if his legs were asleep and he could not move them. Geppetto led him around the room for some time, showing him how to put one foot down in front of the other foot.

Soon Pinocchio began to walk and then to strut. Before long he was running around the room. When he came to the open door, he jumped into the street and ran away.

230

Poor Geppetto ran after him as fast as he could, but he was unable to catch him. Pinocchio ran in leaps and bounds like a rabbit. His two wooden feet, as they beat on the hard road, made as much noise as twenty pairs of little wooden shoes.

"Stop him! Stop him!" Geppetto kept shouting. But the people in the street, seeing a wooden marionette running as fast as a rabbit, stopped to look at it, and laughed and laughed until they cried.

Finally, through good fortune, a soldier appeared. Upon hearing the misleading noise of the wooden feet, he thought that some colt had escaped from its master. The soldier planted himself in the middle of the road to catch the runaway. Pinocchio tried to run past the soldier, but he could not do it. The soldier, scarcely moving his body, seized the marionette by the nose and carried him back to Geppetto.

231

Taking Pinocchio by the neck, Geppetto led him back, saying as he did so, "When we get home, I must punish you."

Pinocchio, at this threat, threw himself on the ground and refused to walk farther. Meanwhile, the curious people began to stop and surround the marionette and Geppetto.

First one said something and then another. "Poor marionette!" said one of them. "He is right not to want to go back to his home. Who knows how hard Geppetto beats him?"

Another person added, "That Geppetto appears to be a kind man, but he is sometimes mean to boys. When he gets that poor marionette in his hands, it is possible that he may break him into pieces."

Because the people made so much noise, the soldier gave Pinocchio back his freedom. Instead, he took to jail Geppetto, who was by now speechless. The poor man could only weep.

Upon reaching the prison Geppetto finally cried out gloomily, "Wicked son! To think I tried so hard to make a good marionette! I ought to have thought of all this at first."

This was only the beginning of the wooden marionette's many adventures—adventures so strange that they are hard to believe.

## Understanding the Author's Words

1. This author uses words cleverly to make word pictures. Find and write the words the author uses to describe

    *a.* what Master Cherry's nose looked like.
    *b.* what color Geppetto's wig was.
    *c.* how Pinocchio ran.
    *d.* how fast Pinocchio ran.

2. Reread page 225, paragraph 2. Write why you think Master Cherry had to *force* a laugh.

3. Reread page 229, paragraph 2. What is the meaning of the words, "He might as well have spoken to the wall"?

4. Reread page 227, paragraph 4. Write what Geppetto meant when he said, ". . . earn for myself a little bread."

5. Reread the last three lines on page 226. What do you think Master Antonio wanted to know when he said, "What brought you here, friend Geppetto"?

6. Reread page 228, paragraph 2. Using the author's word picture, draw your own picture of Geppetto's wall.

# The Little Juggler

**Based on the Story by Ruth Sawyer**

## Act I

READER. A wooden statue fair and lovely,
      Stands smiling above the abbey doorway.
      And people passing by look up
      To see Our Lady's face—calm and sweet.
      They breathe a tiny prayer to her,
      As on their way they go.

      Children sometimes stop to stare
      Because they like to see her smile,
      To see her smile as once she did
      On the juggler—the juggler of Notre Dame.

      "Is it true?" they cry,
      And then they shrug.
      It doesn't matter if it is or not.
      It could be true and that's enough
      To make them dare to hope.

      So they gather in a circle tight
      And listen once again to the story old.
      Their eyes grow bright and round
      And fill with solemn thoughts.
      As the age-old words fall gently,
      The story comes to life.

NARRATOR. It is the month of May; it is market day in the village of Cluny. Look, you can see the square before the Abbey filled with children, with lads and maidens, with farmers selling their wares. You can hear them calling from here, from there.

WOMAN (*calling out*). Onions, turnips, good white cabbages!

FIRST FARMER. Good cheese—cream cheese!

SECOND FARMER. New beets. Strawberries, fine early strawberries!

ALL. Who will buy? Who will buy?

CHILDREN (*suddenly shouting and pointing down the road*). Look who is coming! A juggler . . . a juggler. . . .

FIRST CHILD. May he be a good juggler. May he toss up many golden balls and keep them spinning in the air.

SECOND CHILD. May he twirl the hoops and catch them on the stick.

THIRD CHILD. May he sing lots of songs—gay songs.

NARRATOR. Look with the children, and you will see him coming down the road. He is a little one, a boy still. His stockings are in shreds; his clothes, in tatters. Hunger shows in his cheeks. His body looks as if the wind could blow straight through it.

For many nights he has had nowhere to sleep but under the bushes along the road. He has walked far and eaten nothing. He holds tightly to his bag of tricks. It takes all his courage to laugh boldly at the crowd.

JEAN (*above the shouting and laughter of the crowd*). Hello all! Behold, you see me—Jean, king of the jugglers!

236

FIRST FARMER (*above the crowd's laughter*). Ho-ho! A pretty king! A king of tatters and hunger. Well, what can you do, Jean, king of the jugglers?

JEAN (*leaning weakly against the stone bench*). What can I not do! Tricks—marvelous! Songs—five new ones! But first, my good friends, a penny for my bowl. It brings luck to all who give Jean a penny. I will make music with them . . . if there are enough.

FIRST FARMER (*holding the children back after they have thrown in only two pennies*). First, let us see what he can do. He may not be worth a penny.

NARRATOR. A face the juggler makes at these two pennies. Then carefully he takes from his bag the golden balls. It is a trick all jugglers know—the trick of keeping six balls in the air. He tosses them: one—two—three. He never gets beyond the fourth before he spills them.

FIRST FARMER (*as the crowd laughs*). I could toss cabbages better than that.

237

NARRATOR. The juggler tries the hoops, tossing them, twirling them, catching them on the stick. But his arms, they ache. They are as weak as his legs. He doesn't catch one of the hoops. The crowd laughs. The people start to walk away when a farmer asks the juggler to sing a drinking song, gay and wicked. It is then that the little juggler looks above the Abbey doorway at the statue of Our Lady—the only mother he knows.

JEAN (*praying*). Holy Mother, forgive me. Close your ears for I don't want you to hear this song. I really don't want to sing it, but I am hungry. And the song isn't a sin. It is just not proper for you to hear.

NARRATOR. And who is coming now? Look down the road, and you will see the Father-Abbot coming back from visiting the sick. Just as Jean starts to sing, the Father-Abbot arrives at the square. Quickly he scatters the crowd and lays a tight hand over Jean's mouth. He scolds Jean so harshly that the small juggler's knees begin to knock together, to bend.

Look again, down the road. You will see the good Brother Boniface riding on his small donkey. He is the cook of all the brothers. He has been out in the country gathering food. The baskets on his donkey are filled with fruit, with meat, with vegetables.

BROTHER BONIFACE (*speaking to the Father-Abbot*). Father, look here! Here are lilies, sweet violets for the altar of Our Lady. Here are onions—white as pearls—cheese, cabbages. And, look, two fine fat hens! The better the monks eat, the better they can pray, eh, Father?

NARRATOR. As the monk holds up one good thing
after another, it is too much for Jean, the starved king
of the jugglers. His knees drop from under him. He
falls forward, fainting almost beneath the doorway of
the Abbey. Brother Boniface and the Father-Abbot
lift him very tenderly. Together the three enter the
courtyard of the Abbey, the king of the jugglers sobbing
against the white robe of the cook-brother.

# Act II

NARRATOR. And now, a juggler lives at the Abbey. He no longer wears his tattered clothes. He wears clothes given to him by the monks. He works in the kitchen as a helper to Brother Boniface. As he works he thinks of the beauty at the Abbey. He has forgotten the noisy, dusty, lonely world that he had known. He is really very happy. There is only one thing that bothers him.

JEAN (*speaking to Brother Boniface as they prepare dinner*). It is so beautiful here. All day long there is beauty to touch, to see, to hear. Everyone does something to make things even more beautiful for Our Lady. The painting-brother is making a new holy picture. The carving-brother is making a new holy water font. The singing-brother is composing a new song. But me—what can I do to make something beautiful for Our Lady? Nothing!

240

BROTHER BONIFACE (*holding up a big cabbage*). Look, my little one. This is what I do for Our Lady. I make ready this cabbage. I pare the carrots. I take these pearls of onions and quarter them. I do this to make good soup to feed the brothers. Never mind, little one, we cannot all serve in ways of beauty, but we can serve humbly and lovingly with our hands and our hearts. I think Our Lady finds all our gifts beautiful—the painting by Brother Joseph *and* the soup by Brother Boniface. She loves them all. Now, cheer up!

NARRATOR. But Jean does not cheer up. Finally, he takes his trouble to Our Lady herself. He kneels before her in the chapel.

JEAN (*speaking slowly*). How sad you look, Holy Lady, my Mother! Is it because you are always thinking of your Son Who died on the Cross? I have a great wish to make you smile. That would be wonderful—to have Jean make you smile!

NARRATOR. One day an idea comes to the little juggler. Suddenly he knows how he might truly serve Our Lady. Secretly he hurries to the old tree where he had hidden all his tricks and all his juggler's clothes. When the chapel is empty, Jean puts on his cap with the bells and the long feather and the rest of his juggler's outfit. Then he skips down the aisle and stops before the statue.

JEAN (*making a deep, low bow to Our Lady*). Holy Mother, my Mother, here I stand—Jean, a poor juggler. Once I made many a sad mother smile. Now I beg of you the honor of doing for you all my tricks. I will do them the very best way I can.

NARRATOR. First, come the golden balls. Jean takes them out and keeps the six in the air, each one catching the light of all the candles. Look, they are magnificent. Now for the hoops.

Jean does them all, every trick he has ever learned. How gloriously he performs! Now he takes the drum. He is marching with it, beating time, singing an old French marching song.

JEAN (*singing as he marches and beats his drum*). Tra-la-la-la-la-la . . . tra-la-la-la-la-la!

NARRATOR. That is what he is singing when the musician-brother returns to the chapel. For a moment the musician-brother stares at Jean. Then he is angry.

He hurries out to call the Father-Abbot and all the other brothers. They come rushing into the chapel without a sound. And there is Jean, once a juggler, still marching, still beating his drum, still singing bravely.

JEAN. Tra-la-la-la-la-la.

NARRATOR. Whisperings grow. It is like the gathering of a black, angry storm. Words are spoken harshly.

GROUP OF MONKS (*speaking softly, but angrily*). For shame! For shame! Throw him out! Stop him! Stop him!

BROTHER BONIFACE. No, brothers, no. Look at Our Lady's face. Our Lady is smiling. Look! Look!

JEAN (*kneeling before the altar and laughing aloud with great happiness*). My Mother smiles at last! I have brought happiness this day to Our Lady.

NARRATOR. It is no longer a statue that smiles. It is the living Mother of Christ. She leans down and gathers that small king of the jugglers into her arms. He who has never known a mother's arms in all his life feels a great happiness filling his heart. A bright light fills the chapel. A chorus, unseen, of heavenly music seems to fill the spaces. The monks kneel in wonder and silence. They know that they have seen a miracle.

READER. From that day to this,
So the people say,
Our Blessed Lady of Cluny
Has always worn a smile.


## Was It Kind or Unkind?

The phrases below tell of sad, happy, kind, or unkind things that happened to Jean. Make two lists with the phrases. At the top of one list, write *In the Market Place*, and below it, list all things that happened there. At the top of the other list write *In the Abbey*, and list things that happened there.

To show that you know what the phrases tell of, after each phrase write: *happiness*, *kindness*, *sadness*, or *unkindness*.

    a farmer laughing boldly at a bad juggler
    Brother Boniface trying to cheer Jean
    a juggler who is hungry and weak
    Jean knowing a mother's arms for the first time
    monks giving clothes to Jean
    a juggler in tattered clothes
    Jean performing marvelous tricks
    a farmer calling Jean a "king of hunger"
    Brother Boniface talking tenderly to Jean

# Heidi's Day on the Mountain

### By Johanna Spyri

Heidi was awakened early in the morning by a loud whistle. When she opened her eyes, the sunshine was pouring through the round window so that everything shone like gold. Heidi looked around her in surprise. She did not have the slightest idea where she was.

Then she heard her grandfather's deep voice outside. Now she remembered. Only yesterday she had come to live on the mountain with her grandfather.

Heidi jumped quickly out of bed, and in a few minutes she was dressed. She climbed down the ladder and ran outside the hut. There stood Peter with his flock of goats. Grandfather was bringing his two goats, Little Swan and Little Bear, out of the shed to join the other goats. Heidi ran to say good morning to him and the goats.

"Would you like to go to the pasture with Peter?" asked Grandfather.

Heidi jumped for joy at this wonderful idea.

"But first you must wash," said Grandfather, pointing to a large tub of water that stood before the door of the hut.

Heidi ran to it and began to splash and rub with all her might.

Grandfather went into the hut and called to Peter, "Come here, my lad, and bring your lunch bag with you."

When the surprised Peter entered the hut, the old man pointed to the bag in which the lad carried his bit of lunch. "Open it," said Grandfather.

Then he put a large piece of bread and a large piece of cheese into the bag. Peter's eyes opened wide in wonder. This was almost twice as much food as he had brought for his own lunch.

"Heidi is to go with you to the mountain pasture. Take good care of her and don't let her fall off the cliffs," warned Grandfather.

Just then Heidi came running to the entrance of the hut. She had rubbed her face, neck, and arms so hard that they were red and shining.

Her grandfather smiled. "Go along with Peter," he said.

Heidi went merrily up the mountain toward the high pasture land. The sky was a deep blue, with not a cloud to be seen. Everywhere the blue and yellow flowers smiled and nodded in the bright sunshine. Heidi was

so delighted that she scurried ahead, picking armfuls of blossoms and putting them in her apron.

The pasture where Peter usually went with the goats lay at the foot of the high cliff. The lower part of the cliff was covered with clumps of bushes and fir trees, but it loomed toward heaven quite bare and steep. On one side of the high pasture there were steep drops to the valley far below. Heidi's grandfather had been right in warning Peter to watch out for her.

When Peter reached the pasture land, he stretched out on the ground to rest from the climb. Heidi sat down beside him and looked around her.

The valley lay far below nestled in the full morning sunshine. Heidi saw the great wide fields of snow, stretching high up into the deep blue sky. The child sat as still as a mouse. Everywhere there was a great, deep stillness. Only the wind passed softly and gently over the tender blue bells and the golden rockroses, which were everywhere swaying back and forth on their slender stems.

Heidi drank in the golden sunlight, the fresh air, the sweet smell of the flowers. She wished for nothing more than to stay there forever.

Suddenly Peter began a loud whistling and calling. Heidi couldn't imagine what was going to happen, but the goats must have understood the sound. One after another, they came leaping and bounding down from the high places until the whole flock was gathered on the green pasture. Some nibbled the tender grass, others ran back and forth, and still others playfully butted one another with their horns.

Peter brought out the lunch bag. He arranged their pieces of bread and cheese on the ground in a square, the larger pieces on Heidi's side, the smaller ones on his side. He knew exactly how many he had. Then he took a little bowl, and he milked sweet fresh milk from the white goat and placed the bowl in the middle of the square.

248

"Come, Heidi," he called. "It is time to eat."

She looked happily at the neat square and the bowl in the middle. "Is the milk mine?" she asked.

"Yes," answered Peter, "and the two large pieces of bread and cheese are yours too. When you have drunk all the milk, you can have another bowlful, and then it is my turn."

Heidi began with the milk, and as soon as she set down her empty bowl Peter rose and filled it again. Heidi broke some of her bread into it. The rest, a piece still larger than all of Peter's bread, she handed over to him, together with a large piece of cheese.

"You may have it," she said. "I have enough."

Peter looked at her amazed. Never in his life had he been able to give anything away. He could not believe that Heidi meant it. When he did not take the food, she placed it on his knee. He then knew that she really meant for him to have it. He nodded his thanks and eagerly ate the largest lunch he had ever had in all his life.

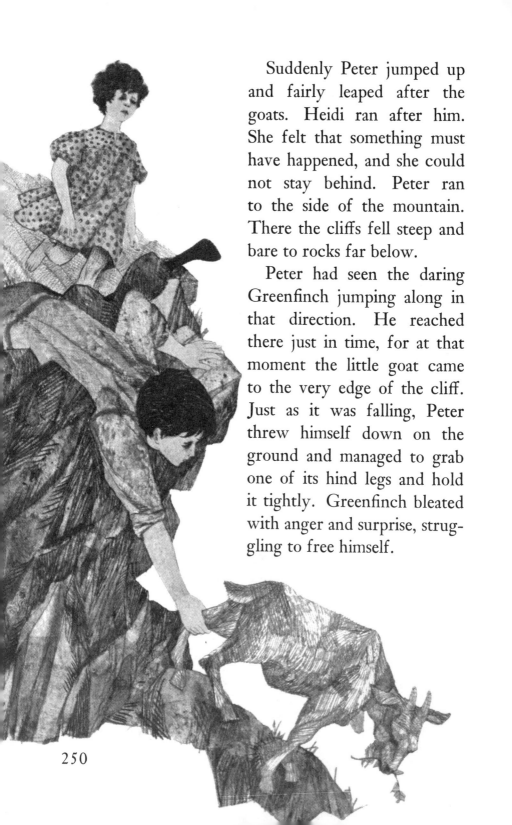

Suddenly Peter jumped up and fairly leaped after the goats. Heidi ran after him. She felt that something must have happened, and she could not stay behind. Peter ran to the side of the mountain. There the cliffs fell steep and bare to rocks far below.

Peter had seen the daring Greenfinch jumping along in that direction. He reached there just in time, for at that moment the little goat came to the very edge of the cliff. Just as it was falling, Peter threw himself down on the ground and managed to grab one of its hind legs and hold it tightly. Greenfinch bleated with anger and surprise, struggling to free himself.

Peter screamed, "Heidi, help me!"

Heidi was already there and saw at once the danger. She quickly pulled some sweet-smelling plants and held them under Greenfinch's nose.

"Come, Greenfinch," she coaxed. "You must be quiet. See, you might fall off and break your bones."

The goat quickly turned its head and eagerly nibbled the green plants from Heidi's hands. At that moment Peter managed to get hold of the cord which held the bell around the little goat's neck. Heidi grabbed the other side, and the two together led the runaway back to the peacefully grazing flock.

When Peter had the goat in a safe place once more, he raised his rod to punish Greenfinch for giving him such a fright. The goat drew back, for he saw what was going to happen.

"No, Peter," cried Heidi. "No, you must not strike him! See how frightened he is!"

"He deserves it," said Peter angrily, raising his rod once more.

But Heidi seized his arm and cried, "You shall not do it. It will hurt him! Let him alone!"

Peter looked in surprise at Heidi, whose black eyes snapped at him. Unwillingly, he dropped his rod.

"I will let him go if you will give me some of your cheese again tomorrow," said Peter.

"You may have it all—the whole piece—tomorrow and every day," agreed Heidi. "I will give you a good part of my bread, too, as I did today. But you must never, never beat Greenfinch or Snowflake or any of the goats."

"It's all the same to me," said Peter, and this was as good as a promise with him. Then he let the runaway go, and the happy Greenfinch leaped high in the air and scampered back to the flock.

In this way the day had passed, and the sun was just ready to go down behind the mountains. Heidi sat down on the ground again and quietly gazed at the wild flowers glowing in the evening light. All the grass seemed tipped with gold, and the cliffs above began to gleam and sparkle.

Suddenly Heidi jumped up and exclaimed, "Peter! It's on fire! Everything, everything is on fire!"

"It's like that every evening," said Peter, "but there is no fire."

"How lovely!" exclaimed Heidi. "See the snow all rosy red, and on the peaks above there are ever so many roses! Oh, now they are turning gray! And now it is all gone!" Heidi sat down on the ground and looked as unhappy as if the world were coming to an end.

"It will be just the same tomorrow," explained Peter. "Get up! We must go home now."

Peter whistled and called the goats together and they all started for home.

"Will it be like that every day when we go to the pasture?" asked Heidi as she walked by Peter's side.

"Perhaps," was the reply.

"But really tomorrow again?" she wanted to know.

"Yes, yes, tomorrow, for sure," Peter answered.

Then Heidi was happy once more. She said nothing more until they reached the hut and she saw her grandfather sitting under the fir trees, awaiting their return.

"Oh, Grandfather! It was so beautiful," she exclaimed even before she had reached him. "The fire and the roses on the cliffs and the blue and yellow flowers! See what I have brought you!"

Heidi shook all of the flowers out of her folded apron, but what a sight the poor little flowers made! They were all dried, like bits of straw. Not one flower cup was open.

"Oh, Grandfather, what is the matter with them?" moaned Heidi. "They were not like that. Why do they look so now?"

"They like to stand out in the sunshine and not to be shut up in your apron," said Grandfather.

Later, when Heidi sat on her high stool with a bowl of milk before her, she told her grandfather about everything that had happened that lovely day. Then she asked her grandfather to tell her where the fire that evening had come from.

"You see," the grandfather explained, "the sun does it. When he says good night to the mountains, he sends to them his most magnificent rays, so that they may not forget him until he comes back again in the morning."

This answer pleased Heidi so much she could hardly wait for another day to come. Then she could go up to the pasture and see once more how the sun said good night to the mountains.

That night she slept soundly, dreaming of bright, shining mountains, in the midst of which little Greenfinch merrily ran and jumped.

## Finding Word Pictures

The author uses words well to describe happenings. Find and write the words in the story which tell

1. how the early morning sun made things look.
2. how the blue and yellow flowers moved.
3. how Peter's eyes opened when he saw so much food.
4. how Heidi sat when they reached the pasture land.
5. how the blue bells and rock-roses moved.
6. how the goat ate the plants that Heidi gave him.
7. how the evening light made the grass look.
8. how unhappy Heidi looked when the sunset was over.
9. how dry the flowers were.
10. how the sun says good night to the mountain.

# The Race

**By Mary Mapes Dodge**

You will read, in certain books, that the Dutch are a quiet people, and so they are, most of the time. But listen! Did you ever hear such noise?

On this clear, cold December day, people from every part of Holland have come to Amsterdam to watch twenty boys race on the ice. The prize for the winner will be a pair of silver skates.

Everyone is here—the rich in silk and velvet; the country folk in wide blue trousers and wooden shoes, in stiff white bonnets and gay skirts. There are beautiful girls, wearing aprons bright with color, their long golden hair held down with bands of gold. Everywhere can be seen tall women, short women, tall men, short men, and children of every age and size.

Upon the edge of the ice, tents have been set up on wooden platforms. Each one is different, but all are gayly decorated. The important people of the town can watch the race in comfort from these tents. The big one with the blue flags flying from the roof is for the musicians.

The tents with peaked roofs, and decorated with streamers of every possible color, are the judges' stands. From there the judges can see the two white poles, twined with evergreens, which form the starting and finishing points of the race. The skaters will race from these poles to the flagstaffs, half a mile off, and back again. The silver skates will go to the lad who can win this mile race twice.

There's the music! Now, where are the racers?

There they are, near the white poles on the ice, near the starting point. It is a wonderful sight—twenty boys, darting here and there on skates, sailing swiftly along the ice, calling, talking, laughing. A few careful boys are giving a last look at their skate straps. Others stand on one leg, glance at a skate, and then dart off again. They cannot stand still.

Holland is a place for skaters, after all. Where else can so many children skate so well? Such jumping, such

spinning, such performing! Their backs are like the springs of a watch. That boy with the red cap amazes everyone. When you think he is up, he is down; when you think he is down, he is up. He drops his glove on the ice, and turns a somersault as he picks it up. Without stopping, he grabs the cap from Jacob's head and claps it on again—backwards!

Lambert, Ludwig, Carl, and Peter are at the starting point now, cool and in good skating order. Hans Brinker is near them. Hans would not be in this race today if it were not for the kindness of Peter. Hans is a poor boy; his only skates were wooden ones he had made himself. Because Carl had laughed at him, Peter bought Hans a pair of steel skates.

Now there are twenty boys on the ice. They are ready for the first run. Two or three bend to give a last pull to their skate straps. Now they have formed a line. They are ready!

See the crier! He is standing between the poles and the judges' stand. Now he reads the rules in a loud voice: *"The skaters are to race until one boy has won twice. They are to start in a line from these posts, skate to the flagstaff line, turn, and then come back to the starting point."*

A flag is waved from the judges' stand and the bugler gives the signal to start. The boys are off!

No! They are back again. Their line was not true as they passed the judges' stand. The signal is repeated!

Off again! No mistake this time. Whew! How fast they go! Cheers go up from the crowd. Hurrah! Halfway to the flagstaff already! Did you ever see the like?

Three hundred legs flashing by, it seems. But there are only twenty boys. No matter! It looks like hundreds of legs. Where are they now? One cannot see.

A cloud of feathery ice flies from the heels of the skaters as they turn at the flagstaffs. Something black is coming now, one of the boys. It is all we know. The crowd fairly roars. Now the racers come nearer. We can see the red cap. There's Peter! There's Hans!

259

Hans Brinker is ahead. Carl is next, then Ben, and then the boy in the red cap. A tall figure passes them. It is Peter! Hurrah, Peter! Hans shoots past Peter. Fly, Hans! Fly, Peter! Carl is close behind you. Carl is mean and selfish. Carl is the one who did not want Hans in the race.

Now it is an even race between Peter and Hans. Hans and Peter, Peter and Hans, which is ahead? We do not care which wins, but not Carl.

Four more strokes of the shining skates will take Hans across the finish line. He is there! Yes, but so is Carl, just a second before. At the last instant Carl had whizzed between Peter and Hans and passed the finish line. Carl has won the first round.

Once more the bugle sounds, and the boys are off like leaves before the wind. Again Peter, Hans, and Carl lead the racers to the finish line, but this time Peter is the winner of the second round.

The crowd buzzes with excitement. Who will win the third round? Will it be Hans, or Carl, or Peter? It is almost time for the boys to line up for the third round. But where is Peter?

Hans looks back. Peter, kneeling on the ice, is working on a skate strap. Hans is beside him at once.

"Are you in trouble?" he asks Peter.

"Yes, Hans, my race is over. I tried to tighten my strap, to punch a new hole, but my knife cut the strap in two," replies Peter sadly.

"You must use my strap," says Hans, at the same time pulling off a skate.

"Not I, indeed, Hans Brinker," cries Peter, looking up, "though I thank you. Go to your place, my friend. The bugle will sound in a minute."

"You have called me your friend," says Hans, "and you have been my true friend. Take this strap—quick! There is not a moment to waste. I shall not skate this time. Peter, you *must* take it!"

"Come, Peter," Lambert calls from the line.

"Be quick," begs Hans. "There, the skate is on. You must go. I could not possibly win. The race lies between you and Carl."

"You are a noble fellow, Hans," says Peter, and springs to his place as the bugle sounds loud and clear.

Off they go! They race like mad. All of them are running like hunters. They are hunting Peter. They will catch him! There's Carl. The race grows faster.

The chase turns into a cloud of mist. It is coming this way. Who is hunted now? It is still Peter! Fly, Peter! Hans is watching you. He remembers your kindness. He is sending all his strength into your feet. Your mother and sister are watching you. Fly, Peter! The crowd is roaring. The other skaters are close behind you. Touch the white post! There, it is near you! Touch it! Touch it!

"Hurrah! Hurrah!" cries the crowd. "Peter has won the silver skates!"

"PETER VAN HOLP!" shouts the crier. But who heard him?

"PETER VAN HOLP!" shout a hundred voices.

"PETER VAN HOLP!" shouts Hans Brinker.

Hurrah! Hurrah! Now the music is heard above the roar of the crowd. It strikes up a lively air and then a booming march. The race is over.

## Reading between the Lines

Show that you can read between the lines by writing answers to these questions.

1. Nowhere does the author say that the Amsterdam race was a big happening in Holland. What two things does the author tell you to show that this is true?

2. The rules do not say that the winner had to skate at *least* two miles. How do you know that this is true?

3. The author does not tell you that the judges kept a very careful and close watch to see that the racers did what they should do. What happened at the beginning of the first race to show that this is true?

4. Nowhere does the author say that Hans was an unselfish boy. What did he do to show that this is true?

5. The author does not say that Hans, Peter, and Carl were three of the fastest skaters of the twenty boys in the race. How do you know that this is true?

6. The author does not say that it wasn't necessary for the crier to announce the winner of the race. How do you know that this is true?

# A Pet for Mr. Popper

**By Richard and Florence Atwater**

## A Visitor from the South Pole

It was an afternoon in late September in the pleasant little city of Stillwater. Mr. Popper, the house painter, was going home from work. He was carrying his buckets, his ladders, and his boards, and so he had rather a hard time moving along.

No one knew what went on inside of Mr. Popper's head. He was a dreamer. He was always dreaming about faraway countries.

He had never been out of Stillwater. Not that he was unhappy. He had a nice little house of his own, a wife whom he loved dearly, and two children, named Janie and Bill. Still, it would have been nice, he often thought, if he could have seen something of the world before he settled down.

How he wished that he had been a scientist, instead of a house painter in Stillwater, so that he might have joined some of the great polar expeditions. Since he could not go, he was always thinking about them.

Whenever he heard that a polar movie was in town, he was the first person at the ticket window. Whenever the town library had a new book about the Arctic or the Antarctic—the North Pole or the South Pole—Mr. Popper was the first to borrow it. Indeed, he had read so much about polar explorers that he could name all of them and tell you what each had done.

One evening, when the little Poppers had been put to bed, Mr. and Mrs. Popper settled down for a long, quiet evening. Mrs. Popper picked up her mending, while Mr. Popper collected his pipe, his book, and his globe.

"What are you reading?" asked Mrs. Popper.

"I am reading a book called *Antarctic Adventures*. It is very interesting. I think the nicest part of all is the penguins. They are the funniest birds in the world. They don't fly like other birds. They walk upright like little men. It would be very nice to have one for a pet."

"Pets!" said Mrs. Popper. "First it's Bill wanting a dog and then Janie begging for a kitten. Now you and penguins! I won't have any pets around. They make too much dirt in the house, and I have enough work now."

Mr. Popper put down his book of *Antarctic Adventures* and turned hastily to the radio.

"This is the night the Drake Antarctic Expedition is going to start broadcasting," he said.

There was a buzz, and then suddenly, from the South Pole, a faint voice floated out into the Popper living room.

"This is Admiral Drake speaking. Hello, Mama. Hello, Papa. Hello, Mr. Popper."

"For goodness sakes!" exclaimed Mrs. Popper. "Did he say 'Papa' or 'Popper'?"

"Hello, Mr. Popper, up there in Stillwater. Thanks for your nice letter about the movie of our expedition. Watch for an answer. But not by letter, Mr. Popper. Watch for a surprise."

"*You* wrote to Admiral Drake?"

266

"Yes, I did," Mr. Popper said. "I wrote and told him how funny I thought the penguins were."

Mr. Popper picked up his little globe and found the Antarctic. "And to think he spoke to me all the way from there! And he even mentioned my name. Mama, what do you suppose he means by a surprise?"

"I haven't any idea," answered Mrs. Popper.

What with the excitement of having the great Admiral Drake speak to him over the radio, and his curiosity about the Admiral's message to him, Mr. Popper did not sleep very well that night.

The next day he settled down with his pipe, his globe, and his book of *Antarctic Adventures*. Somehow, as he read today, he could not keep his mind on the printed words. His thoughts kept straying away to Admiral Drake. What could he have meant by a surprise for Mr. Popper?

That afternoon, while Mrs. Popper was away at a meeting and Janie and Bill had not yet come home from school, there was a loud ring at the front door.

Mr. Popper went to the door. There stood an express-man with a very large box.

"Party by the name of Popper live here?"

"That's me."

"Well, here's a package that's come Air Express all the way from Antarctica. Some journey, I'll say."

Mr. Popper examined the box. It was covered all over with markings. "UNPACK AT ONCE," said one. "KEEP COOL," said another. He noticed that the box was punched here and there with air holes.

You can imagine that once he had the box inside the house, Mr. Popper lost no time in opening it. He had removed the outer boards and part of the packing, when he suddenly heard a faint "*Ork.*" His heart stood still. Surely he had heard that sound before at the Drake Expedition movies. His hands were trembling so that he could hardly lift off the last of the wrappings.

There was not the slightest doubt about it. It was a penguin.

Mr. Popper was speechless with delight.

The penguin was not speechless. "*Ork,*" it said again, and this time it held out its flippers and jumped out of the box.

Although it was about the size of a small child, it looked much more like a little gentleman, with its smooth white waistcoat in front and its long black tailcoat dragging a little behind. Its eyes were set in two white circles in its black head. It turned its head from one side to the other as, first with one eye and then with the other, it examined Mr. Popper.

Mr. Popper had read that penguins are very, very curious, and he soon found that this was true, for the visitor began to explore the house. Down the hall it went and into the bedrooms with its strange, pompous little strut. When it got to the bathroom, it looked very pleased.

"Perhaps," thought Mr. Popper, "all that white tile reminds him of the ice and snow at the South Pole. Poor thing, maybe he's thirsty."

Carefully Mr. Popper began to fill the bathtub with cold water. This was a little difficult because the curious bird kept reaching over and trying to bite the faucets with its sharp red beak. Finally, the tub was all filled, and Mr. Popper picked the penguin up and dropped it in. The penguin seemed not to mind.

## A Curious Bird

When he thought the penguin had had enough of a bath, Mr. Popper drew out the stopper. He was just wondering what to do next when Janie and Bill burst in from school.

"Papa," they shouted together at the bathroom door. "What is it?"

"It's a South Pole penguin sent to me by Admiral Drake."

"Look!" said Bill. "It's marching."

The delighted penguin was indeed marching. With little pleased nods of his handsome black head he was parading up and down the inside of the bathtub.

"For such a big bird he takes awfully small steps," said Bill.

"And look how his little black coat drags behind. It almost looks as if it were too big for him," said Janie.

But the penguin was tired of marching. This time, when it got to the end of the tub, it decided to jump up the slippery curve. Then it turned, and with outstretched flippers, slid down on its white stomach. Janie could see that the flippers, which were black on the outside like the sleeves of a tailcoat, were white underneath.

"*Gook! Gook!*" said the penguin, trying its new game again and again.

"What's his name, Papa?" asked Janie.

"*Gook! Gook!*" said the penguin, sliding down once more on his glossy white stomach.

"It sounds something like 'Cook,'" said Mr. Popper. "Why, that's it, of course. We'll call him Cook—Captain Cook."

"Call who Captain Cook?" asked Mrs. Popper, who had come in so quietly that none of them had heard her.

270

"Why, the penguin," said Mr. Popper. "I was just saying," he went on, as the surprised Mrs. Popper sat down suddenly on the floor, "that we'd name him after Captain Cook. He was a famous English explorer. He sailed all over where no one had ever been before. He didn't actually get to the South Pole, of course, but he made a lot of important discoveries about the Antarctic regions. He was a brave man and a kind leader. So I think Captain Cook would be a very suitable name for our penguin here."

"Well, I never!" said Mrs. Popper.

"*Gork!*" said Captain Cook, suddenly getting lively again. With a flap of his flippers he jumped from the tub and strutted to the washstand and stood there for a minute. Then he marched over to Mrs. Popper, and began to peck her ankle.

"Stop him, Papa!" screamed Mrs. Popper, running into the hallway with Captain Cook after her, and Mr. Popper and the children following. In the living room she paused. So did Captain Cook, for he was delighted with the room.

Now a penguin may look very strange in a living room, but a living room looks very strange to a penguin. Even Mrs. Popper had to smile as they watched curious Captain Cook. His black tailcoat dragged pompously behind his little pinkish feet, as he strutted from one chair to another, pecking at each to see what it was made of. Then he turned suddenly and marched out to the kitchen.

"Maybe he's hungry," said Janie.

Captain Cook marched up to the refrigerator.

"*Ork?*" said the penguin, nibbling at the metal handle of the refrigerator door.

Mr. Popper opened the door for him, and Captain Cook stood very high and leaned his glossy black head back so that he could see inside.

"What do you suppose he likes to eat?" asked Mrs. Popper.

"Let's see," said Mr. Popper, as he took out all the food and set it on the kitchen table. "Now then, Captain Cook, take a look."

The penguin jumped up onto a chair and from there onto the edge of the table, flapping his flippers to keep his balance. Then he walked around the table, and between the dishes of food, examining everything with the greatest interest, though he touched nothing. Finally, he stood still, raised his beak to point at the ceiling, and made a loud, almost purring sound. *"O-r-r-r-r-h, o-r-r-h!"*

"That's a penguin's way of saying how pleased it is," said Mr. Popper, who had read about it in his Antarctic books.

But what Captain Cook wanted to show was that he was pleased with their kindness, rather than with their food. For now, to their surprise, he jumped down and walked into the dining room.

"I know," said Mr. Popper. "We ought to have some seafood for him. Or maybe he isn't hungry yet. I've read that penguins can go for a month without food."

"Mama! Papa!" called Bill. "Come see what Captain Cook has done."

Captain Cook had done it all right. He had discovered the bowl of goldfish on the dining-room windowsill. By the time Mrs. Popper reached over to lift him away, he had already swallowed the last of the goldfish.

"Bad, bad penguin!" scolded Mrs. Popper, glaring down at Captain Cook.

Captain Cook squatted guiltily on the carpet and tried to make himself look small.

"He knows he's done wrong," said Mr. Popper. "Isn't he smart?"

273

"Maybe we can train him," said Mrs. Popper. "Bad naughty Captain," she said to the penguin in a loud voice. "Bad, to eat the goldfish." And she spanked him on his round black head.

Before she could do that again, Captain Cook hastily strutted out to the kitchen.

There the Poppers found him trying to hide in the still opened refrigerator. He was squatting under the ice-cube coils, under which he could barely squeeze.

"I think that's about the right temperature for him, at that," said Mr. Popper. "We could let him sleep there, at night."

"But where will I put the food?" asked Mrs. Popper.

"Oh, I guess we can get another refrigerator for the food," said Mr. Popper.

"Look," said Janie. "He's gone to sleep."

Mr. Popper turned the cold control switch to its coldest so that Captain Cook could sleep more comfortably. Then he left the door open so that the penguin would have plenty of fresh air to breathe.

"Tomorrow I will have the refrigerator company send a service man out to bore some holes in the door, for air," he said. "Then he can put a handle on the inside of the door so that Captain Cook can go in and out of his refrigerator, as he pleases."

"Well, dear me, I never thought we would have a penguin for a pet," said Mrs. Popper.


## Pretending to Be a Popper

Choose one of these things to do. Find ideas in the story, but try to say them as Mr. or Mrs. Popper would.

1. Write a telephone conversation between Mr. Popper and Mr. Jones, the man at the refrigerator company. To Mr. Popper it may *not* seem strange to ask to have holes bored in the refrigerator door and a handle put on the inside of the door. But how do you suppose Mr. Jones would feel?

You may wish to begin the conversation like this:

MR. POPPER: Could you send a service man here today?

MR. JONES: Certainly. What do you need to have done?

2. Reread the things that Mrs. Popper said. Notice how she expressed herself. Pretend that you are Mrs. Popper and write a letter to a friend telling about your new pet.

# Someone

By Walter de la Mare

Someone came knocking
   At my wee, small door;
Someone came knocking,
   I'm sure—sure—sure;
I listened, I opened,
   I looked to left and right,
But nought there was a-stirring
   In the still, dark night;
Only the busy beetle
   Tap-tapping in the wall,
Only from the forest
   The screech owl's call,
Only the cricket whistling
   While the dewdrops fall,
So I know not who came knocking,
   At all, at all, at all.

# The Potatoes' Dance

By Vachel Lindsay

## I

"Down cellar," said the cricket,
"Down cellar," said the cricket,
"Down cellar," said the cricket,
"I saw a ball last night,
In honor of a lady,
In honor of a lady,
In honor of a lady,
Whose wings were pearly white.
The breath of bitter weather,
The breath of bitter weather,
The breath of bitter weather,
Had smashed the cellar pane.
We entertained a drift of leaves,
We entertained a drift of leaves,
We entertained a drift of leaves,
And then of snow and rain.
But we were dressed for winter,
But we were dressed for winter,
But we were dressed for winter,
And loved to hear it blow
In honor of the lady,
In honor of the lady,
In honor of the lady,
Who makes potatoes grow,

Our guest the Irish lady,
The tiny Irish lady,
The airy Irish lady,
Who makes potatoes grow.

## II
"Potatoes were the waiters,
Potatoes were the waiters,
Potatoes were the waiters,
Potatoes were the band,
Potatoes were the dancers
Kicking up the sand,
Kicking up the sand,
Kicking up the sand,
Potatoes were the dancers
Kicking up the sand.
Their legs were old burnt matches,
Their legs were old burnt matches,
Their legs were old burnt matches,
Their arms were just the same.
They jigged and whirled and scrambled,
Jigged and whirled and scrambled,
Jigged and whirled and scrambled,
In honor of the dame,
The noble Irish lady
Who makes potatoes dance,
The witty Irish lady,
The saucy Irish lady,
The laughing Irish lady
Who makes potatoes prance.

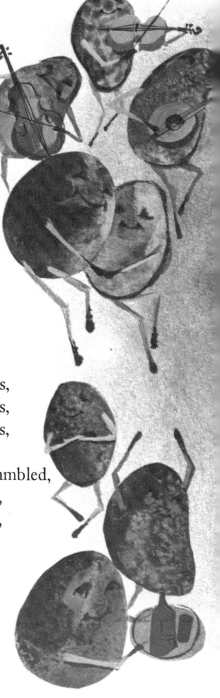

### III

"There was just one sweet potato.
He was golden brown and slim.
The lady loved his dancing,
The lady loved his dancing,
The lady loved his dancing,
She danced all night with him,
She danced all night with him.
Alas, he wasn't Irish.
So when she flew away,
They threw him in the coalbin,
And there he is today,
Where they cannot hear his sighs
And his weeping for the lady,
The glorious Irish lady,
The beauteous Irish lady,
Who
Gives
Potatoes
Eyes."

# Books to Enjoy

*Winnie-the-Pooh*, by A. A. Milne.

The story of Pooh getting stuck in the rabbit hole is only one chapter from this delightfully funny book. In it you will meet all of Pooh's friends as they go on strange expeditions to catch a woozle, to find the North Pole, or to meet a heffalump.

*Adventures of Pinocchio*, by C. Collodi.

The many pranks of Pinocchio lead the wooden marionette from one adventure to another until he finally learns what it means to be a "real" little boy.

*Heidi*, by Johanna Spyri.

This is one of the truly great books written for children. It is long and somewhat hard to read, but by reading it you will gain a colorful trip to the Swiss Alps and a delightful friend in Heidi.

*Mr. Popper's Penguins*, by Richard and Florence Atwater.

The arrival of Captain Cook is only the beginning of Mr. Popper's funny adventures with penguins. Later comes Greta, and then the eggs, and then all the little penguins, and finally fame for their owner.

*The Peterkin Papers*, by Lucretia P. Hale.

The Peterkin family has one hilarious problem after another —problems that may never have been solved if it had not been for the intelligent lady from Philadelphia.

*Charlotte's Web*, by E. B. White.

The barnyard life of the pig Wilbur is lovely and peaceful until he learns that he, as all pigs, will be killed. Amazing things happen when Wilbur's spider friend helps him.

# God Speaks

# The Word of God

By Sister M. Sheila, P.B.V.M.

God speaks in many ways—
Through many things.
Man hears in many ways—
Through many things.

The heavens and the earth
Speak of the glory of God.
All creation sings of His love,
His greatness, and His beauty.

Listen, Man, to all creation.
Listen to the Word that God speaks,
For the Word brings joy and peace;
It brings strength and salvation.

282

*In the beginning God spoke to man. He spoke through creation. He spoke through kings and prophets.*

# A Humble Servant

**From the Old Testament**

The first time God spoke to Moses, He spoke from a burning bush.

On that day Moses was out on the hillside watching over the sheep as they grazed. He may have been thinking of his people who were being held as slaves by the Egyptians, for it was the greatest desire of Moses to free his people.

Now, when Moses saw the flames of fire in the bush, he was amazed. Although the fire was in the middle of it, the bush was not burning.

283

"I will go and see this great sight," Moses said. "I will find out how it is that the bush has fire in the midst of it, but yet is not burning."

As Moses moved forward, out of the bush came the voice of God, calling, "Moses, Moses."

And Moses answered, "Here I am."

And the Lord said, "I am the God of your father, the God of Abraham, the God of Isaac, and the God of Jacob."

Upon hearing this, Moses hid his face, for he dared not look at God.

Then the Lord said to him, "I have seen the great grief and suffering of My people in Egypt. I have heard their cry. Knowing their sorrow, I have come down to free them from the hands of the Egyptians. I have come to lead them out of that land into a good and spacious land.

"Come, and I will send you to the Pharaoh that you may lead My people, the children of Israel, out of Egypt."

It was hard for Moses, the humble shepherd, to believe that he should become the leader of so many people. And he cried out, "Who am I that I should go to the Pharaoh? Who am I that I should lead the children of Israel out of Egypt?"

Comforting him, the Lord said to Moses, "I will be with you."

Then Moses went to the Pharaoh and told him what God had commanded.

Now, although the Pharaoh hated the children of Israel, he found them useful in his country. So he said

to Moses, "Who is the Lord that I should hear His voice and let the Israelites go? I do not know the Lord. I will not let these people go."

Then the Pharaoh became angry with the Israelites because of their desire to leave Egypt. He ordered that they be given harder work than ever and less freedom. He treated them more cruelly in all ways.

So that the Pharaoh might see the wickedness of his acts, God sent punishment to all the Egyptians. Plague after plague came to their country. The horses, the camels, and the beasts of the fields all died. The crops were destroyed. Finally, all of the eldest sons of the Egyptian people died—all in a single night.

This last punishment so filled the Pharaoh with fear that he called Moses and cried out, "Arise, Moses, and leave my people at once. Take with you all the Israelites. Take your flocks, too, and your herds."

And so the Israelites, free at last, went out of Egypt with Moses as their leader.

It was not long before the Pharaoh was sorry that he had let the Israelites go. He decided that he wanted his slaves back, and so he led his great army after them. The children of Israel looked back, and there was the great army of the Pharaoh. And they looked forward, and there before them was the Red Sea.

As the great army drew nearer, the Israelites became more and more frightened. But Moses said to the people, "Fear not. Stand and see the great wonders of the Lord which He will do this day. The Egyptian army which you see now, you will see no more. The Lord will fight for you, and you shall hold your peace."

So, at God's command, Moses gave orders to the people to go forward. Suddenly the Red Sea parted, the water becoming two high walls. In the middle was a dry road. Down this road Moses led his people until all were safe.

Behind them the Pharaoh and his army came. They rushed between the high walls of water. Instantly the walls of water fell back, and the mighty king and his army were drowned.

And so, the Lord saved Israel that day from the hands of the Egyptians. And the Israelites feared the Lord, believing in Him and in Moses, His servant. But their belief was not lasting. Again and again they lost faith in their Lord and in their leader.

Above all things, the Lord wished to save the souls of His people from sin. So it was that again the Lord spoke to His servant. It was on the day when Moses and the Israelites had come to the wilderness of Sinai.

God called to Moses and said, "Now, I will come to you in the darkness of a cloud so that the people may hear Me speaking to you and may believe you forever."

And then on the morning of the third day there was thunder and lightning, and a thick cloud covered the mountain. Fire and smoke rose around the mountain.

The Lord came down upon Mount Sinai on the very top of the mountain, and He called Moses to the top.

The Lord delivered these commandments to Moses.

I, THE LORD, AM YOUR GOD; YOU SHALL NOT HAVE OTHER GODS BESIDES ME.

YOU SHALL NOT TAKE THE NAME OF THE LORD, YOUR GOD, IN VAIN.

REMEMBER TO KEEP HOLY THE SABBATH DAY.

HONOR YOUR FATHER AND YOUR MOTHER.

YOU SHALL NOT KILL.

YOU SHALL NOT COMMIT ADULTERY.

YOU SHALL NOT STEAL.

YOU SHALL NOT BEAR FALSE WITNESS AGAINST YOUR NEIGHBOR.

YOU SHALL NOT COVET YOUR NEIGHBOR'S WIFE.

YOU SHALL NOT COVET YOUR NEIGHBOR'S GOODS.

So it was that Moses received the Ten Commandments of God. And he came down from the mountain with two tablets of stone on which the commandments were written.

For forty years Moses was to the Israelites a teacher and a leader. He did the work that God commanded of him and delivered his people safely to the Promised Land.

There were other prophets to whom God spoke in visions or in dreams. But never again was there a prophet in Israel like Moses, to whom God spoke face to face.

For, as the Lord said, "I speak to him mouth to mouth, and plainly. Not by visions does he see the Lord."

## Saying It Another Way

The story of Moses has been taken from the Old Testament of the Bible. It is written very much as it was in the Bible. Words and phrases that we would not use today are used in Bible stories. Rewrite the following sentences, changing the underlined parts to show that you understand how these things would be said today.

1. The bush has fire in the midst of it.
2. Upon hearing this, Moses hid his face.
3. Who is the Lord that I should hear His voice?
4. Arise, Moses, and leave my people.
5. Moses said to the people, "Fear not."
6. So it was that again the Lord spoke to Moses.
7. So it was that Moses received the Ten Commandments.
8. He delivered his people safely.

# Christmas Morning

By Elizabeth Madox Roberts

If Bethlehem were here today,
Or this were very long ago,
There wouldn't be a winter time
Nor any cold or snow.

I'd run out through the garden gate,
And down along the pasture walk;
And off beside the cattle barns
I'd hear a kind of gentle talk.

I'd move the heavy iron chain
And pull away the wooden pin;
I'd push the door a little bit
And tiptoe very softly in.

The pigeons and the yellow hens
And all the cows would stand away;
Their eyes would open wide to see
A lady in the manger hay,
If this were very long ago
And Bethlehem were here today.

And Mother held my hand and smiled—
I mean the lady would—and she
Would take the woolly blankets off
Her little boy so I could see.

His shut-up eyes would be asleep,
And he would look like our John,
And he would be all crumpled too,
And have a pinkish color on.

I'd watch his breath go in and out.
His little clothes would be all white.
I'd slip my finger in his hand
To feel how he could hold it tight.

And she would smile and say, "Take care,"
The mother, Mary, would, "Take care,"
And I would kiss his little hand
And touch his hair.

While Mary put the blankets back
The gentle talk would soon begin.
And when I'd tiptoe softly out
I'd meet the Wise Men going in.

*When God sent His only Son to earth,*
*He used angels to tell His word. Through*
*angels He spoke to the shepherds.*

# The Shepherd's Coat

By Caryll Houselander

There was never anyone else in the world who could tell such beautiful stories as Benji's grandfather. Of all the stories he told, none was so wonderful as the true story he loved to tell again and again. It was about the night that Benji's grandfather had gone to the cave in Bethlehem and saw the mysterious Baby.

Many nights, when the sheep and the lambs were all in the fold, Benji's grandfather would gather the younger shepherds around him and tell them the story.

The old man would describe the sudden glory and the chorus of angels shouting their joyful song. He would describe the great ropes of stars swinging like golden chains in the sky. He would tell about the one great star that was more beautiful than all the others put together.

Then Grandfather would tell about seeing the little family in the stable—the infant lying in the manger, the poor father, and the very young mother. When he came to this part of the story, the old man's voice shook as if he were near tears—as if the memory was too sweet for him.

Most of the shepherds laughed kindly. It seemed strange to them that the old man should be more stirred by three ordinary people in a stable than he was by a sky blazing with angels. Benji understood. But he kept wondering why the angels took the shepherds to see this child.

When the other shepherds had wrapped their blankets around them and gone to sleep, Benji would ask Grandfather questions long into the night.

"Did you give him anything?" Benji would ask.

"Yes, Benji, I gave him a lambskin. It was a cold night and the poor infant was shivering."

"How long ago was it?" Benji wanted to know.

"It was twelve years ago," the old man answered.

"Then now he would be my age, a boy like me?" Benji questioned.

"Yes."

"Grandfather, he must be *somewhere*. Do you think we could ever find him again?" asked the boy.

"Well, I don't think so, Benji," Grandfather said, shaking his head. "When we went back, they had gone. The stable was empty except for the four-footed beasts."

"How I wish I knew who he was, and where he is!" said Benji.

Several days later, Benji's father came to him and gave him a sheepskin coat.

"You are twelve years old," his father said. "That is grown-up. Now you must be a real shepherd."

He put the sheepskin coat on Benji and the shepherd's staff in his hand. Benji felt the warmth and softness of the coat. He saw how the sheep came up close to him and huddled against the coat. Only then did Benji begin to understand the sheep in a new way and all that it meant to be a real shepherd.

294

Every morning after that Benji took his flock out on the hills, and every evening he gathered them home. As often as he did so, he wondered about the boy who had been an infant in the manger.

Benji thought, "If only I could find him, I would go to him. I would give him my sheepskin coat, the best thing I have. Yes, I would kneel down and put it on him and fasten the belt around his waist. I would serve him forever and ever."

After the sheep were gathered in at night, Benji would pray to God under the stars. "Grant to me, almighty Father, that I may find the wonderful little one and may give him my sheepskin coat."

One windy evening, with a storm coming up and dark clouds driving across the sky, a lamb was discovered missing. Benji had to find it.

As he walked up into the hills, the sky became blacker, and the wind was howling. It was hard to know where to look for the lamb. Benji tried first one path and then another. Often he stood listening for the lamb's bleat.

At last he thought that he heard a poor little frightened cry. "I'm coming," he shouted. "Where are you?"

He hoped the lamb would bleat again so he would know which way to go. But to his amazement, *words* came to him. He heard a tiny shrill voice saying, "Here I am. I'm lost!"

Benji followed the voice along a rocky path. Coming around the corner of a big rock, he saw not his lamb. He saw a tiny boy, shivering with cold and fear. He was weeping pitifully.

"I'm lost. I'm cold. I'm hungry," he wept.

Benji knelt down and put his arm around the boy.
"I will take you home as soon as I find my lamb," he said.
"Tell me where you live."

The little boy was sobbing now in a way that he could
not stop. His poor little ribs were heaving in and out,
and his teeth were chattering.

Suddenly an idea came to Benji. He took off his sheepskin coat and put it on the little boy. It was all warm
with the warmth of Benji's own body. As soon as the
little boy felt the comfort of it, he began to stop crying.

At last the lamb was found, and Benji took the lost
child to his house. Benji did not have the heart to take
back his coat. The child seemed to be such a poor little
boy, and his own coat was so thin. His mother was a
poor woman.

Benji thought, "For a shepherd it is easy to get such a coat. For this little boy it would be nearly impossible. I will let him keep mine."

As Benji went home without his coat, he felt sad. He was not sad because he no longer had the coat for himself. But if he should ever see the wonderful boy of the angels' song, he could not give him his first shepherd's coat.

Benji knew that no other coat would be the same. This first coat had been the sign of his being a shepherd. It had made him friends with the flock. He felt almost as if he had given *himself* to the little lost boy!

The years passed for Benji, and the day came when Grandfather was too old to live out in the hills with the shepherds. Benji was now thirty years old, and it was for him to take Grandfather down to Jerusalem where he would live with some of his relatives.

After walking for many miles toward the city, they came to a hilltop, and it was then that Benji saw a most wonderful sight. Below them in the valley, surrounded by the sunset clouds, lay Jerusalem. His grandfather saw a group of people nearby. The people were sitting on the ground talking, very much as the shepherds themselves often sat talking on the hillside.

Benji had eyes only for the city, and might not have even noticed the group of people. But his grandfather suddenly gripped his arm and whispered in his ear, "Benji, Benji, it is the infant of Bethlehem!"

Benji looked around in amazement. There were just a few poor men there. In their midst there was a young man explaining something. He was about Benji's own

age. It was at this man that his grandfather was looking
so intently. But how could he possibly know?

"How do you know?" Benji asked.

"Do you not see that woman watching him? Do you
see her face and the love in her face? Do you see it,
Benji?"

"Yes, I do."

"Well, Benji, isn't it sure that she is the young man's
mother?"

"Yes, it is, indeed, Grandfather. That's a mother's
look, I'm sure."

"Well then, Benji, it's the baby the angels led us to, for
I can recognize her; she is the mother who was in the
stable. I know him by his mother."

Benji's heart leaped up in joy and love. "Oh, Grandfather," he said, "if only I still had my first sheepskin
coat, the only *great* treasure that I ever had. It was my
dream to give it to him. But I gave it away many years

ago to a cold little stranger I found when I was looking for one of our lambs."

"Hush, lad!" said Grandfather. "Let us listen to what He is saying, for He is surely the Lord." They moved a little closer and listened.

The Lord was speaking slowly while looking at His listeners. He was speaking about sheep. He was saying, "And He shall set the sheep on His right hand, but the goats on the left."

Benji and his grandfather stood like statues. They hardly breathed for fear that they should fail to hear the beautiful voice.

The voice went on telling what we have often heard, but what *they* were hearing for the first time. They learned that on the day of Judgment people would find out with astonishment that little kind things they had done and forgotten were really done to the Lord, Who would never forget.

299

"I was naked," Benji heard, "and you covered Me."

Benji listened and the lovely story went on until the Lord said that the people would ask, "Lord, when did we see You naked and cover You?" And the answer came back, "As long as you did it for one of these, the least of My brothers, you did it for Me."

Just then the Lord looked aside and smiled at Benji. Suddenly Benji saw a cold little boy wrapped in the sheepskin coat again. Then he understood. It was as if joyous bells were ringing in his soul.

Benji went back to his sheep and lived the life of a good shepherd. He knew that his dream had come true. He knew that it came true long before he had seen the Child, of the angels' song, grown to be a Man.

## Finding the Author's Words

The author uses words well to express beautiful thoughts and to help the reader see beautiful pictures. Skim the story to find sentences that show the way the author expresses the following things. For your answers, write the page number, the paragraph number, and the sentence number to show where you found the author's words.

1. Grandfather told of hearing the angels singing.
2. He would describe how the stars looked in the sky.
3. Only animals were in the stable.
4. Below them in the valley was Jerusalem.
5. Benji and his grandfather stood very still.
6. Benji felt a joy very deep within himself.
7. He had seen the Infant after He was grown.

*Then when Christ became a Man, He Himself spoke. He spoke in parables.*

# The Prodigal Son

**From the New Testament, St. Luke, 15**

At that time Jesus said—
A certain man had two sons,
And the younger said to him,
"Father, give me my inheritance
And let me leave to seek my fortune."
And the father was sad, but he agreed.
Not many days later, the younger son left.
He went far away into another country,
And there he spent all he had.
A mighty famine came into that country,
And the boy was very hungry.
He hired himself out as a servant,
But no one shared any food with him.
At last he said, "Those in my father's house
Are clothed well and they eat well. I shall rise
And go to my father and I shall say to him,
'Father, I am sorry for what I have done.
I am not worthy to be called your son.
Let me live in your house as a servant,
And I shall be satisfied.' "
And arising, he started home.

When he was yet a long way off,
His father saw him coming and was glad.
He ran to meet his son and he kissed him.
The boy fell on his knees and said,
"Father, I am not worthy to be called your son."
But his father lifted him up and called to his servants,
"Bring forth fine clothes and put them on him.
Kill the fatted calf and let us make merry,
For my son, who was lost, has been found
And has returned home to all of us.
He, who was dead, is now alive.
Let us give thanks and let us be glad."

302

*Today when God speaks, sometimes He speaks through the love children have for beauty, the love they have for the saints— God's holy ones.*

# The Reward of Love

By Janice Holland

## The Search

Maestro Doni had given the boys a week in which to design their statues of St. Francis. Time flew like the wind for Carlo. One after another he made drawings of his ideas for the figure, and one after another he tore them up. He could not be satisfied with any of them.

Over and over Carlo had heard the beautiful stories of the good friar. Carlo always liked to think of St. Francis as walking the dusty roads, singing to the wide skies his joy in the love of God and all that God had made.

Most saints were rather sorrowful—at least they looked so in the paintings that filled the churches. But St. Francis said that joy was most pleasing to God. Truly, if one loved the sun and the moon, the wolf, the deer, the birds, and even the air itself as St. Francis did, how could he be other than happy?

How could one ever capture such a living spirit in wood and paint? Yet with these alone the statue must be made to sing, to breathe.

If only St. Francis had worn a brocaded cloak! Then there would have been something to add beauty to the statue. Instead, he had chosen the coarse brown robe in which his followers were even now seen on the streets of Assisi. No, there was no outer beauty to show. All the glory of St. Francis was in his golden spirit. Unless one could capture that, the statue would be dead.

On Wednesday afternoon Carlo took the winding road from Assisi to the little church where St. Francis and his followers had so often gone to pray. Perhaps, if Carlo prayed there, he would also feel the spirit of the good saint and could put it into his work.

After praying in the church, Carlo wandered into the little garden just outside. There grew the thornless roses,

brought into being by the great holiness of the saint. Carlo sat down on a stone bench and looked at the bare stalks standing in the hard brown earth. In only a few weeks the miracle of spring would crown them with glorious blooms. Carlo jumped to his feet.

That was it! The lovely flowers, springing from the hard, brown earth, were like the spirit of St. Francis, springing from the plain figure in the coarse brown robe!

At last Carlo knew how he wanted to carve his statue. He would show the friar with his head raised in joyous song, his robes flowing with life. In his arms would be the thornless roses—the glory of his soul.

Carlo hurried back to the studio. In the failing daylight he quickly drew the lines of his statue. So eagerly did he work that one piece of charcoal after another broke under his hand. Carlo hardly noticed.

When the daylight died, he lighted a candle, hardly knowing that he did so, and went on with his work. He sketched the front, the two sides, and the back of his statue. The town clock was striking nine before he sat down. Carlo drew a deep and happy sigh and put out the candle. His sketches were ready for the Maestro.

The next morning Carlo arrived at the studio early, as usual. He began to fasten his sketches to one wall of the studio. Before he had finished, the other boys came in. One after another they arranged their drawings on the wall near Carlo's. Just as they finished, their teacher entered.

"Ah! I see you have all brought your designs," Maestro Doni said.

One by one he studied the drawings. His students watched him closely.

"This one is yours, Giorgio? Very good. Very good, indeed. I see you have chosen to show St. Francis as he preached to the birds."

"Yes, Maestro," Giorgio said quickly. "I hope to show the good saint's love for his 'little sisters,' the birds."

"You have made a good beginning. And now, Pietro, you have chosen St. Francis' taming of the terrible wolf of Gubbio."

"Yes. I hope to show his great love even for those who are fierce and cruel," Pietro answered.

"I believe you will do that, Pietro," the Maestro said. "Now, Marco, tell us what you have in mind."

306

"I wish to show St. Francis when he met the young man who had caught many wild doves and was about to sell them in the market place. St. Francis, you remember, talked the young man into giving them to him. Then, holding them close to his heart, he said, 'Oh, my little sisters, the doves, so simple, so pure, I will save you from death. I will make you nests, so that you may live as God wishes.' "

"You have chosen well, Marco. But you must be careful not to let the birds clutter your design. A statue must be simple, you know.

"Well, Bredo, tell us now about your design."

"I have chosen no single moment from the saint's life," Bredo said. "What I wish to do is group the little animals and birds around him so as to show his love for them all. See, I have sketched in a squirrel, a rabbit, a pigeon, and several others, nestling against the folds in his robe."

"You are a skillful sculptor, Bredo," said his teacher. "But a statue is not made better because of the number of things in it. Won't you try to make your design a little more simple?

"And now, Carlo. I see you have a very simple design. That is good. Tell us about it."

"I have tried to make the figure as I thought St. Francis himself would like it. It seemed to me that nothing could show his gentleness and his love like the beautiful thornless roses that I have put in his hands."

"Good, good," said the Maestro softly, almost as though to himself. Then he looked at his students. "I am well pleased with the way you have all begun your work. Now go into the storeroom and choose for yourselves suitable blocks of wood. You have no time to lose, for it is only seven weeks until the last of May, when the statues will be judged."

The boys rushed through the door at the back of the studio and into the crowded, dusty storeroom. Wooden blocks of all shapes and sizes were standing against the walls and scattered about the floor.

Carlo was the last to make his choice, but finally he found a block that satisfied him. He carried it into the studio and clamped it to a stand. For a moment he stood looking at the beautiful, unmarked block.

"Oh, good St. Francis," Carlo said in a low voice, "in you alone is the spirit that will make this statue live. Please come to me and guide my hand." Then, trembling with excitement, he began to draw his design upon the wood.

308

## The Spirit of St. Francis

For the next few weeks the studio hummed with happy activity. Chips of wood covered the floor, and the rough outlines of the statues began to appear.

One morning Carlo was at the studio as soon as it was light. He was surprised to find someone else had already arrived. It was Bredo who was there before him. Carlo noticed that Bredo's work was moving along faster than that of any of the others.

When Carlo passed Bredo, he saw something that pierced his heart like a knife. Bredo, eager to do a good job of his statue, had a living model to work from. A brown rabbit, half grown, stood on the table before him. The rabbit had been tied with heavy wire so that it could not move.

The fear in the poor dumb creature's eyes called out to Carlo for help. At once Carlo started toward it.

"Oh, Bredo, how could you—how could you?" he moaned. "How can you carve a statue of St. Francis and, in the carving, torture the very creatures he loved?"

"My statue will last a hundred years or more," Bredo answered angrily. "The wonderful, lifelike animals will be admired by everyone. What's the suffering of one little rabbit? The world is full of suffering."

"It is people like you who make it so!" breathed Carlo. He felt in his pocket for a coin he had been saving toward the price of a new jacket. He held the coin out to Bredo. "Sell me the rabbit. You have almost finished your work on it anyway."

With a sneer, Bredo said, "Well! The poor boy has so much money he can throw it around buying rabbits! Give me the coin. I've gotten the best use of the creature anyway. Now take it and get out of here!"

Quickly Carlo untied the rabbit. It was trembling with fright. Tenderly he put it inside his jacket, next to his heart. He would take it out and let it run free.

The work in the studio speeded up as the day of the contest drew closer. Maestro Doni often passed through the room as the boys worked, suggesting a change here or there in one figure or another. If he liked any of them best, he never showed it.

310

Finally all the statues had been finished, and the day
of the judging came. The statues were being set up in
the square. Carlo looked up at his own work. The sun
was slanting across it so that the light caught the joyous
smile on St. Francis' upturned face. The brown robe below fell into shadow, but the light blazed again on the
thornless roses, white as pearls, in his hands. Carlo sighed.
Whoever won the prize, he knew that this was the best
carving he had ever done.

When the judges announced the winner that afternoon, Carlo found that he had not won the prize. Bredo's statue with the lifelike animals was judged the best.

Carlo's head throbbed, his throat ached, he could hardly see. Bredo! Bredo had won! How was it possible? Carlo turned quickly and fled from the square. He had no idea how long he had been walking before he found himself at the door of Maestro Doni's studio.

"Come in, Carlo," said Maestro Doni. "I have been waiting for you."

"Oh, Maestro," Carlo wept. He could not keep from crying any longer. Great sobs shook his shoulders as he knelt before his teacher. "How could it have happened this way? Bredo does not even love the good St. Francis. He tortured the little creatures he carved."

"I know, I know," the Maestro whispered, putting his hand softly upon Carlo's head. "This greatly disappoints me, too, although I feared it might happen. Bredo's skill in carving is rare. But to find a sculptor who can give a statue the simple grace and gladness that your St. Francis has is rarer by far. Do not give up hope. Sometimes it takes greatness to know greatness. The cleverness of Bredo's work is easily seen."

The Maestro stopped suddenly. "Which would you rather have," he asked, "the spirit of St. Francis, or the prize money?"

Carlo realized what the Maestro wanted him to say. "Surely you know the answer to that," he murmured, looking down at the floor.

The Maestro put his arm around Carlo.

"No one can love as St. Francis loved," he said, "without learning that hope and love sometimes are lost in sorrow. You are very like the good saint, my lad. And the cruelty of the world will often make you weep. But St. Francis found the joy that lies hidden beyond the pain—the joy that the world can never take away. Some day that joy will come to you."

Carlo gave his teacher a grateful look. He wanted to speak, to thank him for all he had said, but he could not find the words. With a shy smile he turned and slipped out into the night. The weeks and weeks of work had left him worn out. Joy was only a word—a faraway word. He found his way home in the darkness and fell into bed.

Carlo remembered nothing more until the next morning, when he was awakened by shouts of his friend, Antonio. "Carlo! Carlo! Come at once! You must see! There is a crowd of people in the square, and they are all looking at your statue. Hurry!"

313

Carlo hurried out and followed Antonio. Arriving at the square, Carlo saw men, women, and children standing before his statue. They were hushed and still. All were looking in the same direction. Carlo followed their gaze up, up to the statue. There, in the hands of St. Francis, among the thornless roses, a white dove sat upon her new-made nest.

"Surely the spirit of St. Francis, who freed the captive doves, lives in that statue!" whispered an old woman nearby. "This dove feels that holy love and knows she is safe in his arms!"

Carlo stood for a moment, almost unbelieving. The bird, so delicate and pure, turned her tiny head in his direction. Suddenly the sunlight blazed like a holy fire. For Carlo, the humble friar who had gone into the fields and blessed the birds was no longer only a legend. He was a living spirit, bringing joy and peace to every gentle heart.

"Maestro Doni was right," Carlo said, half to himself. "For the joy of St. Francis is the joy of heaven itself. And there is nothing like it in all the world."

## Noticing the Feelings of Characters

The author often shows the feelings of characters by what they do or say. Reread the paragraphs listed below and tell how characters were feeling at different times in this story. Choose answers from words at the bottom of the page.

1. Write how Carlo felt when
   a. he finished his drawings. (page 303, paragraph 1)
   b. he went into the church. (page 304, paragraph 2)
   c. he went to the studio with an idea for his statue. (page 305, paragraph 3)
   d. he began work on the wood. (page 308, paragraph 7)
   e. Bredo's statue won. (page 312, paragraph 2)
   f. the Maestro finished talking. (page 313, paragraph 2)

2. Write how Maestro Doni felt after he had seen his students' drawings for their statues. (page 308, paragraph 4)

3. Write how Bredo felt when he talked to Carlo. (page 310, paragraph 3)

| | | | |
|---|---|---|---|
| dissatisfied | thankful | satisfied | angry |
| disappointed | hopeful | excited | eager |

# Mary, We Greet Thee
## (SALVE REGINA)

Ma - ry, we greet thee, Moth-er and Queen all mer - ci - ful,
*Sál - ve, Re - gí - na, Má - ter mi - se - ri - cór - di - ae:*

Our life, our com - fort, and our hope, we hail thee.
*Ví - ta, dul - cé - do, et spes nó - stra, sál - ve.*

To thee, we ex - iles, chil-dren of Eve, lift our voic - es.
*Ad te cla - má - mus, éx - su - les, fí - li - i Hé - vae.*

To thee we send our sighs while mourn-ing and weep - ing,
*Ad te sus - pi - rá - mus, ge - mén - tes et flén - tes*

we pass through this vale of sor - row.
*in hac la - cri - má - rum vál - le.*

316

Haste, then, we pray, O our in - ter - ces - sor, look with pit - y,
*E - ia er - go, Ad - vo - cá - ta nó - stra, íl - los tú - os*

with eyes of love and ten - der - ness, up - on us sin - ners.
*mi - se - ri - cór - des ó - cu - los ad nos con - vér - te.*

And Moth - er, when this earth-ly ex - ile shall be end - ed,
*Et Jé - sum, be - ne - dí-ctum frú-ctum vén-tris tú - i,*

show us the Sav - ior thou didst bear, thy Je - sus.
*nó - bis post hoc ex - sí - li - um o - stén - de.*

O_____ clem - ent, O_____ lov - ing,
*O clé - mens, O pí - a,*

O_____ gra - cious Vir - gin Ma - ry.
*O dúl - cis Vír-go Ma - rí - a.*

*God speaks through His creatures—through flowers, animals, birds. Even tiny swallows speak the glory of God.*

# Song of the Swallows

### By Leo Politi

At the foot of the low and soft hills near the sea lay the small village of Capistrano.

The bells of the mission church were ringing on that early morning of spring. Juan came running down the road through the village on his way to the little school near the mission. He ran through the gardens filled with flowers to the patio of the "sacred gardens." There he stopped to speak to old Julian.

Old Julian was the proud bell ringer of this beautiful mission. Many times had he told Juan the story of the mission, but always it seemed new.

318

"Long, long ago," Julian told him, "the good brothers of St. Francis came to this country from across the sea. Father Junipero Serra and the brothers walked along the wild trail through the wilderness. With the help of the Indians they built many mission churches."

"That is Father Junipero Serra," said Juan looking up at the statue in the garden. "He is my friend."

"The missions were like little villages," Julian said. "There the Indians learned to make shoes and harness, blankets and hats, tools and pottery—many of the things they needed in their daily life."

On his way to school and on his way home Juan liked to look at the flowers in the mission garden. They were so gay against the old walls!

Julian was also the gardener of the mission. He took much pride in showing Juan the plants, for he knew and loved each one of them.

Many birds came to the garden to nest, for here they were undisturbed. They flew happily among the trees and drank the fresh water of the old fountain. There were hummingbirds, white pigeons, sparrows, and other kinds of birds.

Julian always carried crumbs of hard bread in his pockets to feed them. The pigeons came and perched on his shoulders and on his hands.

But the most joyous birds were the swallows. There were hundreds of them nesting beneath the roof beams above the arches and their twittering filled the gardens with the sweetest music. They made spring a very happy time in Capistrano.

"Ever since I can remember," Julian told Juan, "the swallows have come in the spring on St. Joseph's Day and have gone away late in the summer."

"But how can little birds know when it is St. Joseph Day?" Juan asked.

"That I do not know," said Julian.

Juan was full of curiosity about the swallows. He watched them build their small mud houses against the beams of the roof. The best time of all was when the old swallows taught the baby birds how to fly.

One morning Juan and Julian watched a family of young swallows seated in a row on an iron bar across the arch. One by one the old swallows gave them flying lessons.

At first, as the little birds tried to flutter, they were so clumsy and awkward! One of them tumbled to the ground.

"Poor little one!" cried Juan as he ran to pick him up. He held the baby bird close and soothed him.

When they found he was not hurt, Julian set him back on the iron bar. The little swallow seemed eager to get back to his nest. Perhaps, he felt that it was feeding time.

One day late in the summer, Julian noticed that the swallows were noisier and more excited than usual. It seemed as if they were getting ready to leave.

"Juan!" he called. "The swallows are leaving us!"

Juan was sad because he knew he would miss them so much. He felt that he knew each one of them and they were like dear little friends to him.

The swallows rose, twittering, in the air, and flew toward the south. Juan and Julian watched, motionless, until they disappeared beyond the horizon.

Julian said, as he always did when the swallows left,

"Farewell little swallows,
For you we will yearn,
May God bless your journey
And guide your return."

"I shall pray for their return," said Juan. The swallows flew down the coastline.

"How wonderful the flight of the swallows is!" said Julian. "Just try to picture, Juan, the hundreds and thousands of miles they travel, high up in the air, looking down over strange and beautiful lands. I believe that, of all the creatures, God has given them the most freedom and happiness."

"But where are they going?" asked Juan.

322

"Some say to a land far south of us—some to a green island in the Pacific Ocean," said Julian.

"No one really can tell, but I do know, Juan, that they will go where there are flowers and fresh water streams and people who welcome and love them."

As the autumn and winter months set in, the colors in the mission gardens became quieter and softer. The mission was still lovely, but there was now a feeling of loneliness without the swallows.

On his way to school Juan often stopped and looked up with sadness at the empty nests. There the joyous swallows had lived and played, but now their little houses were still and lonely.

When the winter months were nearing an end, new buds began to swell and trees to bloom again. Soon the blossoming trees bent gently over the garden walks. They made lovely patterns against the sky and filled the clear air with fragrance. Juan felt he was going through an enchanted garden.

Julian worked hard in the gardens, for St. Joseph's Day was coming soon. He wanted the gardens to look their best for the swallows' return.

The sky was tinted red at early dawn on St. Joseph's Day. Soon the sun rose from behind the hills and cast a golden glow over the valley.

Juan and his friends came early that morning to greet the swallows. The boys wore their best suits and the girls, their newest dresses, with flowers and ribbons in their hair.

They played games, sang, danced, and acted little

plays of olden days. As the gay fiesta went on, every now and then the children would look up at the sky.

Would the swallows come?

Hours of waiting and watching went by. Time dragged into the late afternoon with not a swallow in sight. The children became tired and discouraged. Some of them began to leave.

Then Juan, who was standing high up on the column of a broken arch near the edge of the playground, saw some little dots far off on the horizon.

"The swallows are coming!" he cried.

The children jumped up and down with joy.

The little dots came nearer; they grew bigger and bigger. Soon hundreds of swallows circled over the mission.

Juan ran and hugged Julian. "The swallows are here! I thought they would never come!"

"They came late, perhaps they met a storm on the way, but I told you, Juan, that they would return. See how glad they are!" said the wise old man.

The swallows were very much like little folks who had been on a long journey and were happy to be home again. They fluttered and twittered joyously and filled the gardens with sweet sound.

Juan and Julian went into the garden and rang the mission bells to tell the people of the valley that spring had now begun.

## Can You Help Juan?

Juan was full of curiosity about the swallows. You have already read a story in Unit 4 which gives many facts about swallows. Turn back to the story "How Nature Helps Birds to Fly" on page 175 and reread the parts that tell about swallows. Then write the answers to these questions.

1. If Juan asked you how swallows eat on their long journey, what would you tell him?

2. Maybe Juan thinks that the poor swallows get very tired on this long journey. What could you tell him?

3. Would you tell Juan that the swallows molt before or after the baby birds learn to fly?

4. Juan knows how swallows fly. If he asked you how the bobwhite flies, what would you tell him?

# Prayers from the Ark

**By Carmen Bernos de Gasztold**

## The Prayer of the Butterfly

Lord!
Where was I?
Oh yes! This flower, this sun,
thank You! Your world is beautiful!
This scent of roses . . .
Where was I?
A drop of dew
rolls to sparkle in a lily's heart.
I have to go . . .
Where? I do not know!
The wind has painted fancies
on my wings.
Fancies . . .
Where was I?
Oh yes! Lord,
I had something to tell You:

Amen

# The Prayer of the Little Ducks

Dear God,
give us a flood of water.
Let it rain tomorrow and always.
Give us plenty of little slugs
and other luscious things to eat.
Protect all folk who quack
and everyone who knows how to swim.

Amen

# The Prayer of the Tortoise

A little patience,
O God,
I am coming.
One must take nature as she is!
It was not I who made her!
I do not mean to criticize
this house on my back—
it has its points—
but You must admit, Lord,
it is heavy to carry!
Still,
let us hope that this double enclosure,
my shell and my heart,
will never be quite shut to You.

Amen

*God speaks to us through His Church, through its Sacraments, its priests and its bishops. He speaks through the deep, unselfish love of its faithful members.*

# The Bishop Rides on Horseback

By Mary Synon

Everyone in Burning Bush seemed to take a special interest in all that went on at Sacred Heart Church. Just two years before the Catholic Church Extension Society had helped Father Mills to build his church. Now the Extension Society was sending a bishop to confirm the children of the Sacred Heart Parish.

No one in the small town was more excited than Gloria Gomez. She had looked forward for such a long time to her Confirmation. For many months she had been saying that the bishop would come in the spring when the Texas plains were bright with bluebonnets.

And now the springtime had come.

"How will the bishop get here?" Gloria asked Father Mills.

"He will come by railroad to Five-Mile Stop. There I will meet him in my car," Father Mills answered.

"Oh, then we must shine your car today," cried Gloria. "My brother Frank will help."

Father Mills laughed. "If you wish, Gloria," he said.

That was Tuesday, and Tuesday evening everything was ready for the bishop's arrival on Thursday morning. At least, everyone thought all was ready.

Early Wednesday morning the Seco River began to rise. During the hot, dry months the Seco is a shallow river that is hardly more than a name. Sometimes in the springtime it becomes an angry, threatening river that rises and floods over its banks, breaking down bridges and tearing down homes.

By Wednesday noon the river had risen up to the highway bridge, making the bridge dangerous to cross.

The ranchers' cattle were in danger of the flooding waters. Gloria's father and her brother Frank went with other ranchers out on the plains to round up the cattle.

Then Father Mills was called out of town. An old man at a distant ranch had become very ill and wanted to see a priest. To reach the ranch, Father Mills had to cross one of the little rivers that runs into the Seco. It was no longer a little river, and the priest's car sank down into the soft mud and got stuck. It was dark before he reached the ranch.

Someone else, Father Mills realized, would have to meet the bishop. From the ranch he telephoned Gloria's home. Father Mills told Gloria about his mishap.

"I won't be able to meet the bishop," he said. "Do you think your father would be able to get to the railroad? The train on which the bishop is coming will arrive at Five-Mile Stop at ten minutes past seven tomorrow morning."

"I'm sure my father will do it as soon as he gets home," answered Gloria.

Then she sat down and waited, but her father did not come home. Gloria knew that the men must be having trouble rounding up the cattle. Hour after hour she waited for her father. She had no one else to turn to. Her mother had been dead for several years.

"Someone has to go to the railroad," Gloria thought. She had just heard on a radio broadcast that the highway bridge had been washed out. Only cowboys had been able to cross the river at the Shallows, but they were on horseback.

It would take hours to ride horseback to the railroad. Already it was late and growing dark. Whoever was to meet the bishop must start the trip at once.

Suddenly Gloria knew what she must do. There was only one horse in the corral, but she could ride the horse to the railroad. The bishop could ride the horse back.

Alone and in the darkness, Gloria set out. When she got to the Shallows, she rode cautiously and slowly through the water. The river was not so high here, but it was too high for easy riding. At every step her horse took, Gloria prayed to God for help.

"I hope the bishop can ride well," she said as she reached the bank.

Finally Gloria came to the railroad tracks. Five-Mile was no more than a name on a railroad map. There was no station, not even a platform. There was only a lantern that hung on a pole near the tracks.

By its dim light Gloria could see the outline of two horses standing beside the tracks. There was a rider on one of the horses.

"Hello," Gloria said as she rode up to the rider. "Are you waiting for the train?"

"Yes," replied the boy, "I came to meet my father. We live on a ranch about a mile down the tracks. Do you think the train will be on time?"

"Of course, it will," said Gloria. "The bishop is on it. The Catholic Extension Society is sending him to our town, Burning Bush."

"Then you must have ridden all the way from Burning Bush. Did you come across the Seco? Isn't it flooding?" the boy asked.

As the starlight faded to dawn, Gloria and the boy talked. Gloria told him all that had happened during the last few days.

Finally, Gloria heard a distant noise in the east. "Here comes the train," she cried.

When the train came to a stop, two men, carrying traveling cases, stepped off. One was a tall man with sandy blond hair.

"There's my father," said the boy.

The other was a shorter, older man whose gray hair might once have been red. Gloria saw a tiny touch of purple just below his white collar.

"There is the bishop," she said, wondering what she should say to him.

"I am Gloria Gomez, Father, I mean Bishop. I mean... I do not know what I should call you, Father," Gloria stammered. "I have come with a horse for you because Father Mills could not come to meet you. The Seco River is over its banks, and the bridge has been washed

332

out. And Confirmation will be today at Burning Bush when you get there, and—"

"Well, well," said the bishop, his blue eyes twinkling. "Am I to ride this horse?"

"You can ride, can't you?" Gloria asked. Not for a moment had she thought that the bishop might not want to ride through a rising river.

"Oh, yes," said the bishop, "I can ride. I am lucky to find a horse here. There have been times when bishops have had to walk very great distances. There have been times when bishops have had to swim."

"I certainly hope you will not have to swim the Seco," said Gloria.

"If I ride your horse, how shall you get home, Gloria?" the bishop asked.

"Oh, I will wait," said Gloria. "I can walk to the nearest ranch and get something to eat. Then I will wait here until you come back."

"But, my dear child, I cannot leave you here alone," the bishop said.

"But Father, I mean Bishop, you are the one who has to get to Burning Bush. Everyone is waiting for you."

"Have you been confirmed, Gloria?" the bishop asked.

"No, Father, I mean Bishop, but—"

"Is there no way by which you can come, too?" the bishop asked.

"I know a way," said the young boy who was still standing by the tracks. "You may have my horse. I can ride with my father. We do not have far to go."

"Oh, thank you," Gloria cried happily.

"That's very kind of you," said the bishop.

"Not at all, not at all," said the boy's father. "This is Texas. We do something for you today. You do something for us tomorrow."

"That is life," said the bishop as he strapped his bag to the saddle and started mounting the horse.

The bishop and Gloria said farewell to their friends as they started off toward Burning Bush. The bishop rode very well, much to Gloria's astonishment.

"I didn't know bishops could ride so well," she said as they rode through the Texas plains.

After they had crossed the Shallows, Gloria repeated her praise. "You came through the Shallows like a real cowboy," she said.

Soon Gloria was able to see in the distance the little white church of the Sacred Heart Parish. At last, they were near Burning Bush.

Hours afterward, all of the townspeople who could crowd into the little church were looking at her with a feeling of pride. As she knelt, all in white, Gloria Gomez felt the bishop's hand upon her forehead. She heard him say the words that confirmed her a soldier of Christ.

Afterward, outside the church, the bishop called her. "Father Mills and I have been talking about your confirmation name," he said. "We wonder why you chose Cunegunda."

"St. Cunegunda always did kind things to help her people," explained Gloria. "And besides, I wanted a name that everyone would remember."

"I see," smiled the bishop.

Somehow, though, no one in Burning Bush ever remembers that she is Gloria Cunegunda Gomez. But everyone remembers that she is Gloria Gomez, the girl who rode across the Seco, alone and at night, so that the bishop could come to the little Church of the Sacred Heart.

## When Did It Happen?

1. When you read this story, did you notice the "cue" words that show the passing of time? Look at page 328, paragraph 3. The cue words there are "the springtime had come." On page 329, paragraph 2, the cue words are "Tuesday" or "Tuesday evening." Read the following paragraphs and find and write the cue words.

*a.* Page 329, paragraph 3    *e.* Page 330, paragraph 7
*b.* Page 329, paragraph 4    *f.* Page 332, paragraph 5
*c.* Page 330, paragraph 1    *g.* Page 335, paragraph 3
*d.* Page 330, paragraph 5    *h.* Page 336, paragraph 1

2. Most of the story takes place in a rather short time. How much time passed from the beginning of page 329 to the end of page 335?

# Whatsoever Things Are True

By Emilie F. Johnson

Whatsoever things are true,
Whatsoever things are honest,
Whatsoever things are just,
Whatsoever things are pure,
Whatsoever things are lovely,
Whatsoever things are of good report;
If there be any virtue,
And if there be any praise,
I will think on these things.

# Books to Enjoy

*A Small Child's Bible*, by Pelagie Doane.

Here you will find stories from the Old and the New Testament—stories of Moses, David, King Solomon, the birth of Christ, and parables told by Christ. All of the stories are short, and each is illustrated.

*Stories from the New Testament*, by Piet Worm.

Important happenings in Christ's life are retold from the Bible so simply that they are easy to read and understand.

*The Boy Jesus*, by Pelagie Doane.

The life of Christ from His birth to the age of twelve is told simply and illustrated beautifully.

*The Twelve Apostles*, by Katherine Wood.

Short articles about each of the twelve apostles include both facts and beliefs that exist about them.

*Angelino and the Barefoot Saint*, by Valenti Angelo.

A young Italian boy often visits a statue of St. Francis. One day Angelino discovers that the statue has a look of sadness, and he involves the entire village as he searches for the reason.

*The Story of Mary, the Mother of Jesus*, by Catherine Beebe.

This lovely story tells the complete life of the Blessed Mother from the time of her birth to her glorious Assumption.

*The Mission Bell*, by Leo Politi.

Father Junipero Serra journeyed from Old Mexico to California through desert and over mountains to build his missions. Here the story of the kind priest's journey is simply told and illustrated with many interesting pictures by the author.

338

# Americans All

# The Warm of Heart

By Elizabeth Coatsworth

The warm of heart shall never lack a fire
However far he roam.
Although he live forever among strangers,
He cannot lack a home.

For strangers are not strangers to his spirit,
And each house seems his own,
And by the fire of his loving-kindness
He cannot sit alone.

# Who Built the Bridge?

By Lucy Sprague Mitchell

The new bridge was finished. On each side of the big river stood the broad stone bases. From each stone base rose a high slender steel tower. The steel beams and cross beams made lovely designs against the blue sky. Between the two high slender steel towers hung two great cables in a long, swooping, lovely curve.

Far away those cables looked like threads from a spider's web. Each one was really three feet thick and made of hundreds of smaller cables of twisted wire. Even so, the cables didn't look strong enough to hold up a road for automobiles. Yet there was the road, hung from the great cables.

Today that road was to be opened. Today the first automobiles were to cross the new bridge, for the new bridge was finished.

341

The town was excited and proud. Now the towns-people would be able to whiz across the big river in a few minutes. Why, now you could live over on the other side in the open country with grass and trees and get to your work in the town on time.

The farmers on the other side of the town were excited. They were proud. Why, now you could load your truck with vegetables in the early morning and get them over to the market in a jiffy.

No wonder many people were going to be there for the opening of the bridge. No wonder the morning paper had a picture of the beautiful bridge on the front page and carried big headlines.

EVENING ⚓ CLARION

## OPENING OF NEW BRIDGE
## BUILT BY TOWN AND STATE

Diamond Construction Company
Builds Another Great Bridge

Yes, in a way the town and the state and the construction company built the bridge. But not with their hands. Whose hands had built the bridge, anyway? There were many children in the town who knew. Hadn't their fathers worked on it?

The two Caruso children knew. Their father and mother had come from Italy. Maria Caruso was in the third grade. She had large black eyes and long, black, curly hair. Her brother Luigi was in the fifth grade. He had large black eyes and short, black, curly hair.

Both children had been born in America. They had never seen Italy with their eyes, but they had seen it often through the stories their father and mother had told them. When their parents talked, the children could see a little town in Italy. They knew how the little town's stone quarry looked. They both knew just how carefully the stones from that quarry had been fitted into the walls of many of the town's houses and even into the walls of the town church. For had not their father fitted many of these stones himself with his strong skillful hands?

"Yes, yes," their father would say, shaking his head with its curly gray hair. "I worked with stone in Italy. Then I came to America. Now I am American. I work with stone in America. I helped build the stone walls in the big bridge. You look at my walls. Every stone is in the right place. I helped to make good strong walls for the big bridge."

Yes, the Caruso children were excited and proud that the new bridge was finished. Was not their father's stone work a part of that bridge?

And the Votipka children, too, knew who had helped build the bridge. Indeed, they always called it "Father's bridge." Those steel towers that made a pattern against the sky—those were "Father's towers." For their father was a member of the steel riveters' team. Once, as a boy in the old country, their father had known nothing of steel. He had known only the wooden houses which his own father had built in a little town.

Their father often told them how queer the high houses in New York had looked to his eyes when he was a boy and had stared at them from the ship's deck.

"How could houses be strong enough to stand up so high?" he had asked.

He was told that their beams were made of steel. "Steel!" Then and there the little boy had decided he would grow up and be a steel worker. He would build houses and bridges of steel in this new country that was to be his home.

And in time this actually happened. He became an American and learned to be a skillful worker in steel. He learned sureness of foot. He didn't get dizzy out on a steel beam. Yes, the little boy was now a grown man with a family of his own. Now he was a member of the riveting team that had built the new bridge.

Now here on the front page of the morning paper was a picture of Father's steel towers. Jan, the oldest Votipka boy, looked at it proudly. And so did all the other little Votipkas.

In another part of the town, in the Mulligan kitchen, big and little Mike were looking at the picture of the new bridge in the morning paper. Little Mike was only five. But that was old enough to know that big Mike, his father, was the smartest man on earth. That was old enough to know that the big bridge could never have been built without his father's help.

"Now, isn't it an amazing thing, Mike boy," big Mike asked, "that we Americans can build whatever we want?

"Take this bridge," he said as he tapped the picture with a strong thick finger. "Our townspeople looked across the big river, and they said to themselves, 'Now wouldn't it be fine to drive right across the river?' So they got a smart man to draw some fancy pictures of a fine bridge. Would you believe it, son? Those pictures show just what your father and other sandhogs should do. And we all began to work. Before you know it, here is the morning paper saying the new bridge is to open this very day."

So it was in many families that morning. Booker T. Washington and Mary Frances Washington knew that their father had helped drill the rock on the two sides of the river so that the steel towers could be anchored deep in the rock. They, too, looked at the picture of the new bridge. It was their bridge, too.

The Pulaski children knew that their father had helped mix the cement in the huge cement mixers. They knew that the bridge could not have stood up so big and strong without the cement to anchor the steel beams and cables.

The Macpherson children well remembered the days when their father's tugboat carried first one steel cable and then another giant cable across the river. They had watched the little tug puffing and puffing as the great cable trailed behind it in the water. They felt that the bridge could not have been built without their father, and they were right.

Yes, Americans had built another great bridge. Not only the town and state, not only the construction company, but many Americans had built that new bridge. Americans from many lands. Some had come to America only a short time ago. They still carried memories and customs from the land they had left. Others had never known any land except these United States.

New Americans and old Americans; workers in stone, workers in cement, workers in steel, sandhogs, tugboat captains and bridge engineers; nearby townspeople and faraway steel workers, miners and railroad men—workers of many kinds built that great bridge. The great new road that crossed the big river was the work of many Americans—to be used by all.

## Pretending You Are a Reporter

1. On the day that the new bridge was to be opened, there was a story on the front page of the town newspaper. Pretend that you are a reporter for that newspaper and that you are going to write the newspaper story about the construction of the bridge. Use the headlines on page 342 for your title and then write the newspaper story.

2. Below are some words which describe the new bridge. Be sure you know the meanings of the words. If you don't, look in your glossary or a dictionary for the meaning.

| stone bases | steel towers | bridge road |
|-------------|--------------|-------------|
| cables | | cross beams |

Now make a drawing of the bridge to go with your newspaper story. Label the parts of the bridge. Be sure to use the words above as well as others that you think of.

# A Nation's Strength

By Ralph Waldo Emerson

Not gold, but only man can make
    A people great and strong;
Men who, for truth and honor's sake,
    Stand fast and suffer long.

Brave men who work while others sleep,
    Who dare while others fly—
They build a nation's pillars deep
    And lift them to the sky.

# Anita's Gift of Flowers

By Carol Morgan

*Pablo had moved from a small quiet town on the island of Puerto Rico to live with his father in a crowded apartment building on the busy, hurried streets of New York City. He had come to his new home with his grandmother, his mother whom he called Mamita, and his six-year-old sister Anita.*

*At first life was strange for Pablo in our country's largest city. He and his sister had made many mistakes. But they learned by their mistakes and grew to love their new home more and more each day.*

Pablo burst into the apartment that night without the least idea of what he would find within those four walls of home. He soon found out. A strong sweet odor met him as he opened the door. It wasn't something cooking, he knew. Where did it come from? Then he saw them—the beautiful, big red roses in a pitcher on the kitchen table.

"Wow! Where did those come from?" he shouted. But no voice answered and no one seemed to be around.

"Where's everyone?" he called again.

"In here, son. Come in." It was Grandmother's voice from the bedroom.

Pablo stood in the doorway and looked at the three of them, Mamita, Anita, and Grandmother. Mamita and Anita were sitting on the bed close together. Anita, leaning against Mamita, was crying. Grandmother was rocking back and forth in her chair with her worn black Bible in her hands. She always seemed to find comfort in holding her Bible tenderly when she was frightened.

"What has happened? Tell me." Pablo was frightened. Was something wrong with Papa?

"The flowers, son, the roses. Anita stole them," Mamita said at last.

"Anita—stole—roses?" Pablo was sure he had not heard right.

"I'll tell you, Pablito," Grandmother said. "Anita was down on First Avenue. She saw big cans of flowers on the sidewalk against the side of a house. Because she did not see any store, she thought someone was giving them away and that she could help herself. So, poor little thing, she brought that bunch to us. She did not mean to steal, but no one gives flowers away, not in New York. We know that. These must cost much money. What shall we do? Maybe someone followed her home and knows."

This brought a fresh flood of tears from Anita.

"Where's Papa?" Pablo asked.

"This is the night he works. He will not be home until tomorrow night," Mamita said.

By this time Anita was clinging to Pablo, crying against his sleeve. "I didn't mean to, Pablo, but they were so beautiful. I wanted the flowers for us. They look like the ones in gardens in Puerto Rico, don't they? I didn't steal, did I, Pablo?"

How Pablo wished for Papa to tell them what to do! He went to the front window and looked into the street. No one was there looking up at their apartment. Of course not, he thought. The owner of the flower shop would wait until tomorrow morning and then send the police.

On the other hand, perhaps no one knew Anita had stolen the flowers and would never know anything about it. The flowers would die and be thrown out. That would be all there would be to it. Should he just wait and see and do nothing?

"No, I can't do that," Pablo thought silently. "My family is honest. We do not steal or lie. I must do something about this right now."

Then Pablo exclaimed, "Anita, you come on with me. Mamita, we'll be back soon. Don't worry."

He went to his drawer and got all the money he had, the ten-dollar bill that he was saving for Christmas. Taking Anita by the hand, he led her to the street.

"I'm afraid, Pablo. What will they do to me? Where are we going?"

"I don't know what they will do, little sister, but we will see. We are going to the shop. Just keep hoping the flower man is a kind man."

It had been dark for some time. Days were getting shorter now. Stores were closed or closing with great banging of doors and shutters. Shopkeepers were saying good night to each other in many languages as the children passed by.

Pablo felt the first coolness of fall blow down First Avenue as they walked along. He pulled the collar of his cotton shirt together. He felt a shudder run through Anita and put his arm across her shoulders to keep her warm.

"There is the place, Pablo, right there," she said. "Against that wall they stood. Cans and cans of them. Hundreds, I'll bet. There were all kinds, and no one was sitting there to sell them. But they're all gone now."

They stopped while Pablo looked at the place. It was a florist's shop, all right, facing First Avenue on the corner. Whoever was selling the flowers on the street must have stepped inside at the moment Anita came along. Looking at the dark sign outside, Pablo realized that the shop was closed for the night.

"There's nothing we can do now, Anita. It's too late. The store's closed. There's nothing to do but go home and go to bed. I have money to pay for the flowers. If he's a kind man, it may be all right. But you must never, never take anything again without paying for it, little sister. Promise?"

"Yes, you know I promise," Anita answered in a low voice. "I'll never, never do it again. Pablo, you're the most wonderful brother."

Pablo was able to smile a little in the dark as he led his sister home.

Pablo was restless all night, wondering between dreams what tomorrow would bring. The little family was very quiet at breakfast and did not seem to be hungry.

As Pablo, with Anita, started out again for the florist shop, he found her little hand very cold. There was no jumping around this morning and no whistling. They walked in silence, and each step seemed to Pablo to be bringing them near something serious. He wished they were running the other way.

At last they reached the florist's corner. The door of the shop was open. A gray-haired man was setting cans of flowers on the sidewalk where Anita said they had been yesterday. The two stood behind him as he

354

pushed the cans this way and that and arranged blossoms in several of the cans. Would he never see them? Suddenly he turned, almost stepping on them.

"Mister, did you lose any flowers yesterday?" Pablo began. "I mean, did any disappear from here?" He pointed to the sidewalk.

The man frowned. "What? I don't understand. What do you two want this early in the morning?"

Pablo had to begin again. At last the story was out. He offered his ten dollars if the man would not arrest Anita.

The man listened closely and looked from one to the other. "You're Puerto Rican, aren't you?"

"*Si, senor,*" Pablo answered, not realizing he spoke in Spanish.

"Good, and I am, too," the man answered with a smile. "We have flowers all year in the beautiful gardens of our beloved island, don't we, children? We give them away just as little sister here thought people, in New York do."

He looked off down the street and took a long breath. "Every house table has its bright bouquet, and at night, ah, at night the air is filled with sweet jasmine. Ay, yes, yes," and he took a long breath again. "I grow homesick for Puerto Rico."

Pablo thought, too, of the many flowers on porches and in gardens in Puerto Rico.

"Here, we pay and pay for every flower." The man looked at the ten dollars Pablo held. "I will take just the cost of the roses. They are a dollar and a half.

"Now, my name is Don Antonio," he added, as he handed Pablo the change, "and if you ever want to buy flowers, remember Don Antonio. If Anita will come sometimes on Saturday nights at six, I will give her a few blossoms to take to her mamita, blossoms that will not keep in the shop over Sunday. Then you will have flowers to remind you of our beautiful Puerto Rico, with the love of Don Antonio."

356

Again the children were silent as they walked home, but it was very different this time. Pablo wondered if Anita was as grateful for kind people as he was. Grandmother and Mamita almost cried when the children told them about Don Antonio and the dollar-fifty only.

"Of course, he was kind. Is he not from Puerto Rico?" Mamita asked.

Grandmother answered quickly, "Not because he is from one place or another is anyone kind, but because kindness is in his heart toward all peoples. Children, remember today well, and be kind to everyone, always."

## Reading between the Lines

Can you hunt out hidden ideas? Sometimes the author tells us things about characters without saying it in so many words. Read these paragraphs and sentences and answer the questions.

1. Read page 350, the last two sentences of paragraph 1. What kind of person was Grandmother?

2. Read page 352, paragraph 3; read page 356, the last sentence of paragraph 1. What kind of person was Pablo?

3. Read page 354, paragraph 5 and the last two sentences of paragraph 6. How do you think Pablo was feeling?

4. Read page 357, the last sentence of paragraph 1. How do you think Grandmother and Mamita felt?

5. Read page 351, paragraph 5; read page 354, paragraph 3. How do you think Anita felt about her brother?

6. Read page 350, paragraph 4; read page 353, paragraph 2. How do you think Pablo felt toward his little sister?

7. Read page 351, paragraph 7; read page 352, paragraph 1. How do you think Pablo felt?

# House of Singing Windows

**By Nan Gilbert**

## A New Home

Johann Riehl lay flat on his stomach behind the low stone wall and peeked out at the children going by.

There were two of them. There was a boy who might match Johann's own ten years and a girl who was a little younger. Every morning they passed Johann's home on their way to the white frame schoolhouse down the road. And every morning Johann huddled breathlessly behind the stone wall and watched them.

358

"Strange Americans!" he whispered when they were safely gone.

Johann did not really think the two children looked so strange, but he kept thinking of his great-uncle's words.

In Germany, across the sea, Johann's mother and father had begged the old man to come to America with them. He had said that he was too old to go and battle goblins.

Johann had been confused, but his mother explained it to him. "Your great-uncle speaks of a different goblin than you are thinking of. He means only the strange customs we will meet, the unfamiliar people, and the strange, new language. To him, these are as frightening as goblins. But remember, Johann, he is an old man now —a man no longer young and strong of heart."

Well, Johann's heart was young and strong, but now it hid a deep growing worry. Oh, he didn't fear the new language. He had spent a whole year taking English lessons. But strangers, other boys his age, that's what he feared.

Before he left Germany, he had asked his great-uncle about them, trying to act as if it didn't really matter.

Under his great bushy eyebrows, his great-uncle's eyes had twinkled secretly. "Oh, such creatures! They do nothing but play baseball, eat apple pie and ice cream, and dream of being cowboys! And their talk is worse! 'Jumping catfish,' they say."

Soon after that Johann had come to America with his mother, his father, and the twenty-two canaries Mother could not leave behind. Spring reached America almost as soon as the Riehls did. Johann learned to love his new land as they crossed the number of miles to Iowa—their new home.

Johann hoped with all his heart that America's people would love him. But for the first week, he didn't have time to find out. Mother kept him too busy. They scrubbed every inch of the snug farmhouse that was to be their home. It was an old, old house, built of stone.

In it Johann could almost believe himself back in Germany. Mother had set up her many little pots of plants against the living-room and kitchen walls. She had spread the familiar braided rugs over the floors. Father had screened the front windows inside and out so that the windows made fine big cages for the twenty-two canaries.

"Next week," Mother decided briskly, "you must start to school, Johann."

Johann's heart dropped straight to his boots. School! To Johann it meant many strange American children like the two who passed his hiding place each morning. Now surely Johann was up against the biggest goblin of them all.

Soon after eight o'clock, the following Monday morning, Johann's mother was pleased with the way her son looked. His short tight jacket and pants were freshly pressed. His bare knees, like his hands and face, shone pink with scrubbing.

"Now shall your father go with you, Johann?" his mother asked kindly. "Or shall I?"

"No, neither!" Johann said quickly. "Let me go alone, Mother."

"Alone?" she looked at him doubtfully. "Do you have the school report? And the letter from the schoolmaster? . . . Ah, well, go then, little one."

Once outside, Johann went quickly to the barn.

His heart beat fast. If he hadn't been ten years old, he would have thought he was scared. Soon now he must face the American children. But, oh joy, he had found the right outfit for his first day at school.

He had discovered it yesterday, hanging dusty and forgotten in the barn. It was a very old, very large pair of overalls!

Just such a pair of overalls, though smaller, was worn by the American boy who'd passed Johann's house each morning.

With great care, Johann smoothed out the precious overalls. He put them on and pinned them to his size with many, many safety pins. The overalls bulked out a little strangely when he was finished.

"Even so," Johann said anxiously, "they look better and more American than my own suit."

Carefully he hung his own jacket and pants on the hook and walked quickly out to the road.

The same girl and boy were walking just ahead of him. The boy was first to hear Johann. He looked back and stopped, waiting for Johann to catch up with them.

Then, finally, he spoke. "Hi!" he said to Johann.

The careful how-do-you-do Johann had learned from his English lessons choked in his throat. He swallowed hard and faintly echoed, "Hi!"

"Are you going to school?"

Johann nodded. They fell into step.

"My name's Peter Janus, and this is Paula. What's your name?"

"Jo—" An idea suddenly came to Johann, and boldly he cut off the rest of his first name. "Joe Riehl."

Then Johann motioned back toward the stone farmhouse to show where he lived.

The little girl squealed suddenly, "Oh, Peter, he lives in the house with the singing windows! I *told* you somebody nice must live there!"

Peter looked back at Johann. "They said some Germans bought that house. Are you German?"

Johann took a deep breath and gathered the words well in his mind before trying them. "Jumping catfish, no! I'm American!"

## A Real American

When they reached the school, Peter led Johann to the teacher's desk. "We have a new boy, Miss Iverson," he said. "His name's Joe. Joe—what did you say?"

"Riehl."

Miss Iverson held out her hand. "Hello, Joe. We're glad to have you." She had a smiling face and corn-yellow hair. Johann knew at once that he wanted to please her above all else.

There was no time then to find out what class Johann would belong to. He took a seat in the back of the room and listened and looked with all his might. Here all about him were American children, real Americans. Already they accepted Johann as one of them. But if they found out he *wasn't*—

When the recess bell rang, Peter came straight to Johann. "What do you want to play?"

Johann said bravely, "Baseball."

"Baseball," Peter's face brightened. "What's *your* act? Do you pitch or catch?"

Johann gulped, his eyes searching for help. Miss Iverson chose just that moment to come up to them and say, "You run out and play, Peter. I must find out what class to put Joe in."

"Now, Joe," she asked, "have you a report card from your last school?"

Johann reached into his pants pocket beneath the bulky overalls. Then his hand stopped. His face became a picture of worry.

"You forgot it?" Miss Iverson smiled. "Well, never mind. Tomorrow will do. Now, what were you studying in your other school? Reading, I suppose?"

"Oh, yes!" Johann said briskly. "And script and French and political science—" He stopped short, and stared at the puzzled look in Miss Iverson's eyes. Now what had he said wrong?

Slowly, Miss Iverson said, "I believe we'll wait for the report card after all. I'll put you with Peter today."

The rest of the morning went smoothly. Johann was able to read with Peter's group. His sums were correctly done, too. He went out to lunch very satisfied with himself.

The afternoon got off to a bad start. Miss Iverson opened it by talking about a party—an all-American party. Everyone's parents were invited. It was going to be a big evening.

Johann's heart curled into a tight little ball. All-American! Then it would be just for those who were completely American. Johann felt suddenly cold and left out.

Afternoon classes didn't go as well as the morning ones. Then, it was recess again, and Peter was pushing a great long kind of club into Johann's hand and shouting, "First bat! Joe has first bat!"

He was pushed around until he faced a boy with a ball. Johann's eyes were huge and black with fright. He didn't know what was coming next. It turned out to be the ball that was coming—coming right at him and fast!

Johann gave a frightened yell and put up the strange club to keep the ball from hitting him. The ball cracked against the club and was hurled back above the boy who had thrown it. Everybody was yelling and screaming. Children's hands pushed Johann wildly. "Run, Joe! Run!"

Johann was confused. What had he done? What must he run from? His pounding heart took his breath away; he tried to push more speed into his shaking legs. Something tangled with his feet and almost made him fall. An open pin stuck sharply into his side. Then he felt his overalls slipping, slipping from his shoulders. And the tangle was getting greater around his feet.

Still he ran. Still hands pushed at him, turning him in a big circle until suddenly he fell flat, right where he had started.

"Home run! Home run!"

Johann thought his poor ears would split. Peter pounded him on the back. He tried to get up, and now the cause of his tangle could be easily seen. The pins in his overall legs had come loose. Terrible folds of blue overalls rolled like elephant flesh around his ankles. Even the sides of the suit hung open.

The roar around him was sharpened by laughter. "Hey!" the big boy who had thrown the ball called. "Are you shrinking, kid?"

Suddenly Peter spoke up. "Maybe he likes his clothes that way," he said. "Maybe he likes room to grow!"

The recess bell cut across the playground. Peter hurried to Johann and helped him with the pins. "Don't you worry about anything!" Peter said strongly. "You are swell!"

The spreading warmth around Johann's heart cooled quickly at four o'clock. At that time Miss Iverson closed the schoolhouse door and joined Johann and Peter and Paula.

"I believe I will just walk home with you," she told Johann in a friendly manner. "It'll be a good time to pick up your report card!"

Johann couldn't say a word at first. Finally, he said hurriedly, "I'll go ahead! I—I'll tell Mother you're coming."

He tore away from them, running faster than he had when he made the home run. Panting, he crossed the fields and rushed to his house.

"Mother! Mother! They are coming!" he called.

His mother hurried anxiously out of the kitchen, wiping her hands on her big apron. "What is it? Who's coming?"

"The teacher, Mother! Oh, you must hurry. Hurry —make yourself fine in the good dress. And talk only American. Oh, Mother, you do understand, don't you?"

"Yes, yes!" She ran up the steps, too hurried to notice Johann's strange costume. He trotted quickly back to meet the others. Now if Mother put on the American dress! It was just a kitchen work dress, but it was *American!* Then, maybe his secret would still be safe.

Slowly, slowly, Johann led his new friends through his front gate.

"See, Miss Iverson!" Paula cried. "See the windows! Hear the singing birds!"

"Oh, beautiful!" Miss Iverson exclaimed. Then she said softly again, "Beautiful . . ."

But her voice was different. And she wasn't looking at the windows now. Johann followed her glance to the front door.

His mother stood there. Her face was flushed pink from hurry, but its gentle pride shone through. She had done what her son asked. She had put on her very finest outfit—the full, embroidered skirt and tiny jacket, the fine-tucked lovely blouse of her Sunday best back in Germany.

Her eyes went to Johann to see if she had pleased him. Proudly, now she held out her hands to the guests. She said in her careful English, "Welcome!"

Johann's throat choked with a great love for her. Oh, it didn't matter that she had torn his poor secret wide open! She had tried hard to please him. They'd just better like her! They'd just better!

Fiercely he bounded to her side and faced them. "Miss Iverson, this is my mother, Frau Riehl!" And just so there'd be no mistake, he added, "And my name's not Joe, either. It's Johann!"

But strangely enough, nobody seemed upset. Paula and Peter had run over to look at the canaries in the screened windows. Miss Iverson said in her friendly way, "I'm sure your name will be Joe soon enough. The boys will see to that."

Then she started to follow his mother into the house. Johann said questioningly, "But we're not Americans like you. We come from across the sea—"

Miss Iverson smiled. "Don't we all, Joe? Isn't that what America is? Isn't it a gathering place for everybody with the courage to cross the sea and find it? Why, that's why our country is big and strong, Joe. It takes big, strong people to leave all that's dear and familiar behind them, and to strike out to find a new world! It takes people like you and your parents—like Peter's grandfather who came from Greece, like my own mother and father who left their home in Norway."

She smiled and went on, "Oh, you'll see us all, dressed in our own special Old World clothes at the all-American party! Your mother must be sure to come and wear that lovely costume."

Johann's head was swimming with happiness. "But all-American — I thought it meant . . ."

"Just that we, who are from Norway and Greece and Germany, are all Americans now, Joe. That's what it means." Miss Iverson went into the house, and Johann swung around with outstretched arms to Peter and Paula.

"Come on in!" he invited warmly. "The windows look much prettier from inside!"

Proudly he led them into his home, and sunshine poured into his heart through a thousand singing windows.

## Working with the Story

1. The author uses words well to describe things. Find and write the words in the story which tell
   a. the color of Miss Iverson's hair.
   b. how Johann felt when he first heard about the all-American party.
   c. how the overalls rolled around Johann's ankles.
   d. how Johann's good feeling began to leave at four o'clock.
   e. how Johann's mother gave away his secret.
   f. how Johann felt at the end of the story.

2. Pretend that you are Johann and write to your great-uncle in Germany to tell him about your first ball game in America. Try to think of how Johann would feel about it. Remember that he had never played baseball before and knew nothing about it. You may wish to start your letter like this:

Dear Great-Uncle,

Now, I can tell you what an American baseball game is like. First, you hold a great long kind of club in your hands.

# Mothers

**By Rt. Rev. Hugh F. Blunt**

Mothers have a way with them
Only mothers know;
Just a secret heavenly
God has taught them so.

Arms that know the way to make
Softest cradle bed,
Giving shelter from the world
To a baby's head.

Mothers have a way with them
Only mothers know,
For to take His place on earth
God just made them so.

# Maile's Lei

By Mary Dana Rodriguez

Maile, the little Hawaiian girl, awakened before dawn the day of the fair. She was so excited, for this was the first year she was old enough to enter the lei-making contest.

For months Maile had been planning the kind of lei she would make. It would be a two-tone lei, made of the lovely white ginger blossoms that grew high in the mountains by the waterfall and the creamy, yellow ginger blossoms from the valley. With such a lei, she should win third prize, at least.

"But today," she scolded herself, "is not the day to dream. It is the day to *do*."

With that, she hopped out of bed, ate a quick breakfast, and then started up the mountain.

What a wonderful day for a fair! What a wonderful day just to be alive, thought Maile, watching the sun cast a rosy mist over the mountain. The dew, glistening on the forest of dark green fern, was like tiny diamonds.

Maile knew she shouldn't but she couldn't help planning how she would spend the prize money. Maile thought how nice it would be to buy something for her aunt, with whom she lived. She would get her a *good* straw hat—one she could wear to church with her best dress. The only hat her aunt owned now was very old.

Then if there were enough money left, she would buy some new rope so that Uncle Solomon could mend his fishing nets.

If there were *still* some money left over, she would take Keoki, her younger brother, down to the village. They would buy a big ten-cent bag of candy and two cups of crushed ice with delicious pink strawberry syrup poured over it.

While Maile planned how she would spend her prize money, she gathered the delicate, white ginger blossoms. Soon she had filled a large bag. She hurried down the valley to the house where Tutu lived. There she would pick the yellow ginger blossoms.

In the Hawaiian language Tutu means *grandmother,* but Tutu was not really Maile's grandmother. She was a kind old lady who was called Tutu by all the children who lived nearby.

Reaching Tutu's door, Maile was surprised to hear no singing and to smell no fragrance of a cake baking. Each year since the fair had first started, Tutu had entered a big, fresh coconut cake. And each year Tutu's cake had won the first prize!

Tutu was sitting in her rocker, her hands over her face, when Maile entered. Everything needed to make the cake was on the table. The oven was lighted. But Tutu just sat, rocking back and forth.

"Tutu, what's the matter?" Maile cried.

"Oh," moaned Tutu. "It's no use, Maile. For the first time since the fair began, I will not have a cake to enter. I have tried so hard to mix, but my hands are old and stiff. They hurt so, I can hardly move them."

Maile looked sadly at the old hands. Tutu needed the baking contest money especially this year. There had been little rain, and her garden had failed.

"Tutu," Maile said, "let me rub your hands with coconut oil. Then I will help you make your cake. All you have to do is tell me, step by step, exactly what to do."

Much later, when Maile was putting the cake into the oven, she glanced at the clock. Tears clouded her eyes, for there was no time left to gather the yellow ginger or to make the lei. Still, Tutu was looking so much happier that everything seemed worthwhile.

Wrapping the beautiful cake very carefully, Tutu said, "I wish I felt strong enough to go with you." Then giving Maile a good-by kiss, she said, "There's a nice lunch for you in the paper bag by the door."

Maile picked up the bag, and then ran to the bus stop as fast as she could, trying as she did not to jar the cake. The bus came along at the exact moment she reached the corner. Sitting down in one of the few empty seats, she realized that this was the first moment she had sat still since morning.

"Whew!" she sighed.

"Whew!" went the bus, only louder.

"Flat tire," the driver announced. "Everybody out."

Sitting by the side of the road, Maile decided to eat the lunch Tutu had sent with her. Imagine her surprise when, upon opening the bag, Maile discovered white ginger blossoms. Why, she had picked up the wrong bag!

Her string and needle were there, too. Maile began at once to make a lei. It could not be the two-tone one she had dreamed of making, of course, and she could never finish it in time. Nevertheless, the cool white buds were fresh as the dew still on them. Maile worked gently and steadily with them. Her lei was nearly half finished when the driver called, "All aboard!"

It was no use trying to string flowers on such a crowded, jiggling bus. So Maile just held the cake box carefully upright on her lap and sighed again.

"Whew!" she said.

"Whew!" went the bus again. Another flat tire!

The other passengers grumbled, but Maile sat underneath a shady tree and finished her lei. The tire fixed at last, everyone boarded the bus, and in half an hour's time they arrived at the fair.

First of all, Maile entered Tutu's cake in the baking contest. Then she found the flower booth where leis were to be kept hidden until time for the judging. There she entered her lei. It would not receive even so much as an honorable mention, she thought. It was just a plain white ginger blossom lei.

"Well," Maile thought, "there's fun to be had at a fair, prize or no prize."

She walked around looking at all the other booths. Here were some Hawaiian men making mats and bags from straw. There was a weathered old man hollowing out a canoe from a log. Maile looked at the lovely dolls in one booth for a long time.

She returned to the bakery booth in time to see Tutu's coconut cake take first prize. Happily she accepted blue ribbon and money for her good friend. She had almost

378

forgotten the flower booth and her lei until she heard her name being called over a loudspeaker. Someone at the flower booth was calling for Maile!

Back to the booth she went, her heart pounding like a hollow drum. To her great surprise, there was her lei hanging among the prize winners. On it was a lovely white ribbon with the words *Honorable Mention* printed on it in glistening gold letters.

She noticed that first prize had gone to a fancy two-tone white and yellow ginger lei such as she had planned to make.

However, Maile did not feel unhappy that it was not hers. She thought mostly about how pleased her beloved Tutu would be with her first prize and the money she needed so badly.

Maile did not receive a cash prize with the honorable mention award. Even so, she was thrilled that her white ginger lei had pleased the judges. As she took it from the booth, she heard someone call her.

She turned around. It was the Mayor. She had heard him speak at meetings she had gone to with her aunt and uncle. She had heard him over the radio, but he had never spoken to her like this before.

"Young lady," he said, "white ginger is my wife's favorite flower. Your lei is so beautiful and fresh that I would like to buy it for her."

He held out two crisp dollar bills for Maile.

Maile thanked him, and following an old Hawaiian custom, she reached up, placed the lei around his neck, and kissed him.

The Mayor smiled and said, "I hope you are awarded first prize next year."

Two crisp dollar bills—not enough to buy the presents she had planned, thought Maile. Nevertheless she had plenty to buy a treat for the family for dinner. She would stop by the poultry stand in the market on the way home and pick out the nicest hen.

Maile knew that Tutu, of course, could explain how everything that day had happened. The Hawaiian elves, the little people, had arranged everything. They switched the bags in the first place, and later arranged for the flat tires on the bus. They did it all to make sure that Maile would have good fortune because she had been kind to Tutu.

## Finding the Author's Words

1. Read these paragraphs and answer the questions.
   - *a.* Page 373, paragraph 2. Which word tells you that Maile's lei would be made of more than one color?
   - *b.* Page 377, paragraph 2. Which word tells you that the bus ride was not smooth?
   - *c.* Page 378, paragraph 4. Which word tells you that Maile willingly took the blue ribbon?
   - *d.* Page 380, paragraph 1. Which word shows that Maile was happy?
   - *e.* Page 373, paragraph 5. Which two words tell how the dew drops looked?

2. Write six sentences to tell how each of the following things might be used in Hawaii.

| | | |
|---|---|---|
| ginger blossoms | string | logs |
| coconut oil | straw | rope |

# Snow Is Your Friend

By Alice Curtis Desmond

## Arctic Adventure

Taku squatted before a cabin near Nome in Alaska.
His white-haired grandfather, Karen, sat nearby.

Today the old man was teaching his grandson how to
build an Eskimo snowhouse. This was a new thing to
the twelve-year-old boy. His people no longer used
snowhouses. Taku and his family and friends now lived
in wooden cabins built around a mission and a general
store. The men hunted the seal no longer with harpoons,
but with rifles. They had almost forgotten how to build
the old-fashioned snow shelters.

382

Taku's grandfather had been a famous sealer. The boy listened eagerly to tales of the old man's adventures. Taku especially liked to hear about snowhouses. He liked to hear how they kept the Eskimo warm even in zero weather and how they had saved many a sealer's life.

"The bear sleeps in snow caves during the winter. Other animals live underneath the soft snow," old Karen told the boy. "Snow is also man's friend. Why doesn't he learn to use snow, and not to fear it? Gone would be his fear of cold and death in the Arctic."

Where Taku lived the snow was never deep. Now in April it had begun to melt into the brown tundra. So the building of a snowhouse was not easy. The boy was wishing that he was old enough to go to the Arctic regions where there was real snow and ice.

Suddenly Taku stood up, his snowhouse forgotten. His father Navook stood at the cabin door talking with visitors—a tall man and a fair-haired boy, about Taku's age.

Karen and his grandson joined the group at the cabin door. They wondered who these white-skinned strangers were. It seemed that Captain John Horne had come from Minnesota to ask Taku's father to take him seal hunting.

"Fine!" said the Captain, when things were decided. He turned to Taku. "And why not take your boy with us? He would be company for my son, Dick."

The young Eskimo gasped with excitement, but Navook shook his head. "Taku is too young," he replied.

"Oh, please take me!" Taku begged. "I can look after the dogs. I'm not too young. I'm big now, twelve years old."

"Why, I'm twelve, too, and I'm going sealing!" exclaimed Dick Horne.

"At twelve I began to learn to be a sealer," old Karen added. "My grandson should go."

Slowly Navook was won over. It was decided that Taku should go on his first seal hunt.

On a bright, sunny morning, with the ice of the Bering Sea turning mushy, they started north. The sled was packed high with tents, rifles, canned goods, and hunting equipment. Taku helped his father hitch the dogs to the sled. The big huskies were so eager to go mushing that they gave little howls of pleasure.

Dick Horne rode on the sled. Taku ran along beside him as they started off. "How do you like this?" he panted. The young Eskimo was proud of his mission English.

The white boy grinned. "It's swell!"

As they went north, the air became colder. Soon the snow was so deep that Taku sank in to his knees as he helped push the sled. The dogs liked the deep snow. It made easier pulling.

Without a mishap, the party reached the sealing grounds. The weather had turned mild. This was best for sealing. The seals had dragged their sleek bodies from the water, up onto the ice—the same ice which had roofed them in all winter. Everywhere, they were napping in the warm sun.

Taku now learned the seal hunter's first lesson. "You must get near enough to a seal to shoot him," Navook told Captain Horne. "Seals are cautious animals. Every few minutes a seal wakes and looks all about him. At the least sign of danger, he disappears through a hole in the ice."

Navook explained how the nearsighted seal can be fooled into thinking that a hunter is only another seal. Captain Horne and Navook lay down on the ice. They crawled cautiously up to the sleeping herd until they were near enough to shoot.

Dick and Taku had no guns, but the boys wriggled over the slippery ice, too. They pretended they were seals.

As soon as the hunt was over, the sealing party started home. They planned to travel down the coast, for Navook's dogs were tired. The route by the water was the easiest and the shortest.

The next morning they came to the wide mouth of the river. Navook went ahead to test the ice.

"It's solid," he said. "We'll save many miles by taking this shortcut across the ice."

At first the dogs were frightened. Their feet skidded on the ice, which was lightly covered with snow. Soon they lost their fear. The sled runners fairly flew over the smooth white surface. It was the easiest traveling they had had on the trip.

"Too bad we can't go on ice all the way," said Captain Horne.

They were a half mile from land when Navook cried out, "Black ice, Taku! Look out!"

The young Eskimo's heart pounded at those dreaded words. They were on new, thin ice, which was very dark because of the water close beneath it. Snow had covered the "black ice," and so Navook had not seen the danger. Now they could not turn back. Taku felt the thin ice give beneath the heavy sled. The shore, so near a minute ago, now seemed far away.

Crunch! Crunch! The ice was breaking. Water splashed up. The sled was cutting through!

"Mush! Mush!" Taku yelled at the dogs to pull hard.

It was too late. There was another sound of breaking ice, and the sled lunged deeper into the water. Navook rushed back, a long knife in his hand.

"Cut the dogs loose!" he cried.

As the team lunged to safety, the men worked wildly to save what they could from the sinking sled. Then sadly they watched the rest of their equipment being dragged down into the sea.

Once on the riverbank, Navook nodded. "Ice and snow are always dangerous. They cannot be trusted. We saved time coming by this route, but we almost lost our lives."

Taku remembered what his grandfather had said. Snow was man's friend if he would learn to use it and not to fear it. The Eskimo boy wondered about that.

# Arctic Shelter

Well, here they were on dry land—and safe! Or were they? They had their dogs, but the sled with most of their equipment was lost in the sea. They were far from any village. And stronger and stronger came icy wind and snow. A late spring blizzard was brewing!

To make matters worse, Dick had turned his ankle in the mad scramble for shore. It was swelling and becoming painful. They could not push on.

"We'll camp here overnight," Navook said.

Shelter for the night was needed. Their tents had gone down with the sled. Navook began to dig a cave in a snowdrift, using a stick for a shovel. It was slow work.

"Why not build a snowhouse?" Taku suggested. "I know how. Grandfather taught me."

"Just the thing!" his father replied. Whipping out his long knife, he cut into the snow.

Navook decided the snow had enough "sticking power" to make a house. He set to work cutting blocks with his long knife. But Taku's father had never built an Eskimo snowhouse. Many of the squares of ice broke. Navook also made the mistake of placing the first layer in a circle flat on the ground.

"No, Father, like this," Taku explained.

The young boy showed the men what his grandfather had taught him—how each block must be cut so that it slants toward the center of the circle. The very bottom layer, too, must be slanted. Each of the following layers are slanted farther and farther inward. The circle gets smaller and smaller and finally comes together at the top. But each block must be placed just right so that the walls will lean inward without falling.

Navook and Taku made mistakes. In the second layer, several blocks fell.

"See, it's impossible!" exclaimed Captain Horne.

But as they worked, Taku remembered all that his grandfather had taught him. He showed his father how to make a strong wall. Proudly, he stood inside the snowhouse beside Navook. Since the walls leaned inward, the builder must stand within the circle of blocks, facing out. Slowly, the domed shelter took shape.

"Marvelous!" cried Captain Horne.

He and Dick stood on the outside of the walls. They could not see what Taku and Navook were doing.

Everyone knows that two handfuls of snow can be packed together to make one. In the same way, each piece of ice in the snowhouse sticks to the one next to it. When Navook and Taku laid a block high up on the roof, they made it stick like this. It was one of the tricks in snow building. Taku took the knife and shaved the corner of each block until it melted. Then it would stick to the block beneath it.

It was growing dark as they worked. They must hurry! Captain Horne and Dick were put to work gently pushing soft snow into the cracks between the blocks.

By dark, the last block had been shaved and fitted into the roof. The snowhouse was finished!

They were just in time. It was very cold, and the blizzard was growing worse. Navook fed the dogs, and they curled up in the snow to sleep. The two men and their sons crawled through the long tunnel which they had shoveled into their new home. This opening was lower than the floor. The cold air would flow down into the tunnel leaving the warm air in the dome. Navook made a small air hole in the roof. He closed the door with a big piece of snow. They unrolled their sleeping bags and were snug for the night.

Pulling a thermometer from his pocket, Captain Horne took a reading of the temperature in the snowhouse. It was twenty degrees below zero. Outside the wind was howling, but they could no longer hear it. Ten minutes later, Taku opened his parka and pulled off his fur gloves. It was getting warm! Later, the Captain took another temperature reading. He stared at the thermometer.

"Believe it or not," he said, "it's thirty-four degrees—two above freezing!"

This had been done in twenty minutes, by means of their body heat. Let the storm rage outside, Taku thought. They weren't going to freeze to death!

With a shelter over their heads, it was time to think about supper. Hot tea and crackers would taste mighty good. Captain Horne had been able to take his small gas stove from the sinking sled. Filling a pail with snow, Navook put it over the flame on the stove to melt. In a few minutes the rise in temperature caused by the flame made fur caps and mukluks uncomfortable. It was almost too warm in the snowhouse!

Captain Horne looked at his thermometer again. "I can't believe it. It's fifty-five degrees!"

That night Taku slept comfortably, his sleeping bag unfastened. The others rolled up and slept well, too.

The next morning snow was still falling, and Dick's ankle was worse.

"We'll stay here," Navook said. "A boat will pass and rescue us."

His father looked serious and worried, and Taku knew why. What boat would pass at this time of year?

If they had to live in the snowhouse for several days, the shelter must be "iced." Navook did this by first closing the door. Then he turned up the gas lamp. When the walls were melting, he removed the door block. Cold air rushed in and the hot air rose. In a few minutes the walls were coated with a thick solid ice. This made the snowhouse stronger and even more windproof.

The men and boys talked, drank tea, and rested for the rest of the day. By the second day the storm had ended. They took turns standing on a high rock to look across the sea for a boat.

On the fifth day, with food getting low, Taku heard an airplane overhead. He waved wildly, but the plane continued on its way.

Had the plane seen them? Anxiously, they waited. But the fog closed down over them. If a ship came into the bay looking for them, it could pass close by and not see them.

Two days later, their hopes of rescue began to grow very dim. Suddenly Taku's sharp ears heard a sound. "Oooooo—"

It was a foghorn, and it was close. Taku caught sight of a Coast Guard ice cutter coming through the fog and into the bay. With a shout, he raced down to the shore. He jumped up onto a rock, where he could be seen. He waved and waved.

393

The Coast Guard boat stopped.

An hour later, the men and boys were safely aboard the ice cutter, headed toward home. "It was a lucky thing the pilot of that plane saw you," the skipper told them.

"But it was your snowhouse that saved our lives, Taku," Captain Horne said. This made the Eskimo boy feel proud. The man turned to the skipper and asked, "Why doesn't every soldier in Alaska, every pilot and mountain climber, learn to build snowhouses, instead of carrying heavy tents?"

Taku wondered, too.

"And how about Boy Scouts?" asked Dick. "When I get back to Minnesota, I'm going to teach my scout troop how to build an Eskimo snowhouse."

"Perhaps snow is man's friend, after all," said Navook.

Taku nodded with pleasure. It might have been his grandfather speaking.

## A *Runner* Is a Person or Part of a Sled

Many words in this story have more than one meaning. Skim to find each of the following words on the page listed after it. Read the sentence in which you find the word. Then think of another meaning for the word and write a sentence using the word with that meaning. The first word is in the glossary. Find the word and read its meanings. This will help you to get started.

| | | |
|---|---|---|
| mush (387) | whipping (389) | rose (392) |
| seal (382) | blocks (389) | dim (393) |
| team (388) | reading (391) | skipper (394) |

# Our Land

ETHEL CROWNINSHIELD

FOLK TUNE

1. Land of the moun-tains, land of the riv - ers,
2. Hearts that are grate - ful, hands that are will - ing,

Land where the sea rolls in from east and west:
Ea - ger to serve to keep our coun-try free.

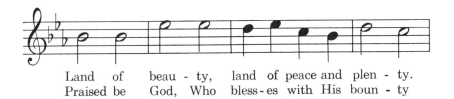

Land of beau - ty, land of peace and plen - ty.
Praised be God, Who bless - es with His boun - ty

This is our land, The land we love the best!
This, our dear land, Sweet land of lib - er - ty.

# Books to Enjoy

*Candita's Choice*, by Mina Lewiton.

Candita Rivera comes from her home in Puerto Rico to live in New York City and is faced with the struggle of learning new customs and a new language. With the help of friends and an understanding teacher, the shy young girl overcomes many difficulties and learns to love her new country.

*Johnny Texas*, by Carol Hoff.

This is the thrilling story of a young boy who came from Germany to settle in Texas. There is much adventure in the new country for Johnny, especially when he has to become the man of the family and care for his mother and baby sister.

*First Book of Hawaii*, by Sam and Beryl Epstein.

Here you will learn what it is like to live in Hawaii and many interesting facts about our new state. You will even learn to pronounce the longest Hawaiian word.

*Benny's Flag*, by Phyllis Krasilovsky.

This is a true story about a young boy in an Alaskan mission school who designed the Alaskan flag.

*Life in America: Alaska*, by Stuart R. Tompkins.

You will learn many interesting things about citizens of our forty-ninth state in this book. Many photographs show how the people live and what their state looks like.

*Honk: The Moose*, by Phil Stong.

Minnesota is the setting for this story about two boys whose parents came to this country from Finland. Their town was quiet and rather uneventful until a sad, hungry moose comes to town and doesn't want to leave.

# Glossary

The glossary will help you to pronounce and to understand the meanings of difficult or unusual words used in this book.

The pronunciation of each word is shown just after the word, in this way: **ab bre vi ate** (ə brē′vi āt). The letters and signs used are pronounced as in the words below. The mark ′ is placed after a syllable with primary or heavy accent, as in the example above. The mark ′ after a syllable shows a secondary or lighter accent, as in **ab bre vi a tion** ( ə brē′vi ā′shən).

| | | | | | |
|---|---|---|---|---|---|
| a | hat, cap | j | jam, enjoy | u | cup, butter |
| ā | age, face | k | kind, seek | u̇ | full, put |
| ã | care, air | l | land, coal | ü | rule, move |
| ä | father, far | m | me, am | ū | use, music |
| | | n | no, in | | |
| b | bad, rob | ng | long, bring | | |
| ch | child, much | | | v | very, save |
| d | did, red | o | hot, rock | w | will, woman |
| | | ō | open, go | y | young, yet |
| e | let, best | ô | order, all | z | zero, breeze |
| ē | equal, be | oi | oil, voice | zh | measure, seizure |
| ėr | term, learn | ou | house, out | | |
| | | | | | |
| | | p | paper, cup | | |
| f | fat, if | r | run, try | ə | represents: |
| g | go, bag | s | say, yes | | a in about |
| h | he, how | sh | she, rush | | e in taken |
| | | t | tell, it | | i in pencil |
| i | it, pin | th | thin, both | | o in lemon |
| ī | ice, five | ᴛʜ | then, smooth | | u in circus |

The pronunciation system and key employed in this publication are from the Thorndike-Barnhart Dictionary Program and are used by permission of Scott, Foresman and Company. Copyright © 1962.

## A

**ab bey** (ab′i), the building or group of buildings where monks or nuns live and lead a religious life; a monastery or convent.

**ab bot** (ab′ət), the person at the head of a group of monks.

**A bra ham** (ā′brə ham), in the Bible, the first leader of the Jewish people.

**ache** (āk), suffer pain; be in pain.

ac tiv i ty (ak tiv′ə ti), action or motion.

ad mi ral (ad′mə rəl), 1. the officer in charge of a group of ships. 2. in the navy, an officer of the highest rank.

aisle (īl), a passage between rows of seats, as in a church, hall, or school.

A las ka (ə las′kə), the 49th state of the United States located in the north-western part of North America.

a lert (ə lėrt′), watchful, especially against danger; on the lookout; wide-awake.

Am ster dam (am′stər dam), a large city and the capital of the Netherlands.

an chor (ang′kər), 1. fasten or fix firm-ly; hold in place. 2. hold a ship in place by means of a piece of heavy iron or steel, also called an *anchor*.

Anchor

an cient (ān′shənt), belonging to times long past; also, very old.

A ni ta (ä nē′tä), a girl's name.

Ant arc tic (ant ärk′tik), the body of land around or near the South Pole. This area is covered with snow and ice.

An to nio (än tō′nyō), name of an old man in the story "Pinocchio's First Adventure."

A pol lo (ə pol′ō), in the religion of the ancient Greeks, the god of youth and beauty and of music, poetry, and prophecy. He was also called the sun god.

arch (ärch), an opening with a curved or rounded top, such as a doorway.

Arc tic (ärk′tik), the region around or near the North Pole.

ar rest (ə rest′), take by force and hold; take to court or jail: *Did the police arrest the thief?*

As si si (ə sē′zi), a city in Italy and the birthplace of St. Francis.

as ton ish ment (əs ton′ish mənt), great surprise; sudden wonder; amazement.

Aus tine (ôs tēn′), a girl's name.

a ward (ə wôrd′), something given after careful thought; a prize or an honor: *He won an award as the best swim-mer.*

### B

bal ance (bal′əns), to be steady because all parts are the same size and weight.

base (bās), 1. a goal or station in some games. 2. a thing on which something else rests; the bottom of something: *the base of a statue.*

bay (bā), a part of a sea or lake that reaches into the land. A bay is like a gulf but is usually smaller.

Bay

beam (bēm), a long thick piece of timber or metal used to help hold up or strengthen a building or the roof of a building.

bea ver (bē′vər), 1. a small animal with a broad flat tail that lives both in water and on land. Beavers dam streams and build their homes of mud and branches in water. 2. the fur of this animal.

be hold (bi hōld′), see; look; watch; take notice.

**be lov ed** (bi luv′id or bi luvd′), much loved; very dear.

**Ben ji** (ben′ji), name of a boy in the story "The Shepherd's Coat."

**Ber ing Sea** (bēr′ing sē), the northern part of the Pacific Ocean between Alaska and northeastern Asia.

**Beth le hem** (beth′li əm or beth′lə hem), a town in the Holy Land where the Christ Child was born.

**Be thune, Al ber tus** (bə thūn′, al bėr′-təs), the man whom Mary McLeod married.

**Bil ly the Kid**, a leader of a group of dangerous outlaws of the West in the nineteenth century. His real name was William H. Bonney.

**birch** (bėrch), 1. a slender tree with hard wood and having a smooth bark that can be peeled off in thin layers. 2. the wood of this tree.

**Blan di na** (blan dē′nə), a Sister of Charity who was a great citizen of the Western frontier.

**bleat** (blēt), make the cry of a sheep, goat, or calf, or a sound that is like such a cry.

**bliz zard** (bliz′ərd), a forceful storm of snow and wind; a very cold snow-storm with a strong wind.

**boar** (bôr), 1. a wild pig or hog. 2. a male pig or hog.

**Bob ry** (bob′ri), name of an otter in the story "A Sea Family."

**bob white** (bob′ hwīt′), an American quail about ten inches long. It is named for the sound it makes.

**Bon i face** (bon′ə fās), a man's name.

**booth** (būth), 1. a small, closed place for a telephone, for voters at elections, etc. 2. a covered stand where goods are sold at a fair or market.

**bore** (bôr), make a hole in something, especially with a tool that turns.

**Bra zil** (brə zil′), the largest country in South America.

**Bre do** (brā′dō), a boy's name.

**bri dle** (brī′dəl), 1. the part of a horse's harness that goes over the head and is used to hold back or turn the horse. 2. put a bridle on.

Bridle

**brisk** (brisk), quickly; very active.

**bris tle** (bris′əl), 1. a short, stiff hair of an animal, especially that of a hog. 2. rise or stand up straight, as the bristles of an animal do when it is angry and ready to fight: *The porcupine's quills bristled.*

**bro cade** (brō kād′), a cloth with a raised design, usually of gold, silver, or silk, or all three, woven into it.

**bulk** (bulk), swell; take up more space; also, have a full, clumsy appearance.

**but tress** (but′ris), 1. on a tree, a part of the root or stem that grows outward close to the ground and gives strength to the tree and helps to hold it upright. 2. something built against a wall or a building to strengthen the sides of the building.

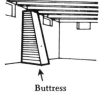

Buttress

---

cap, āge, cāre, fär; let, bē, tėrm; pin, fīve; hot, gō, ôr; oil, out; cup, fůll, rüle, ūse; takən

# C

**ca ble** (kā′bəl), a very strong and heavy rope, wire, or chain. Cables are often made of wires twisted together.

Cable

**Ca pi stra no** (kä′pə strä′nō), a short name for **San Juan Capistrano** (san hwän′), a mission in California; also the village surrounding the mission.

**cap tive** (kap′tiv), kept shut up; held as a prisoner.

**cap ture** (kap′chər), seize and take by force, surprise, or skill; make a prisoner of.

**Ca ru so** (kə rü′sō), a family name.

**cast** (kast), throw: *cast a shadow on a wall; cast a fishing line.*

**cau tious** (kô′shəs), very careful; careful to stay away from danger.

**ce ment** (sə ment′), a mixture which becomes hard like stone when mixed with sand and water. It is used in the building of walls, floors, and walks.

**cen tu ry** (sen′chə ri), 1. a period of one hundred years. 2. one of the 100-year divisions, counting from the birth of Christ. The twentieth century is from 1901 to 2000.

**char coal** (chär′kōl′), 1. a black or very dark piece of wood which has been burned in a special way. 2. a pencil made of charcoal and used for drawing.

**char i ty** (char′ə ti), 1. love of God and one's fellow men. 2. giving of aid to the poor or needy.

**chink** (chingk), a small, narrow opening; a crack: *The chinks in the log cabin were being filled with mud.*

**cin na mon** (sin′ə mən), 1. a spice made from the dried bark of certain trees of the East Indies; also, the tree itself. 2. made with cinnamon.

**clan** (klan), a group of people from related families; of the same family.

**clear** (klēr), cut down the trees on a piece of land so that the land may be used for homes and farms.

**clear ing** (klēr′ing), an open space of cleared land in a forest; land from which trees have been removed.

**Clu ny** (klü′ni), a village in the eastern part of France. Cluny is the site of a famous Benedictine abbey.

**clut ter** (klut′ər), make messy or disorderly with many things placed about in a disorderly way: *to clutter a room with papers, toys, or trash.*

**coarse** (kôrs), 1. made up of parts that are fairly large; not fine: *coarse gravel.* 2. of a poor kind or type; rough: *a coat of coarse cloth.*

**Coast Guard** (kōst gärd), a group of men whose job it is to guard the coast and take charge of the lifesaving stations along the coast.

**coax** (kōks), make another willing by gentle words or pleasant ways; talk another into something by soft and gentle asking: *coax a child to sing.*

**coil** (koil), 1. a wire or pipe that has been wound round and round. 2. anything wound round and round in a pile or curl: *a coil of wire.*

Coil

**col umn** (kol′əm), 1. a slender, upright structure, used to help hold something up; a pillar. 2. anything that is like a column in shape, position, or use: *a column of numbers.*

**com pose** (kəm pōz′), put together parts to make something new: *compose a poem.*

**con dense** (kən dens′), make or become more close; more closely packed together. Milk is condensed by removing most of the water.

**cone** (kōn), 1. a solid body that is round at the bottom and comes to a point at the top. 2. anything that is like a cone in shape, such as a holder for ice cream. 3. the part that holds the seeds of certain trees, such as the pine or fir.

**con fuse** (kən fūz′), to be mixed up; mistaken.

**con struc tion** (kən struk′shən), 1. the building or putting together of something: *the construction of a schoolhouse.* 2. something built or put together; a building, a bridge, or a highway.

**con ven ient** (kən vēn′yənt), easily reached; suited for a person's use; handy to use.

**cor ral** (kə ral′), an enclosed place for animals, such as horses; a pen.

**court yard** (kôrt′yärd′), a space enclosed by walls within, or attached to, a large building: *the courtyard of a castle.*

**crab** (krab), an animal with a broad, flat shell, two claws, and eight legs.

Most crabs are sea animals, but a few kinds live on land.

**crafts man** (krafts′mən), a man who is able to work well in using his hands or tools.

**cre a tion** (kri ā′shən), 1. all things that God has brought into being; the world. 2. the making of something that has not been made before.

**crouch** (krouch), stoop low or bend legs like an animal that is ready to spring or is in hiding.

**Cun e gun da** (kun ə gun′dä), wife of the Holy Roman Emperor St. Henry II, who lived a very holy life and was made a saint.

**cu ri os i ty** (kūr′i os′ə ti), an eager desire to find out something.

**cus tom** (kus′təm), the usual way of doing things: *the custom of saying "Good morning."*

**cut worm** (kut′wėrm′), a caterpillar that eats or cuts off young plants near the ground.

### D

**Daed a lus** (ded′ə ləs), in a Greek myth, a man who escaped from the island of Crete by means of wings which he made of feathers.

**de clare** (di klār′), say; make known; announce.

**de gree** (di grē′), 1. a unit for measuring temperature. 2. a space or a division marked on a thermometer.

**de liv er** (di liv′ər), 1. set free; save from danger or trouble. 2. carry and give out: *deliver a package.*

---

cap, āge, cāre, fär; let, bē, tėrm; pin, fīve; hot, gō, ôr; oil, out; cup, fůll, rūle, ūse; takən

**de sign** (di zīn′), 1. make something; especially following the plan of a drawing, or sketch. 2. make a drawing of; plan out. 3. a drawing, sketch, or plan of something.

**di rect ly** (də rekt′li), 1. at once; immediately. 2. in a direct line or way; straight: *She went directly home.*

**dome** (dōm), 1. a large rounded roof of a building. 2. anything that is shaped like a dome.

Dome

**Don An to nio** (don än tō′nyō), title and name of a man in the story "Anita's Gift of Flowers." *Don* is a Spanish title that means *Mr.* or *Sir.*

**drain pipe** (drān′pīp′), a pipe used to carry off water or other liquid.

**dumb** (dum), 1. silent; not speaking. 2. lacking the natural power of speech: *a dumb person.* 3. by nature, not able to speak: *dumb animals.*

**Dutch** (duch), 1. of or having to do with Holland, its people, or their language. 2. the people of Holland. 3. the language of Holland.

### E

**E gypt** (ē′jipt), a country in the northeastern part of Africa.

**E gyp tian** (i jip′shən), 1. the people of Egypt. 2. of or having to do with Egypt: *the Egyptian pyramids.*

**eld est** (el′dist), oldest: *the eldest son.*

**em broi der** (em broi′dər), trim or add stitches to make a design or pattern.

**en gi neer** (en′jə nēr′), 1. person who plans and builds such things as roads, railroads, bridges, canals, and the like. 2. person who runs an engine, such as a steam engine.

**Eng lish** (ing′glish), 1. the language of England which is spoken also in the United States, Canada, Australia, New Zealand, and many other parts of the world. 2. the people of England. 3. of or having to do with England: *the English government.*

**e quip ment** (i kwip′mənt), supplies or things needed for a special reason; an outfit, as for camping.

**Es ki mo** (es′kə mō), 1. member of a race of people who live on the arctic coasts of North America. 2. of or having to do with the Eskimos: *an Eskimo house.*

**ev er green** (ev′ər grēn′), 1. a tree or other plant that stays green all the year, such as a pine, spruce, or fir tree. 2. *in the plural,* **evergreens,** twigs and branches of evergreen trees or plants that are used for decoration.

**ex pe di tion** (eks′pə dish′ən), a journey for a special purpose, as for exploring an unknown part of the world.

**ex press** (eks pres′), make something known by words or action; show: *express pleasure by smiling.*

**ex press box** (eks pres′ boks′), a strong box for shipping something, such as mail or money. In the early days of the West, large amounts of gold were put in these boxes and carried by stagecoaches.

**Ex ten sion So ci e ty** (eks ten′shən sə-sī′ə ti), a Catholic organization which helps home missions of our nation.

**famine**

**F**

**fam ine** (fam'ən), a very great lack of food in a place; a time of great hunger and starving.

**fee ble** (fē'bəl), weak; lacking strength; *a feeble person; a feeble voice.*

**fetch** (fech), get; go and bring back: *fetch a pail of water.*

**fi es ta** (fi es'tə), 1. a festival, especially, a religious festival. 2. any holiday or time of making merry.

**fig ure** (fig'yər), 1. find out the answer to a problem by using numbers. 2. the mark which stands for a number, as 2, 4, and 6. 3. a form or shape: *to see a figure in the distance.*

**firm** (fėrm), 1. not easily changed; determined: *a firm voice.* 2. tightly fastened; not easily loosened: *a firm hold on a rope.*

**fleck** (flek), mark with patches of light or color; spot.

**flip per** (flip'ər), a broad, flat wing-like part of an animal, used in swimming. Seals and whales have flippers.

Flipper

**fold** (fōld), 1. bend and bring close to the body: *fold one's arms.* 2. bend or double over: *fold a napkin.* 3. a layer of something that has been folded: *a fold of a blanket.* 4. a pen for sheep. 5. a flock of sheep.

**font** (font), 1. a wide bowl used for holding holy water. 2. a bowl or basin to hold water for baptism: *a baptismal font.* 3. a fountain.

**gloomy**

**fra grance** (frā'grəns), a pleasant odor; a sweet smell.

**Frau** (frou), a German word that means a married woman; a wife. As a title, it is equal to *Mrs.*

**French** (french), 1. of or having to do with France. 2. the people of France. 3. the language of France.

**fri ar** (frī'ər), a man belonging to a religious order.

**fron tier** (frun tēr'), the edge of the settled part of a country which is next to the wilderness.

**G**

**Gar de nia** (gär dēn'yə), 1. name of a goat in the story "Gardenia and the Pies." 2. *not capitalized,* a sweet-smelling white flower.

**gen er al** (jen'ər əl), not special; not only one kind or class. A general store is one that usually has a number of different kinds of things for sale.

**Gep pet to** (jə pet'tō), an Italian name.

**Ger man** (jėr'mən), 1. the people of Germany. 2. the language of Germany. 3. of or having to do with Germany: *the German scientist.*

**Ger ma ny** (jėr'mə ni), a country in the central part of Europe.

**gin ger** (jin'jər), 1. a plant that grows in warm places and has a sharp-tasting root that is used for flavoring. 2. a spice made from this root.

**Gior gio** (jôr'jō), an Italian name.

**gloom y** (glüm'i), 1. sad; low in spirits. 2. dark; dim: *a gloomy house.*

---

cap, āge, cãre, fär; let, bē, tėrm; pin, fīve; hot, gō, ôr; oil, out; cup, fůll, rüle, ūse; takən

403

**glo ri ous** (glô′ri əs), 1. delightful: *a glorious afternoon.* 2. splendid; magnificent: *a glorious sunrise.* 3. worthy of praise and honor: *a glorious deed.*

**goal** (gōl), 1. place at which a race is to end. 2. something for which an effort or struggle is made; a purpose: *His goal is to be President.*

**gob lin** (gob′lən), an elf or ugly-looking imaginary creature with many mischievous ways.

**Go mez** (gō′mās), a family name.

**gov er nor** (guv′ər nər), person elected to rule or govern a state of the United States.

**graze** (grāz), feed on growing grass, as cattle and sheep do.

**Greece** (grēs), a country in the southeastern part of Europe.

**ground squir rel** (ground skwėr′əl), any one of several burrowing animals that belong to the squirrel family; especially, the chipmunk.

**Gub bio** (güb′byō), a small town in the central part of Italy near Assisi.

**guide** (gīd), 1. direct the movements of; control. 2. show the way; lead.

## H

**hal lo** (hə lō′), hello; a call of greeting; also, a call to attract attention.

**hare** (hãr), a gnawing animal with long ears, long hind legs, and a short tail. A hare is much like a rabbit, but is larger.

**har poon** (här pün′), a barbed spear used for striking whales, seals, and other large sea animals.

Harpoon

**Ha wai ian** (hə wī′yən), 1. the people of Hawaii. 2. the language of Hawaii. 3. of or having to do with Hawaii: *the Hawaiian Islands.*

**head long** (hed′lông), 1. with haste, speed, and force. 2. headfirst.

**heave** (hēv), rise and fall again and again, as one's chest does when breathing deeply.

**Hei di** (hī′dē), a girl's name.

**hem lock** (hem′lok), an evergreen tree of the pine family.

**hes i tate** (hez′ə tāt), pause or stop for a moment; show that one is uncertain or undecided about something.

**Hol land** (hol′ənd), a small country in Europe, west of Germany. Holland is known also as the Netherlands.

**hol low** (hol′ō), 1. make a hole in, especially a bowl-shaped hole. 2. having a hole inside: *a hollow tree.* 3. a hollow place; a hole.

**ho ri zon** (hə rī′zən), the line where the land or sea appears to meet the sky.

**Hud son** (hud′sən), a river that flows through New York State. The city of New York is located at the mouth of this river.

**Hu ron** (hūr′ən), name of a tribe of Iroquois Indians who once lived in the region between Lake Huron and Lake Ontario.

**husk y** (hus′ki), an Eskimo dog, used to pull sleds.

## I

**Ic a rus** (ik′ə rəs), in a Greek myth, the son of Daedalus.

**in her it ance** (in her′ə təns), something inherited; something received from a parent or ancestor, such as money or property.

**inn** (in), a public house where travelers may eat and spend the night; a hotel, especially a small one.

**in tent** (in tent′), giving careful attention to something; thinking or looking at something very carefully.

**Ir o quois** (ir′ə kwoi), name of a powerful group of Indian tribes that once lived mainly in what is now New York State.

**I saac** (ī′zək), in the Bible, the son of Abraham and Sarah.

**Is ra el** (iz′ri əl), 1. the Jews; the Hebrews. 2. an ancient kingdom in Palestine; now a republic in part of Palestine.

**Is ra el ite** (iz′ri əl īt), a Hebrew or Jew.

**It a ly** (it′ə li), a country in the southern part of Europe.

**I ver son** (ī′vər sən), a family name.

## J

**Ja cob** (jā′kəb), 1. a boy's name. 2. in the Bible, the son of Isaac.

**Ja nus** (jā′nəs), a family name.

**jas mine** (jas′mən), a shrub with shiny leaves and clusters of small, sweet-smelling flowers.

**Je ru sa lem** (jə rü′sə ləm), the ancient and present capital of Israel; once the capital of Palestine.

**Jes u it** (jezh′ü it), a priest who belongs to the Society of Jesus.

**Jogues, I saac** (zhōg, ī′zək), in the seventeenth century, a Jesuit missionary

who worked with the North American Indians and was martyred.

**Juan** (hwän), a boy's name.

**jug gler** (jug′lər), a person who does tricks with his hands, such as tossing objects into the air and catching them quickly one after another.

## K

**Ke o ki** (kā ō′kē), a Hawaiian name.

## L

**Lam bert** (lam′bərt), a boy's name.

**land lord** (land′lôrd′), 1. the owner of land, houses, or buildings that he rents to others. 2. a man who runs an inn or boarding house.

**lan guage** (lang′gwij), 1. the words and expressions used by any large group of people: *the English language.* 2. human speech.

**lan tern** (lan′tərn), a case to protect a light from wind, rain, etc. Lanterns are usually round or boxlike in shape with sides of glass.

**lar der** (lär′dər), a place or room where foods are kept; a pantry.

**law yer** (lô′yər), a person who knows about laws and acts for another person in court.

**leg end** (lej′ənd), a story that has come down from the past that may or may not be true.

**lei** (lā), a wreath or garland of flowers or leaves for the head or neck.

**lil y of the val ley** (lil′i, val′i), a small plant with sweet-smelling, bell-shaped white flowers.

cap, āge, cãre, fär; let, bē, tèrm; pin, fīve; hot, gō, ôr; oil, out; cup, fůll, růle, ūse; takən

**Lin coln, A bra ham** (ling'kən, ā'brə-ham), from 1861 to 1865, the 16th president of the United States.

**lodge** (loj), 1. den of an animal, such as a beaver. 2. a place in which to live, especially a small house or a house to live in for a short time.

**loom** (lüm), come into sight in a form that looks unnaturally large, out of shape, or not clear, as through a haze.

**Lud wig** (lud'wig), a boy's name.

**Lu i gi** (lü ē'jē), a boy's name.

**lunge** (lunj), make a sudden forward movement; plunge suddenly forward.

**lurk** (lėrk), stay or hide in or about a place without attracting attention; wait out of sight.

**lynx** (lingks), a wildcat found in the northern part of the United States and in Canada. A lynx has long legs and a short stubby tail.

## M

**Mac pher son** (mək fėr'sən), a family name.

**Maes tro Do ni** (mīs'trō dō'nē), title and name of a teacher in the story "The Reward of Love." *Maestro* is an Italian word that means *master; master of an art;* also, *teacher.*

**maid en** (mād'ən), a young woman who is not married; a girl.

**Mai le** (mī'lā), a Hawaiian name.

**Ma mi ta** (mä mē'tä), a Spanish word that means *dear mother.*

**Mar co** (mär'kō), an Italian name.

**mar i o nette** (mar'i ə net'), a doll made to move by means of strings or by the hands, often on a little stage; a puppet, such as Pinocchio.

**marsh** (märsh), soft wet land; a swamp.

**may or** (mā'ər), a man who is the head of a town or city government.

**Mc Leod, Mar y** (mə kloud', mãr'i), girlhood name of an American Negro educator. After her marriage she was known as Mary McLeod Bethune.

**meek** (mēk), not easily angered; mild in temper; patient; also, easily managed or controlled.

**mis hap** (mis'hap), an unfortunate happening; an unlucky accident.

**mis lead** (mis lēd'), 1. lead to believe something that is not so; deceive. 2. lead or guide the wrong way.

**moc ca sin** (mok'ə sən), a soft heelless shoe of leather worn by North American Indians.

**molt** (mōlt), 1. shed the feathers, outer skin or hair, before a new growth. 2. act or time of molting.

**mor sel** (môr'səl), 1. a very small amount or quantity; a little piece. 2. a small bite of food.

**Mo ses** (mō'ziz), the great prophet, lawgiver, and leader of the Israelites.

**mound** (mound), 1. in baseball, the place from which the pitcher throws the ball. 2. a bank of earth or stones.

**mount** (mount), 1. a mountain or very high hill. 2. get up on something; especially, to seat oneself on the back of a horse.

**moun tain li on** (moun'tən lī'ən), a large American wildcat; a cougar.

**Muir, John** (mūr, jon), an explorer, writer, and nature lover who, through his writings, saved from destruction many of the forest and scenic areas in the United States.

**muk luk** (muk′luk), a type of sealskin boot worn by Eskimos.

Mukluk

**Mul li gan** (mul′ə gən), a family name.

**mush** (mush), 1. a kind of food made of meal, especially corn meal, boiled in water. 2. something soft and thick like mush. 3. travel on foot across snow, especially with a sled pulled by dogs.

### N

**name sake** (nām′sāk′), one who has the same name as another; especially, a person who has been named after another person.

**nar ra tor** (na rā′tər), a person who tells a story or gives an account of something.

**Na vook** (na′vùk), an Alaskan name.

**near sight ed** (nēr′sīt′id), seeing clearly at short distances only; not able to see far.

**nes tle** (nes′əl), settle or be settled in a comfortable and snug way; lie snugly and cozily, as a bird in a nest.

**Nome** (nōm), a city in western Alaska, on the Bering Sea. Nome is the site of the famous gold rush of 1898–1899.

**Nor way** (nôr′wā), a mountainous country in the northern part of Europe.

**No tre Dame** (nō′trə däm′), the French words for *Our Lady.*

### O

**or di nar y** (ôr′də ner′i), usual; regular; of a common kind; not special.

**ot ter** (ot′ər), a water animal that is a very good swimmer and feeds mainly on fish. It has webbed feet and is hunted for its valuable fur.

**owl.** *See* **Snowy Owl.**

### P

**Pab li to** (pä blē′tō), a form of the Spanish name *Pablo,* meaning *little Pablo* or *dear little Pablo. Pablo* is the name of a boy in the story "Anita's Gift of Flowers."

**Pa cif ic** (pə sif′ik), the large ocean that lies between America and Asia.

**Pal es tine** (pal′is tīn), the Holy Land where the Christ Child was born.

**pal i sade** (pal′ə sād′), 1. a fence of strong wooden stakes set firmly in the ground, sometimes used to keep enemies out. 2. a line of steep cliffs.

Palisade

**par a ble** (par′ə bəl), a short, simple story that teaches a truth or a lesson. Jesus often taught in parables.

**pare** (pãr), cut or trim off the outside of something; peel.

**par ka** (pär′kə), 1. a fur jacket with a hood, worn in Alaska. 2. a long, warm shirt or jacket with a hood.

**pat i o** (pat′i ō), 1. an inner court or a yard that is open to the sky; courtyard. Old Spanish houses were often built around a patio. 2. a paved area just outside a house, used especially for outdoor meals.

cap, āge, cãre, fär; let, bē, tèrm; pin, fīve; hot, gō, ôr; oil, out; cup, fùll, rüle; ūse; takən

**pat tern** (pat′ərn), 1. an arrangement of colors or shapes; a design. 2. a model or guide for making something.

**peer** (pēr), look closely in order to see clearly.

**pen guin** (peng′gwin), a sea bird found mainly in the antarctic region. A penguin cannot fly. In place of wings, it has flippers for diving and swimming.

**Phar aoh** (fãr′ō), a title or name given to the rulers of ancient Egypt.

**Pie tro** (pyā′trō), an Italian name.

**Pi noc chio** (pē nŏk′kyō), name of a wooden marionette.

**pin to** (pin′tō), 1. spotted in two colors. 2. a horse spotted in two colors.

**plague** (plāg), 1. a disease that spreads easily and rapidly and often causes death; an epidemic. 2. anything that causes much trouble or suffering.

**plain** (plān), usual; not pretty; ordinary; also, simple and natural in manner: *a plain person.*

**plot** (plot), a small area of land; a small piece of ground: *a garden plot.*

**po lar** (pō′lər), of, near, or having to do with the North Pole or the South Pole: *the polar regions.*

**po lit i cal  sci ence** (pə lit′ə kəl sī′əns), the study that has to do with government and political affairs.

**pom pous** (pom′pəs), acting very proudly; self-important.

**Pooh.** *See* **Winnie-the-Pooh.**

**por cu pine** (pôr′kū pīn), an animal with stiff, sharp spines or quills.

**pos sum** (pos′əm), 1. a short name for opossum, a small animal, with dark

grayish fur, that lives in trees. When attacked or caught, an opossum acts like it is dead. 2. **play possum,** put on a false appearance; pretend to be ill, ignorant, dead, etc.

**prai rie** (prãr′i), a large area of level or rolling land with grass but with few or no trees.

**prod i gal** (prod′ə gəl), 1. spending too much; spending in a careless way; wasteful of one's money or other belongings. 2. a person who is wasteful: *The father was happy to see the prodigal returning home.*

**pro pel ler** (prə pel′ər), blades that are made to move in circles, or turn very fast. Propellers are used to move airplanes forward.

**proph et** (prof′it), in the Bible, a person inspired by God to speak in his name, giving a religious message or a warning of some kind.

**Puer to Ri co** (pwer′tō rē′kō), an island of the West Indies, located between Florida and South America.

**Pu las ki** (pû las′ki), a family name.

**pyr a mid** (pir′ə mid), something built usually having a square base and four triangular sides that meet at a point. In ancient Egypt, the pyramids were used as tombs.

Pyramid

## Q

**quail** (kwāl), game bird about ten inches long. In America, this bird is known as the *bobwhite* because of the sound it makes.

**quar ry** (kwôr′i), an open place dug into the earth from which stone is cut or blasted for use in building.

**quill** (kwil), 1. a sharp, stiff hair or spine of an animal, such as the porcupine. 2. a large, stiff feather.

Quill

## R

**raft** (raft), logs or boards fastened together to make a rough boat or floating platform.

**ram** (ram), a male sheep.

**reck on** (rek′ən), 1. *in common use*, think; suppose. 2. count; find the number, amount, or value of.

**red wood** (red′wùd′), 1. a very tall evergreen tree, found in California. 2. the brownish-red wood of this tree.

**re gion** (rē′jən), any large part of the surface of the earth: *the cold regions.*

**rein** (rān), one of a pair of long, narrow straps fastened to the bit of a bridle, used to guide and control a horse or other animal.

**re lief** (ri lēf′), the lessening of, or freeing of a burden, pain, discomfort, or difficulty.

**re sist** (ri zist′), stand up against; fight against; prevent.

**Riehl, Jo hann** (rēl, yō hän′), boy's name in "House of Singing Windows."

**ring** (ring), 1. a circle that can be seen in a cross section of the trunk

Ring

of a tree. Each ring marks one year in the life of a tree. 2. a thin circle of metal: *A wedding ring.*

**riv et er** (riv′it ər), in building, person whose work is fastening steel beams together with metal bolts called *rivets.*

**root** (rüt), 1. the part of a plant that grows underground and holds the plant in place and feeds it. 2. take root and begin to grow. 3. become firmly fixed to a spot: *to stand rooted in surprise.*

**route** (rüt or rout), a road or way to go: *the southern route to California.*

**rus tle** (rus′əl), stir or move so as to make light, soft sounds, as the leaves of trees do when moved by wind.

## S

**Salt Riv er** (sôlt riv′ər), a river in northern Kentucky that flows into the Ohio River.

**Sam u el** (sam′ū əl), in the Bible, a leader and prophet for the Hebrew people.

**sand hog** (sand′hog′), *Slang.* a man who does construction work under water, as in driving a tunnel under a river or making a pier for a bridge. Such work is done usually in a watertight box or tube.

**San ta Fe** (san′tə fā′), a city and the capital of New Mexico.

**sap ling** (sap′ling), a young tree.

**Sar ah** (sãr′ə), 1. in the Bible, the wife of Abraham and the mother of Isaac. 2. name of a girl in the story "Keep Up Your Courage."

cap, āge, cãre, fär; let, bē, tèrm; pin, fīve; hot, gō, ôr; oil, out; cup, fùll, rüle, ūse; takən

**saw mill** (sô′mil′), a place where machines saw logs into boards, planks, etc.

**scent** (sent), 1. odor; smell: *the scent of roses.* 2. sense of smell: *a keen scent.*

**script** (skript), 1. handwriting. 2. a special kind of type used in printing that looks like handwriting.

**sculp tor** (skulp′tər), person or artist who designs and carves figures. A sculptor may make statues of wood, marble, or granite.

**seam** (sēm), 1. line made by sewing together two pieces of material. 2. any line, groove, or ridge that looks like a seam.

Seam

**Se co** (sā′kō), a Spanish word meaning *dry;* also the name of a river in "The Bishop Rides on Horseback."

**seed ling** (sēd′ling), a young plant that has been grown from a seed; especially, a young and small tree.

**seize** (sēz), 1. take hold of suddenly or with force; grasp. 2. take control of by force: *The army seized the town.*

**se nor** (sā nyôr′), a Spanish title of courtesy equal to *Mr.* or *sir;* also, a gentleman.

**Ser ra, Ju ni pe ro** (ser′rä, hü nē′pä rō), a Franciscan missionary who lived from 1713 to 1784 and built many missions in California.

**set tle ment** (set′əl mənt), a place newly settled; a village newly built in the wilderness or on the frontier.

**shal low** (shal′ō), not deep.

**She ba** (shē′bə), an ancient country in the southern part of Arabia.

**shed** (shed), 1. a building, usually of only one story, used for shelter or storage. 2. throw off; cast aside: *The snake shed its skin.*

**sheet** (shēt), 1. a single piece of paper. 2. any broad, flat surface, as of water. 3. a broad piece of cloth used as an article of bedding.

**shell fish** (shel′fish′), an animal that lives in the water and has a shell, such as an oyster, clam, crab, or lobster.

**si** (sē), a Spanish word meaning *yes.*

**Si nai** (sī′nī), 1. in the Bible, the mountain where the Ten Commandments were given to Moses. 2. also, the peninsula on which this mountain is located.

**skip per** (skip′ər), the captain of a ship or a small fishing or trading boat.

**sleek** (slēk), smooth and glossy.

**slow poke** (slō′ pōk′), a slow person; one who takes more than the usual time in moving or acting.

**smart** (smärt), 1. fashionable; stylish: *a smart suit.* 2. quick to learn; clever: *a smart child.*

**sneer** (snēr), a look or words that show scorn, contempt, or strong dislike.

**Snow y Owl** (snō′i oul), a large white owl that lives in cold regions of North America. It sees well in daylight and often catches its food while other owls are sleeping.

**soar** (sôr), fly upward on wings or as if on wings.

**sol emn** (sol′əm), 1. very serious; earnest. 2. celebrated with religious rites; sacred: *a solemn feast day.*

**Sol o mon** (sol′ə mən), 1. in the Bible, son of David and a king of Israel, noted for his wisdom. 2. name of an uncle in the story "Maile's Lei."

**soothe** (süᴛʜ), 1. calm, quiet, or comfort: *soothe a crying baby.* 2. make less painful.

**spa cious** (spā′shəs), having much space; large with plenty of room: *the spacious castle.*

**Span ish** (span′ish), 1. language of Spain. Spanish is also the language of most Spanish-American countries, such as Mexico and countries in Central and South America. 2. the people of Spain. 3. of or having to do with Spain: *the Spanish building.*

**sprout** (sprout), start to grow.

**square** (skwãr), 1. a flat figure with four equal sides and four right angles. 2. having the shape of a square. 3. an open place in a city or town where two or more streets meet.

**squir rel.** *See* **ground squirrel.**

**stage coach** (stāj′kōch′), a horse-drawn coach or carriage carrying passengers, mail, and parcels.

**stretch** (strech), 1. make too large; go beyond the truth in telling something: *stretch the truth.* 2. open or spread to full length and width: *stretch out on the ground.* 3. spread out one's body, legs, or arms. 4. spread out over a distance; fill space, as an area of land.

**stretch er** (strech′ər), a light, bed-like arrangement for carrying sick or wounded persons. It is usually made of canvas stretched on a frame.

**strut** (strut), walk in a proud, important way.

**stu di o** (stü′di ō), the room in which a painter or sculptor works.

**sus tain** (səs tān′), keep up; keep from giving way, as in a time of trouble: *to be sustained by hope.*

**swal low** (swol′ō), 1. take into the stomach through the throat: *to swallow food.* 2. a small bird with long wings. Swallows are noted for their swift and graceful flight.

**switch** (swich), 1. a thing used to turn an electric current on or off. 2. change by using a switch: *switch on a light.* 3. put or take one thing in place of another.

**swoop** (swüp), 1. rush down suddenly; come down in a sudden swift attack. 2. a sudden, swift descent.

## T

**tab let** (tab′lit), a flat sheet of wood, stone, or ivory, used to write on. In olden times, such tablets were used as we use pads of paper.

**tail coat** (tāl′kōt′), a coat with deeply-forked tails; a swallow-tailed coat, such as are worn by men at formal parties.

Tailcoat

**Ta ku** (tä′kü), an Alaskan name.

**tan nin** (tan′ən), substance in the bark of some trees which helps to keep them from burning. It is also used in tanning, dyeing, and making ink.

---

cap, āge, cãre, fär; let, bē, tėrm; pin, fīve; hot, gō, ôr; oil, out; cup, fůll, rüle, ūse; takən

**tap root** (tap′rüt′), on a plant, a main root that grows downward and from which small side roots grow.

Taproot

**ther mom e ter** (thər mom′ə tər), a thing used to measure temperature. A thermometer is made up of a glass tube with mercury sealed in it, and with a scale on the outside marked in degrees.

**thrift y** (thrif′ti), careful in spending; saving.

**Till a mook** (til′ə mük), name of a street in "Ellen Rides Again."

**tor toise** (tôr′təs), a turtle; especially, a turtle that lives on land.

**tor ture** (tôr′chər), cause very great pain to others: *He tortures animals.*

**tow el-horse** (tou′əl hôrs), a towel rack; a rack with bars used for drying towels or other articles.

Towel-horse

**trad er** (trād′ər), person who makes his living by trading; one who buys and sells goods.

**Trin i dad** (trin′ə dad), 1. a city in Colorado. 2. an island in the West Indies.

**trudge** (truj), walk; especially, walk in a tired way or with an effort.

**tun dra** (tun′drə), a very large, treeless plain of the northern arctic regions.

**Tu tu** (tü′tü), 1. Hawaiian word meaning *Granny.* 2. a Hawaiian name.

**twine** (twīn), 1. wind or coil; wind around; twist. 2. a strong thread or string made of smaller parts twisted together.

**U**

**un fa mil iar** (un′fə mil′yər), not familiar; not well known; strange.

**u ni corn** (ū′nə kôrn), an imaginary animal much like a horse but with a single long horn in the middle of its forehead.

**V**

**Van Holp** (van hôlp′), a family name.

**vi sion** (vizh′ən), 1. something seen as in a dream; something made known, as to a prophet. 2. power to see; sense of sight.

**Vo tip ka** (vô tip′kä), a family name.

**W**

**war bler** (wôr′blər), any of several kinds of small, bright-colored songbirds.

**wares** (wãrs), 1. goods for sale: *The peddler sold his wares.* 2. utensils: *tinware; silverware.*

**Wa wo na** (wô wō′nä), the Indian name for a tree in "Big Tree."

**wil der ness** (wil′dər nis), a wild large area where no one lives. A wilderness may be bare of growth or it may have a dense growth of trees or bushes on it.

**Win nie-the-Pooh** (win′i, pü), name of a toy bear.

**wrig gle** (rig′əl), turn and twist; wiggle; also, move along by turning and twisting: *The snake wriggled along.*

**Y**

**yearn** (yėrn), have a strong wish or desire for something: *The boy yearns for his mother.*

412

# To the Teacher

*This Is Our Land*, Revised Edition, is the fourth-grade reader of the FAITH AND FREEDOM BASIC READERS and may be used after the completion of the advanced third reader, *This Is Our Valley*, Revised Edition, or after *The Story Tree*, the transitional reader between third and fourth grades.

In order that pupils may have an opportunity to apply the techniques of independent word-recognition developed in the word-study program of the primary grades, only a limited vocabulary control has been instituted. A full explanation of the method used is given in the introduction to the Manual, *Teaching the Fourth-Reader Program*. The following 762 words are considered unfamiliar at this level and are so treated in the manual lesson plans. Those words which are introduced in *The Story Tree* and which occur in this book are included in the following list. A heavy black dot indicates the words which are listed in the glossary.

## WORD LIST

**UNIT I**

10 (*Poem*)
11 . . .

12 firm•
13 . . .
14 booth•
   demanded
   whimper
   howl
15 expected
   counter
   tongue
16 curb
   discovered
17 . . .
18 wiggled
   squirmed
   passengers
19 . . .
20 siren
   squad car
   arrest•
21 . . .

22 imagination
   taxi
   alley
23 . . .
24 drainpipe•
   tomato
25 sofa
   snooze
   zigzag
   disturb

26 baldheaded
   Blondie
27 smart•
28 . . .
29 wobble

30 (*Poem*)

31 pitching
   mound•
32 practicing
33 election
   vote
   base•
34 inning
35 umpire
36 . . .
37 silence
   echoed
38 celebration
   victory

39 Austine•
   couple
   truth
40 pretended
   saddle
   mislead•
41 Tillamook•
   holiday
   corral•
   scrambled
   bridled•
42 . . .
43 palm
   boosted

   pinto•
   rein•
44 anxiously
   steer
   guide•
   suggested
45 panted
46 curved
   doubt
47 hikers
48 gratefully
   meekly•
   grip
49 manage
   range

50 (*Poem*)
51 (*Poem*)

52 Gardenia•
   vacation
53 cinnamon•
   excitement
54 odor
   poked
   flavor
   clamped
   lickety-split
55 fireplug
56 harness
57 repeated
   address
   collect
58 gulped
59 . . .

60 . . .
61 . . .

62 (*Book List*)

**UNIT II**

63 . . .

64 widow
   feeble•
   fetch•
   behave
   search
65 morsel•
   starve
   content
66 inn•
   scarcely
   bid
67 . . .
68 ram•
   coin
69 exchanged
70 . . .
71 cord

72 hare•
   tortoise•
   goal•
   steady

73 trudge•

413

group
74 awful
struggle

75 (*Poem*)

76 prairies•
77 seams•
flecked•
78 fluttered

79 (*Poem*)

80 tailor
stroke
favorite
grumbling
81 stretched•
snipping
82 spied
clump
adventures
scornful
83 soared•
84 crouched•
seized•
outcome
85 . . .
86 destroy
spears
87 rage
battle
forth
unicorn•
discouraged
88 boar•
89 . . .

90 Icarus•
Daedalus•
island
escape
gulls
91 fastened
efforts
glorious•
glide
youth
freedom
92 fog
blazing
upward
Apollo•
93 sense
warning
94 grief

95 mild
pod
human
96 . . .
97 provide
wearily
patiently
98 propped
windowsill
twine•
99 delicate

100 pigeons
gutter
glow

101 (*Poem*)
102 (*Book List*)

**UNIT III**

103 . . .

104 courage
quilt
Noble
wilderness•
Connecticut
trail
105 solemn•
steep
coarse•
106 clung
misty
107 birches•
108 coast
plots•
sloped
hollowed•
109 Bible
namesake•
Isaac•
entrance
110 Samuel•
rustling•
peering•
chink•
palisade•
111 . . .
112 English•
impatience

113 (*Poem*)

114 raft•
Ohio
115 Kentucky
furniture
frontier•
116 partners
army
stolen
117 rifles
bullets
118 deck
task
119 . . .
120 settlement•
121 sank
trembled
drooped
prove
122 ached•
moccasins•
123 rescue
124 wounded
nation

125 studies

French•
admire
precious
126 Jogues•
hardships
Jesuit•
languages•
Huron•
127 mush•
128 difficult
attacked
Iroquois•
fought
tortured•
warriors
carved
Hudson•
129 recognize
humbly
130 slave

131 (*Poem*)

132 narrator•
Indiana
surrounded
lurking•
133 . . .
134 simple
German•
135 swelling
pauses
136 dull
ma'am
flings
137 . . .
138 Washington
President
United States
139 . . .
140 students
friendship
141 governor•
Abraham
Lincoln•
142 stagecoach•
Santa Fe•
143 Trinidad•
Colorado
144 Blandina•
mayor•
lawyers•
dreaded
145 . . .
146 jolted
distance
147 California
148 express•
149 . . .
150 gaze
glanced
entered
151 charity•

152 figuring•
column•
owe

McLeod•
hesitated•
flickering
153 depended
harvest
Negro
South
Carolina
154 autumn
relief•
arithmetic
155 declare•
156 thrifty•
157 soil
forehead
sweat
158 chills
stomach
159 reckon•
160 silently
pupil
generous
amazement
education
161 murmured
162 desire
college
Albertus
Bethune•
Florida

163 (*Poem*)
164 (*Book List*)

**UNIT IV**

165 nature

166–167 (*Poem*)

168 wisdom
Jerusalem•
Solomon•
fame
Sheba•
169 skilled
craftsmen•
bouquet
perfectly
perfume
170 camels
musicians
entertained
designed•
171 difference
swayed
172 . . .
173 guest

174 (*Poem*)

175 warbler•
Alaska•
fuel
muscles
rarely
propeller•
176 amazing
graceful

414

darts
Brazil•
177 quail•
repaired
molting•
178 balanced•
crippled
sprout•
continues
completed
179 insects
180 scientists

181 protect
Bobry•
hump
otter•
Bering Sea•
182 swoop•
183 alert•
dived
surface
184 downward
paddled
185 hushed
186 sheltered

187 (*Poem*)

188 creation•
seedling•
sapling•
ancient•
clan•
189 Wawona•
190 shivered
taproot•
moisture
handsome
191 lightning
torch
192 tannin•
resists•
buttresses•
pyramids•
Egypt•
193 loomed•
Pacific•
Moses•
Palestine•
194 nineteenth
century•
metal
lumbermen
platforms
195 wedge
slanting
196 Muir•
grove
graze•

197 (*Poems*)

198 slender
possum•
199 examples

female
200 liquid
reported
otherwise
awkwardly
millions

201 distant
beaver•
202 lodge•
dam
formed
marsh•
203 quills•
porcupine•
bristled•
204 scent•
scurried
lynx•
205 slyly
snarled
206 hemlock•
pity
hurled
207 thrash
withdrew
respectfully
shuddered
208 . . .

209 (*Poem*)
210 (*Book List*)

UNIT V

211 . . .
212 (*Poem*)

213 Pooh•
stoutness
exercises
properly
214 scuffing
215 hallo•
216 mugs
condensed•
larder•
directly•
217 sternly
218 Christopher
slightly
waste
219 towel-horse•
convenient•
gloomily•
220 sustaining•
221 relations

222 (*Poem*)

223 Pinocchio's•
Antonio•
224 dumb•
stammering
ordinary•
225 . . .
226 Geppetto•

227 service
marionette•
moaned
guilty
228 misfortune
ruined
229 argument
230 hastily
glared
strut•
231 bounds
232 threat
curious
possible
233 speechless

234 juggler•
abbey•
Notre Dame•
235 Cluny•
maidens•
wares•
236 twirl
shreds
tatters
hunger
boldly
behold•
237 marvelous
238 Abbot•
scatters
harshly
Boniface•
pearls
monks
239 fainting
tenderly
240 font•
composing•
241 pare•
outfit
aisle•
242 magnificent
performs
243 . . .
244 chorus

245 Heidi's•
246 cliffs
247 nestled•
248 arranged
249 . . .
250 Greenfinch
bleated•
251 rod
deserves
252 . . .
253 peaks
awaiting
254 rays
midst

255 Holland•
Amsterdam•
decorated
streamers
256 flagstaffs
257 somersault

Jacob's•
Lambert•
Ludwig•
steel
258 . . .
259 bugler
260 instant
punch
261 . . .
262 . . .
263 Van Holp•

264 . . .
265 polar•
expeditions•
Arctic•
Antarctic•
explorers
globe
penguins•
266 broadcasting
Admiral•
267 mentioned
curiosity•
straying
examined
268 flippers•
269 pompous•
tile
reminds
faucets
270 slippery
sleeves
underneath
glossy
271 actually
regions•
suitable
ankle
272 refrigerator
273 squatted
carpet
274 coils•
temperature
275 control
switch•
bore•

276 (*Poem*)
277–279 (*Poem*)
280 (*Book List*)

UNIT VI

281 . . .
282 (*Poem*)

283 prophets•
Egyptians•
284 spacious•
Pharaoh•
Israel•
commanded
285 Israelites•
punishment

415

plague•
eldest•
286 arise
herds
287 . . .
288 Sinai•
thunder
Mount•
delivered•
commandment
289 visions•

290–291 (Poem)

292 Benji's•
Bethlehem•
mysterious
infant
manger
memory
293 . . .
294 warmth
huddled
295 . . .
296 heaving•
chattering
297 impossible
relatives
298 intently•
299 judgment
astonishment•
300 naked
joyous

301 parables•
prodigal•
inheritance•
famine•
302 . . .

303 reward
Maestro Doni•
friar•
capture•
304 brocaded•
Assisi•
305 studio•
charcoal•
sketched
306 Giorgio•
Pietro•
Gubbio•
Marco•
307 pure
clutter•
Bredo•
308 sculptor•
309 activity•
outlines
pierced
310 model
sneer•
contest
311 . . .
312 throbbed
fled
313 cruelty

shy
314 captive•
315 legend•

316–317 (Hymn)

318 Capistrano•
patio•
Julian
319 Junipero
Serra•
pottery
pride
320 beams•
arches•
twittering
321 clumsy
soothed•
322 motionless
horizon•
farewell
yearn•
323 patterns•
fragrance•
tinted
dawn
cast•
324 fiesta•
325 . . .

326–327 (Poems)

328 Extension
Society•
Gloria Gomez•
Texas
329 arrival
Seco•
shallow•
330 mishap•
331 cautiously•
lantern•
332 faded
333 . . .
334 . . .
335 . . .
336 Cunegunda•

337 (Poem)
338 (Book List)

UNIT VII

339 . . .
340 (Poem)

341 broad
cables•
342 jiffy
construction•
Caruso•
Italy•
Luigi•
343 quarry•
344 Votipka•

riveters'•
345 dizzy
Mulligan•
fancy
sandhogs•
346 drill
anchored•
Pulaski•
cement•
Macpherson•
347 customs•
engineers•

348 (Poem)

349 Anita's•
Pablo
Puerto Rico•
Mamita•
350 . . .
351 Pablito•
avenue
clinging
352 honest
353 shutters
354 florist's
serious
355 mister
356 si•
señor•
Spanish•
beloved•
jasmine•
Don Antonio•
357 . . .

358 Johann Riehl•
359 Germany•
goblins•
confused•
unfamiliar•
eyebrows
canaries
360 Iowa
snug
braided
screened
361 briskly•
overalls
362 bulked•
choked
Janus•
363 Iverson•
accepted
recess
364 . . .
365 script•
political
science•
sums
correctly
366 . . .
367 shrinking
368 costume
369 flushed
embroidered•
fine-tucked

blouse
Frau•
370 Greece•
Norway•
371 . . .

372 (Poem)

373 Maile's•
lei•
Hawaiian•
two-tone
glistening
fern
374 Keoki•
crushed
Tutu•
375 coconut
especially
376 . . .
377 nevertheless
aboard
jiggling
378 . . .
379 . . .
380 cash
award•
thrilled
crisp
381 . . .

382 Taku•
Nome•
general•
seal
harpoons•
old-fashioned
383 zero
tundra•
Navook•
Minnesota
384 equipment•
huskies•
pleasure
385 sleek•
386 wriggled•
387 route•
solid
skidded
lunged•
388 trusted
389 blizzard•
snowdrift
shovel
390 domed•
391 shaved
thermometer•
degrees•
parka•
392 mukluks•
windproof
393 bay•
394 pilot
skipper•

395 (Song)
396 (Book List)

BCDEFGHIJ069875
PRINTED IN THE UNITED STATES OF AMERICA